THE
YOUNG ACTORS'
WORKBOOK

Judith Roberts Seto

Grove Press
New York

Published simultaneously in Canada
Printed in the United States of America

Library of Congress Catalog Card Number 83-49383
ISBN 0-8021-5082-9

Grove Press
841 Broadway
New York, NY 10003

00 01 02 03   20 19 18 17 16 15 14 13

The following are the sources of the sections of the plays and other works included in this book:

From *The Young and Fair* by N. Richard Nash. Copyright 1948, 1949 by N. Richard Nash. Renewed 1975, 1976 by N. Richard Nash. Copyright 1944 by N. Richard Nash (under the title *Class Day*). Renewed 1971 by N. Richard Nash. Reprinted by permission of the author and of Dramatists Play Service, Inc.

From *"Me, Candido!"* by Walt Anderson. © 1958 by Walt Anderson. Copyright 1950 by Walt Anderson (under the title *The Little Screwball*). Renewed 1977 by Walt Anderson. Reprinted by permission of the author and of Dramatists Play Service, Inc.

From *David and Lisa* by James Reach (adapted from the book by Theodore Isaac Rubin and the screenplay by Eleanor Perry). Copyright © 1967 by Samuel French, Inc. Reprinted by permission of Samuel French, Inc.

From *All the Way Home* by Tad Mosel. Reprinted by permission of William Morris Agency, Inc. Copyright © 1961 by Tad Mosel.

From *I Too Speak of the Rose* by Emilio Carballido. Translated by William I. Oliver. Copyright © 1971 by Emilio Carballido. Reprinted by permission of Professor George Woodyard, Department of Spanish and Portuguese, the University of Kansas.

From *Junior Miss* by Jerome Chodorov and Joseph Fields. Reprinted by permission of International Creative Management. Copyright © 1942 by Jerome Chodorov and Joseph Fields. Copyright renewed 1969 by Jerome Chodorov and Joseph Fields. Copyright © 1944 revised by Jerome Chodorov and Joseph Fields. Renewed 1974 by Jerome Chodorov and Mrs. Marion Fields.

From *The Effects of Gamma Rays on Man-in-the-Moon Marigolds* by

TO MY HUSBAND,
MOTHER, FATHER
AND MY CHILDREN—BILL, MARC, DANIEL AND MARIANNE

Preface

Acting can bring you joy, excitement and a sense of fulfillment if you approach each role creatively, with your entire self—mind, body and feelings all working in unison. This workbook-anthology is designed to help you do that. Your goal as an actor should be to merge your whole self with another whole self, another "you"—the character you play. The "Suggestions for the Actor" immediately following each selection help you to "step into the shoes" of that other person. These specific suggestions include stimulating thought questions about your role, relevant acting games, exercises and improvisations to play, either as yourself, the actor, or as "you," the character. (Improvisations are situations which you enact spontaneously, inventing your own words and physical actions "on the spot.") It is important to play yourself sometimes, to discover what you, the actor, would do in various situations, to become more aware of your own feelings, attitudes and values. After all, you cannot know another human being intimately, from the inside out, unless you first know yourself.

The acting suggestions may of course be followed, ignored or altered as you or your teacher sees fit. They are intended only as guidelines. By all means invent your own games and improvisations too! I hope that after you have worked on a number of these parts and used some of the listed suggestions, you will be able to approach other roles, not represented here, in a similar manner.

At the back of this book you will find an "Actor's Check List" containing general thought questions about the character you play and the circumstances of the scene. I recommend thinking carefully about these questions whenever you work on a role, no matter how small it may be. These questions are meant to help you create a living, three-dimensional human being with a past, a present and a future.

The Young Actors' Workbook is geared for use in any acting or speech class devoted to scene study for young people, or in an English class in which acting is part of the curriculum. Acting is an incomparable way of making the printed page come to life. Many of the thought questions regarding the various characters and their relationships may be used as topics for group discussion or for creative writing, since you, the actor, need to invent a host of details about the life of the characters from your own vivid imagination. This book may be used by those of you participating in a workshop, those preparing audition material or those of you simply acting for your own pleasure,

These are young roles, chosen to reflect the interests of young performers. The easiest parts for you to play truthfully are most often those fairly close to you in age. You have enough to handle, concentrating on all the circumstances of a scene, without the difficult added problem of portraying age. You need roles with which you can identify. You also need material worth working on —pieces of excellent literary quality. Many of our finest playwrights are represented here, as well as outstanding authors. The selections are divided into two main categories according to age: those for girls and boys over twelve and those for young adults (sixteen and older). These divisions, however, are not hard and fast; it would be worth your while to browse through both categories before choosing your monologue or scene.

There is wide variety in the number of characters appearing in the selections. *The Young Actors' Workbook* contains a great many monologues and dialogues, but in addition it has numerous group scenes. You will find a large number of black roles as well as those of other ethnic groups. You should not feel that you must limit yourself to roles of your own race but, on the other hand, you should be able to play such parts if you desire to do so. Included also are excerpts from books and plays which dramatize the aspirations of young women and the significant contributions women have made to our society.

Each selection is preceded by an introduction describing character, setting and the plot up to that point in the story. The background of each scene has been provided in detail in case some of you are unable to obtain the play script. It is extremely important, however, to study the entire play. No plot summary can ever take the place of the playwright's own words. Nearly all the plays excerpted in this volume are available in inexpensive paperback form—singly or in play collections. Many of the paperback acting editions are sold by Samuel French, 25 West 45 Street, New York, New York 10036. Others are sold by Dramatists Play Service, 440 Park Avenue South, New York, New York 10016. Most plays and other theatre books in print are available in paperback or hard-cover editions, or both, at The Drama Book Shop, 723 Seventh Avenue, New York, New York 10019. The novels, journals, etc., from which material is taken, are widely available in libraries and bookstores, and may be purchased from the original publishers.

Deletions in the quoted material are indicated by asterisks throughout this book.

In order to understand the meaning of stage directions, you should learn the following technical theatre terms. Some of these may be abbreviated in play scripts. (See diagram of the acting areas of the stage on page 334.)

Downstage Left* (*D.L.*) means "toward the audience and to the actor's left." It does *not* mean "to the audience's left."

Downstage Right (*D.R.*) means "toward the audience and to the actor's right."

Upstage Left (*U.L.*) means "away from the audience and to the actor's left."

Upstage Center (*U.C.*) means "away from the audience and in the center."

Downstage side of table means "the side of the table closest to the audience."

Cross above *table* means "walk behind the table, upstage of it."

Cross below *table* means "walk in front of the table, downstage of it."

One final word about acting: Even though the roles in this anthology are close to you in age, a given character may be utterly unlike you in some other ways. By putting yourself in that character's place, you may gain tolerance and perhaps even appreciation

---

* In some scripts (as in this book), this term (and others) may not have first letters capitalized.

of viewpoints radically different from your own. Have you ever
wondered what it would be like to lead someone else's life for a
little while? Now is your chance to find out!

My warmest thanks to my friend Julia Yarrow for all her help.
Without her good advice and welcome assistance, this project
might never have gotten off the ground. My most grateful appreciation to Professor Margaret Linney of the Brooklyn College
Theatre Department for her useful advice, her continual encourage-
ment and for all she taught me in her improvisational drama
courses. My thanks to Wilson Lehr and to actress Ann Spettell for
some valuable observations I used in the text. Thanks also to
Leota Diesel and to my friend Sandra Slipp for helpful suggestions. I would like to thank artist Geraldine Roberts for her illus-
tration. My thanks to all the authors, agents and publishers who
allowed me to reprint these selections. My immense gratitude to
Jim Menick, my editor at Doubleday, whose perceptive comments
and corrections invariably hit the mark.

                                              Judith Roberts Seto

Contents

Monologues for Boys

Part II: Dramatic Selections for Young Adults
(Age Sixteen and Older)

Scenes for Young Adults

Monologues for Young Women

Monologues for Young Men

PART I

DRAMATIC SELECTIONS
FOR GIRLS AND BOYS
(Age Twelve and Older)

Scenes for Girls and Boys

From *The Young and Fair* by N. Richard Nash.
Act II, Scene 2

INTRODUCTION

"The action of the play takes place in the Brook Valley Academy, a fashionable Junior College not far from Boston," shortly after World War II. Frances Morritt, a young woman, an alumna with fond memories of the school and its owner, Sara Cantry, arrives with her sixteen-year-old sister and charge, Patty. She is seeking a position as teacher of English and personnel director. Fran is tactful and diplomatic rather than open or impulsive. She wants to play it safe. Patty Morritt "enjoys everything, especially the fact that she is learning to think. A forthright, impetuous girl with warm impulses." Since their father's recent death has left them without money, Fran has been looking for a "genteel" position, without much success until now. She hopes that Patty will be enrolled as a freshman here as part of the arrangement. Miss Cantry is delighted to hire her. She confides in Fran about her hopes for an endowment so that she will no longer be insecure in her own position, dependent upon trustees.

Patty is given Fran's old bedroom. She makes friends with her new roommate, Lee Barron, "a sensitive, dark girl, about seventeen," who is "friendly, amiable, generous." She also meets some of the other girls, including Nancy Gear, "a small frail girl, nervous, anxious," Drucilla Eldridge (Dru), "about nineteen * * * proud and hard-driven, resourceful, intelligent," and Mildred Cheever (Mil), "about nineteen. She is an athletic girl of spare physical strength" and Dru's devoted follower. Dru and Mildred are seniors and members of a Vigilante Committee, known as the "Vidge." The Vidge makes life miserable for the freshmen during Hell Week, the first week of school. Dru, an overbearing girl who enjoys lording it over the freshmen, wants to continue the Vidge even after Hell Week ends, supposedly to catch the thief who stole an eighty-five-dollar gold fountain pen and a fraternity pin.

Dru posts a notice of a meeting to discuss continuing the Vidge, but she makes it as inconspicuous as possible so that the freshmen won't see it. Patty attends the meeting and opposes the Vidge on principle. Fran also attends but she objects on the grounds of undemocratic procedure. The girls, mostly seniors, vote to disband the Vidge despite Dru.

Patty's roommate Lee is Jewish, but she lied about her religion on her application for admission to the school. She had been a victim of vicious anti-Semitism the previous summer, and still suffered the effects. After telling Patty the truth, she confesses her lie in a written autobiography submitted to her English instructor, Fran. Lee and Patty go to see Fran, hoping that Fran will advise Lee to tell all to Miss Cantry, but Fran urges playing it safe by telling nothing.

Fran is more forthright about Nancy Gear's problems. As personnel director, Fran expresses concern to Miss Cantry about Nancy Gear's mental stability, but Miss Cantry rejects Fran's suggestion to send Nancy elsewhere or to employ the services of a visiting psychiatrist. Miss Cantry fears offending the Gears, whose money she desperately needs for an endowment. Fran interviews Nancy, who is afraid that her mother will be terribly angry if she learns that Nancy has been in the infirmary for headaches. Nancy cries, "Mother thinks I'm a—coward. But I'm not! I can do things that take a lot of courage—!" Fran then questions her gently about the thefts, but when she denies everything, Fran believes her.

Inadvertently, Nancy reveals to Fran that Dru has been making secret plans to reorganize the Vidge because one hundred dollars of Dru's is missing. Fran sends for Dru at once, without implicating Nancy. When Dru refuses to give up the Vidge, Fran punishes her by forcing her to remain on the campus grounds until she changes her mind. Furious, Dru is determined to get even. She notices Lee's autobiography on Fran's desk and reads it while Fran's back is turned.

The ensuing scene takes place in Patty's bedroom. The characters include Dru, Mil, Nancy, Lee and Patty (a small part).

"PATTY MORRITT'S bedroom is a cheerful, sunny room in Fairchild Hall. The furniture is pastel-painted; the beds and bureaus are paired for two occupants. There are two doors; one leads to hallway and stairs; the other, to a vestibule in which there is a clothes closet, and through which one enters the bathroom."

The right side of the stage is illuminated quickly and we see:

THE BEDROOM

No one is there. A knock on up center hall door, then DRU *streaks into the room, wild-eyed and out of breath. She looks about her disconnectedly, then goes quickly to one of the bureaus and opens a drawer. Abruptly, hallway door opens and* MIL, *also breathless, stands on threshold.*

MIL: Dru! For Pete's sake, what are you doing?

DRU: I'm going to search every bedroom—until we find the thief. I'll show Miss Morritt the Vidge can do what she can't!

MIL: Dru, you'd better get out of here!

DRU: No! I'm going to show them all that there's a *need* for the Vidge ——

MIL: But you'll get in trouble!

DRU: I'll risk it!

MIL: Do you have any idea who the thief is? You said you had a suspicion.

DRU: I had to say that, stupid—to show the girls I knew what I was doing. [*Going toward bureau again*] Come on—let's get started.

MIL: Oh Dru! I'm sure Lee didn't take anything—and if you suspect Patty, you're off your trolley!

DRU: I don't suspect anybody, I told you! I only hope—I hope Patty did do it!

MIL: Don't talk so crazy! You know darn well she's not the kind to ——

DRU: How do we know she *didn't* steal those things? And I tell you—if she did—she and her sister will be out of here so fast ——!

MIL: You're doing this out of spite! You're just trying to get back at Miss Morritt!

DRU: Why shouldn't I? She's trying to trim me down to a nobody! It's her against me! She's got to leave this place—or I've got to! And anything I can do to get her out ——

MIL: [*Frightened*] I don't want to have anything to do with this! [*She starts for up center door*]

DRU: Wait a minute! [*Sincerely affected*] You're walking out on me . . . ?

MIL: [*Unhappily*] Dru, let's call it off—forget about it!

DRU: [*Quietly*] What are we calling off? Our friendship?

MIL: No, of course not! I mean *this*—all this sneaking around and ——

DRU: Miss Morritt was right. When it comes to a showdown, I've got nobody. I've got to do it alone!

MIL: [*Desperately*] Dru, don't you understand? All this business —it makes me feel scared and—sick. If you gave a rap about me you wouldn't ask me to ——

DRU: I do ask you! [*Then, quietly*] I ask you to prove that Miss Morritt was wrong—that I do have friends—that they'll stick to me!

MIL: Oh, Dru!

DRU: Well?

MIL: [*Quietly, trembling*] No . . . [*With an outcry*] No! It costs too much to be your friend, Dru—it costs too much! [MIL *rushes out of room up center.* DRU *stands there, immobilized, in an agony of loss and frustration. What to do? She paces, starts for up center door as if to make it up with* MIL—*and give up the whole project. But she can't. At last, quieting the turmoil inside her, she makes her decision:* DRU *goes toward bureau and resumes her search. . . . Suddenly, offstage, the sound of running footsteps.* DRU *shuts drawer, frightened. She freezes as she hears knock on up center door*]

NANCY'S VOICE: Lee! [DRU *looks around for an escape, she races toward closet down right. At this precise moment,* NANCY *enters and sees closet door closing*]

NANCY: Lee! Lee—is that you? [DRU *comes back into room cautiously. She is about to make an excuse for her presence here when* NANCY, *who is carrying some objects in her hand, makes a panic-stricken movement to hide them behind her back.* DRU *sees this*]

DRU: [*Measuredly*] Hello, Nancy.

NANCY: [*Tense*] Hello. I heard voices in here. I thought it was Lee.

DRU: What do you want Lee for?

NANCY: I—just wanted some—some advice. But it's nothing—I'll come back. [*She makes a jerky movement toward up center door.* DRU *steps quickly into her path*]

DRU: Wait a minute. . . . There's no rush, is there?

NANCY: [*Stopping tensely*] I'm in a hurry—I ——

DRU: What for? What are you so nervous about?

NANCY: I'm not nervous. Please let me go by.

DRU: [*Quickly*] What have you got behind your back?

NANCY: [*Retreating*] Nothing.

DRU: Let me see it, huh? You'd better give it to me, hadn't you?

NANCY: [*Breaking away in panic*] It's not yours!

DRU: [*Suddenly making a grab for* NANCY] Give it to me!

NANCY: [*Struggling—crying out*] Please—let me alone! [*She tries to break away but* DRU, *stronger, subdues her. The struggle is over—and* DRU *has objects in her hand*]

DRU: [*With a gasp*] My God! The pen and the fraternity pin and my money—everything! [*As* NANCY *collapses on bed*] So you've been doing the stealing . . .

NANCY: [*In a frenzied confusion*] I don't know—I don't know —— [*She begins to sob*]

DRU: You'd better come along.

NANCY: [*Resisting*] Where? Where are you taking me?

DRU: Miss Cantry. [*She tries to shepherd* NANCY *toward up center door*]

NANCY: No—please—she'll send me home!

DRU: I'm sorry, Nancy. But the Vidge set out to find the thief. Well, we've found her.

NANCY: Please ——! I won't take anything again—I promise! My mother—I don't know what she'll do to me! Please help me out!

DRU: Look, I can't go protecting a girl who ——

NANCY: I'll do anything you say—anything!

DRU: I'm sorry it's you, Nancy—but it had to be somebody. [*Suddenly, struck by inspiration, she drops* NANCY'S *arm*] Wait a minute. . . . Why does it have to be you?

NANCY: You will help me, won't you?

DRU: Be quiet—let me think! [*Suppressing her excitement*] What did you come into this room for?

NANCY: Miss Morritt asked me if I'd taken the things. And I said no ——

DRU: [*Quickly*] Did she believe you?

NANCY: I think so. But then I got scared. I didn't know what to do. I thought Lee would tell me what to do.

DRU: [*Quietly—with studied friendliness*] Nancy, you know you're in a tough spot. Not only could you be sent home—you could be arrested.

NANCY: Please help me ——

DRU: If I do, it's liable to get me in trouble.

NANCY: No—no, it won't!

DRU: If I protect you, you've got to back me up. Because I'd be taking a big chance for your sake.

NANCY: [*Snatching at the straw*] Of course—I understand—I'll back you up.

DRU: And you'll have to stay in with me until the very end. It would be bad for both of us if something went wrong. [*With elaborate solicitude*] And it would be still worse for you, Nancy.

NANCY: I know—I'll do whatever you say.

DRU: All right. . . . Here—take this stuff. [*As* NANCY *obeys,* DRU *quickly moves to* PATTY'S *bureau. She opens second drawer, searches around, then comes up with a stationery box*] Put the things in this stationery box.

NANCY: But it's Patty's!

DRU: Never mind that—do as I tell you! [*As* NANCY *complies*] Now put the box in this bottom drawer.

NANCY: It's Patty's bureau—I couldn't do that!

DRU: [*Impatiently*] All right—if you don't want me to help you ——! [NANCY *puts box in drawer*] Shut the drawer. [*As* NANCY *shuts drawer, we see* PATTY *and* LEE *enter the Main Hall from right.* LEE *starts up center, through archway*]

PATTY: [*Calling*] Hurry up, Lee. We'll miss the main feature.

LEE: I'll only be a minute.

NANCY: [*Frightened*] Lee's coming in!

DRU: Oh, dammit! [*Quickly improvising*] Go round the bend in the hallway. When Lee comes in here, stand outside the door. Listen to everything that goes on in here. [NANCY *goes*. DRU *quickly surveys room. In Main Hall* PATTY *has picked up a book and is reading.* LEE *breezes into bedroom up center. On seeing* DRU, *she halts. As if in slow motion, she puts down the books she is carrying*]

LEE: What are you doing in our room?

DRU: I'm making a search of all the rooms in Fairchild.

LEE: Did you get Miss Morritt's permission to do that? Or Miss Cantry's?

DRU: I have the permission of the Vidge. That's enough.

LEE: The Vidge doesn't exist. And you can't search in here. [DRU *smiles*] Oh, for goodness' sake, do you think we stole your money?

DRU: I don't think anything. But I'm going to fine-tooth-comb this school. Every single room.

LEE: I won't allow you to touch a thing in here.

DRU: Then you make the search while I watch.

LEE: You won't get me to search anything!

DRU: If you're innocent, why do you object to it? [*A moment*] Now don't waste time or I'll make it pretty tough for you. [*Quietly*] And believe me, I can!

LEE: [*Apprehensively—in a strained voice*] It's useless anyway —none of the stolen property is here!

DRU: [*Casually*] All right—let's see. Why don't you start with that bureau ——?

LEE: I can't go rummaging in Patty's things ——

DRU: [*With studied impatience*] Oh, don't be silly. You're *clearing* her by doing it.

LEE: [*Opening top drawer of* PATTY'S *bureau*] There! There's nothing in any of these drawers. You can see for yourself. Scarves—sweaters—three blouses—nothing else.

DRU: [*Offhandedly*] Okay—try the next one.

LEE: [*Opening second drawer*] It's all her art stuff. Brushes, paints —— [*Suddenly she comes upon the stationery box. She opens it and, seeing its contents, gasps. Quickly collecting herself, she closes drawer. In a tight voice*] Nothing there.

DRU: [*Quickly*] What was in that box?

LEE: Nothing. I tell you—nothing! [*But* DRU *has now opened drawer herself. She pulls out box. Opens it*]

DRU: Holy ——!

LEE: [*Quaking*] She—but—where did they come from?

DRU: They came from Abby and Selma and me!

LEE: Patty can't—she doesn't know anything about those things!

DRU: Maybe they just sneaked in by themselves!

LEE: Or maybe they were sneaked in by somebody else! By you, perhaps! [*Abruptly moving toward up center door*] I'm going to ask Patty whether she knows anything ——

DRU: Wait, Lee! [*Suddenly her tactics change. Almost sympathetically*] I had no intention of searching the rest of the school. I knew the search would stop here.

LEE: [*Infuriated*] Of course you did!

DRU: [*Building, block by block*] I knew it would stop here because I was tipped off about Patty.

LEE: [*Savagely*] Tipped off! By whom—Mil Cheaver?

DRU: [*Measuring each word*] No—by somebody else. Somebody in this school saw Patty with that fountain pen this morning!

LEE: You're a liar!

DRU: The girl came into this room without knocking. Patty was standing in front of this bureau—with the pen in her hand. When Patty saw the girl she quickly opened that drawer. And then she was furious at the girl for barging in!

LEE: I don't believe it!

DRU: If I ask the girl who saw her with the pen to come in here will you believe *her?*

LEE: No, I won't!

DRU: Maybe you will when you see who the girl is. [DRU *goes swiftly to up center door, looks down the hall and beckons to* NANCY. *Without an instant's pause*] I know how you feel about this, Lee—and I don't blame you. But somebody did steal that stuff ——

LEE: Not Patty ——

DRU: Listen, you can never be sure of anybody! Who can tell what's eating Patty? Maybe there's something wrong with her—something we don't know about ——

LEE: Don't say that! [NANCY *is now at up center door.* LEE'S *back is to* NANCY, *but* DRU *sees her*]

DRU: [*Indicating* NANCY] All right, Lee—look! [LEE *turns and sees* NANCY]

LEE: [*Shaken*] Nancy!

DRU: [*Gently, to* NANCY] Nancy, tell Lee what you told me. Didn't you see Patty with that pen this morning?

NANCY: [*Her eyes down—faltering*] Yes.

DRU: Where was she standing?

NANCY: It was—I—in front of the bureau ——

LEE: [*Going to pieces*] Nancy, you must be wrong! Are you sure it was this fountain pen? Don't make a mistake, Nancy!

DRU: [*As* NANCY *hesitates*] No—don't make a mistake.

NANCY: Yes . . . it was that one. I'm sure of it.

LEE: Nancy—listen ——

DRU: Don't, Lee. Can't you see how this is getting her all upset? She didn't want to have to tell, did you, Nancy? [NANCY *shakes her head. She is unstrung*] Go on back to your room, Nancy. [NANCY *leaves, up center*]

LEE: [*Breaking out*] I can't believe it! Something must be wrong ——!

DRU: Of course! Something is wrong—with Patty. Otherwise, I couldn't believe it myself. . . . Now, what are we going to do about it?

LEE: [*Crying out*] I'm not going to do anything!

DRU: But we've got to! You and I have got to take that box to Miss Cantry!

LEE: Me?—I won't!

DRU: I'm not asking you to lie or anything. I just want you to ——

LEE: You're asking me to call Patty a thief!

DRU: You needn't call her anything! Just tell Miss Cantry that you and I discovered the stolen property in Patty's stationery box.

LEE: [*Desperately*] I won't!

DRU: What if you're asked? Will you lie?

LEE: If I have to—yes!

DRU: Lee, don't be a fool! Why make yourself her accomplice? [*In a movement of flight,* LEE *starts for up center door.* DRU *stops her. Ominously*] If you lie, you know what'll happen, don't you?

LEE: You can't do anything to me.

DRU: Oh, yes, I can! I'll show them what a liar you really are! You lied to get into the school! You know you people aren't allowed at Brook Valley! I'll expose you—as a liar!

LEE: [*Wildly*] What's Patty got to do with that? You can't perse-
cute Patty because of me!

DRU: [*Quietly*] Look here, Lee. The stolen articles were found
in this room. This is Patty's room—but it's also *yours!* [*Insinuat-
ing*] If Patty didn't steal those things, who did?

LEE: You don't think I did?

DRU: No, but there might be others who'd think so. There are
lots of people around here who wouldn't throw you out because
you're a Jew—but they'd jump at the chance to throw you out
as a thief!

LEE: [*She grips two ends of bureau center, and hangs over it,
shaking*] Oh, God!

DRU: Now, remember. All I'm asking is that you tell the truth.
That's all—the truth—you discovered the box in Patty's bu-
reau. If Patty's innocent, she'll be able to prove it! [*In hallway,*
PATTY *walks to arch up center and calls*]

PATTY: Lee, where are you?

DRU: [*Rapidly—in a whisper*] Now listen to me—don't sacrifice
yourself!

PATTY: Lee!

DRU: You don't want to see her now, do you?

LEE: [*At wit's end*] What'll I do—what'll I do ——

DRU: Come on. Come into my room. She won't see you. Come
on—we'll talk about it some more—come on —— [LEE *hardly
hears* DRU. *She behaves as though she were sleep-walking.* DRU
gets stationery box, takes LEE *gently by the arm, leads her
out*]

SUGGESTIONS FOR THE ACTOR

1. This gripping scene is a particularly good one to use to learn
how to break down a scene into the actions and objectives of each

character. A character's "objective" is *what that character wants to do*. I am defining "actions" as *everything the character does or says in order to get what he or she wants*. (Terminology varies among teachers of acting; the above definitions strike me as easy to understand.) Of course any scene can really be analyzed in this way. This one is particularly suitable for illustrative purposes, however, because each of the major characters has many objectives and sometimes performs a number of actions to reach a particular objective.

Each of the characters also has one main objective in the scene. Dru, your main objective might be phrased, "I want to get even with Miss Morritt." Mil, yours might be, "I want to stop Dru from carrying out her evil plan." Nancy, yours might be, "I want to avoid punishment." Lee, yours might be phrased, "I want to avoid hurting my friend Patty." But the lesser objectives and the actions change because of what the other person in the way (the "obstacle") says or does. Dru, one of your objectives during the course of the scene might be phrased, "I want to find out what Nancy is holding behind her back." Your actions—what you do or *say* to get what you want—are 1) you step into Nancy's path, 2) you verbally menace Nancy and 3) you physically struggle with her. The number of actions required to reach a given objective obviously depends on the *reactions* of the other character(s). Therefore, each character must carefully observe the reactions of the others and proceed accordingly.

What are your character's various objectives and actions? Precisely when do they each occur in the scene?

2. Improvise a scene as *yourself*, using the character's objectives. For example, you, the actress playing Nancy, might improvise a scene as yourself, in which your main, over-all objective would be to avoid punishment. Other students might take part.

3. Improvise a scene as the character you portray, a scene not in the play. Other students might take part, as other characters. For instance you, the actress playing Nancy, might depict one of the actual thefts. These thefts are merely referred to in the play itself; none of them is shown onstage.

4. The dialogue beween Mil and Dru might be played as an independent short scene between two girls. Another possibility might be to divide this long scene in two at Lee's entrance,

thereby giving two different actresses the opportunity to play the part of Dru.

5. For Dru: When you first enter the room, you look about "disconnectedly." You do not yet know where you will begin searching. Then you quickly make a decision. You are familiar with the layout of the room; this had been your room last year.

6. For Mil: You adore Dru and desperately want to keep her friendship, but you are in terrible inner conflict. You also desire to rid yourself of this terrifying sense of pervading *evil*. What is the basis for your decision?

7. For Dru: Certainly you must be truly menacing in order for Nancy and Lee to react with such fright. Yet surely in your own mind you find a way to justify your ugly behavior. How do you justify your actions to yourself? Nobody is all bad. What are your positive personality traits? Answering all the questions on the "Actor's Check List," beginning on page 336, will help you, the actress, to create a living human being rather than a stereotyped, cardboard villain.

8. For Nancy: Anyone in your position would be frightened, but your reactions are always more extreme than a normal person's would be. You are highly unstable now, and by the end of the play you have a complete mental breakdown. You fear as if your very life were at stake; you are deathly afraid. The real object of your terror is your own mother, whose disapproval impelled you to prove your courage by stealing in the first place.

9. For Patty: According to the stage directions, you sit in the Main Hall during the latter part of the scene. If you follow these directions, you must remain in character, seated in an inconspicuous place, reading. Actually read a book, without distracting the audience in any way from the important action "onstage." Up right (away from the audience and far to the actor's right) and up left (away from the audience and far to the actor's left) are commonly considered the least conspicuous stage positions, but what is most or least conspicuous varies with the particular circumstances of the scene, the set, etc. It would be a simple matter to restage the scene so that the Main Hall where you are seated is situated offstage, so long as you, the actress, are able to hear all your cues and the audience is able to hear your offstage voice. In a play production that sort of decision would, of course, be made by the director.

From *"Me, Candido!"* by Walt Anderson.
Act I, Sequence 1

INTRODUCTION

This charming, touching "modern fable" takes place in a poor working-class neighborhood of New York City, a "melting pot" of many nationalities and ethnic groups. Candido is a homeless Puerto Rican orphan, struggling to support himself as a shoeshine boy, sleeping where he can, sometimes in cellars, sometimes on the floor of a restaurant on 116th Street. He has run away from the police because he does not want to be taken to an institution. He is fiercely proud. His favorite expression is "Me, Candido!" meaning, "I am Candido! I am somebody special! Nobody has to feel sorry for me!" He tries to conceal his longing for a home and family, but the Gomezes see through him. The play concerns the struggle of this loving but poor Puerto Rican family to adopt Candido legally, with the help of friends and neighbors.

The play begins on a late afternoon in September. Adelita and Chea Gomez are jumping rope outside their tenement on 116th Street.

"ADELITA, 13, is a sensitive creature, lovely and prim in a newly starched dress of pink. When she is around, there is no question who is boss. CHEA, 6, is the imaginative one. She sports a Wild West gun in a holster and holds a lariat in her hand."

They look forward to Candido's arrival. Candido is now their hero, since he defended them the previous day against "Beefy," a bully who had started a fight with them because they were Puerto Rican.

Candido arrives, "complete with castoff clothes and shoeshine box * * * He is a fierce dark lad of eleven with a patch of black hair that hangs down over bottomless eyes."

Beefy's mother, Mrs. McGinty, appears on the stoop and yells at Candido because he fought with her son. Two other neighbors, however, sympathize with Candido, including Beefy's father. The neighbors enter the tenement. Chea starts to repeat gossip about Mrs. McGinty, whom they all dislike, but Adelita tells her to keep quiet. (We learn later in the play that everyone knows Mrs. McGinty is a "slut.") Chea says that Mr. McGinty gave his wife a black eye. The children giggle and Adelita begins to dance.

Adelita is psychic: she sometimes senses events before they happen. She also mysteriously knows about past events. In this scene she senses that Candido is lying about his uncle, who is really dead.

CHEA: * * * [ADELITA *pirouettes and* CHEA *applauds.* CANDIDO *is intrigued*] Do it again! [ADELITA *repeats it*]

CANDIDO: What's that?

ADELITA: Ballet. I take lessons in the Neighborhood House.

CHEA: Adelita is going to be a great dancer.

ADELITA: You like it?

CANDIDO: It's silly. [*The children sit on the stoop.* CANDIDO *watches them uncertainly.* CHEA *motions for him to join them. He draws back*]

ADELITA: What is your name?

CANDIDO: I am Candido.

ADELITA: I mean your family name.

CANDIDO: [*Angrily*] I am just Candido!

CHEA: [*Taking* CANDIDO's *hand*] He saves all our lives, like Sir Galahad.

CANDIDO: I don't never hear about him. Is he from Puerto Rico?

CHEA: He is in a story that Adelita reads us. He is a knight in shining armor.

CANDIDO: What does that mean?

CHEA: I don't know. But when somebody is in trouble, right away he comes and helps them. Like Superman.

CANDIDO: There ain't nobody like that.

CHEA: There is too!

CANDIDO: He does this for a living?

ADELITA: Stories are not for real. They never talk about that.

CHEA: All the same, that "Beefy" better not start up with you.

CANDIDO: [*Disdainfully*] I can lick him easy. I ain't afraid of nobody.

CHEA: You are not from 116th Street. Where do you live?

CANDIDO: No place.

CHEA: Everybody must live some place. Haven't you got a lot of brothers and sisters?

CANDIDO: [*Picks up his shoeshine box, starts to exit stage left*] You got to know everything! [ADELITA *goes after* CANDIDO, *puts a detaining arm on him, gives him an understanding smile*]

ADELITA: Hey! Don't go away. . . . [*To* CHEA] And you keep quiet.

CHEA: I only ask . . .

ADELITA: You got to open your big mouth.

CANDIDO: I don't have to stay on 116th Street. Sometimes I go down to Times Square. I can go where I like. My uncle he has a big car and we go all over. One time I go with him in an airplane.

CHEA: A real airplane?

CANDIDO: With three motors.

CHEA: My father takes me to New Jersey on the ferry boat.

CANDIDO: New Jersey! Huh. . . . You know where I go with my uncle? In Chicago I go. And one time to California, over the Rocky Mountains. I go every place. Me, Candido!

CHEA: The Rocky Mountains?

CANDIDO: They are very high.

CHEA: The Rocky Mountains are higher than the sky!

ADELITA: What do *you* know!

CHEA: You see cowboys, real cowboys with guns?

CANDIDO: I see plenty cowboys. [*The youngster from the tenement mounts the stoop and enters the house.* CHEA *sees him and shoots at him, and he answers in kind*]

CHEA: Bang! Bang! [To CANDIDO] Here, I let you hold my Wild West gun.

CANDIDO: [*Examines the gun dispassionately, hands it back*] That's for kids.

CHEA: [*With disbelief*] You don't like guns?

CANDIDO: The Rocky Mountains are like . . . like . . . You can look down and see the whole world, and at night are a hundred million stars.

ADELITA: How wonderful! Like in Puerto Rico. [MAMA GOMEZ *is heard calling from house*]

MAMA: [*Off*] Adelita! Come up and bring Chea!

ADELITA: All right, Mama. Upstairs, Chea. You too, Candido. You come upstairs. [CHEA *takes* CANDIDO *by the hand*]

CANDIDO: I don't have to go in no house. I don't need nobody! [CANDIDO *flings off* CHEA'S *hold and starts out.* CHEA *begins to sob.* CANDIDO *turns*] Girls! What are you crying for? I don't do nothing to you. . . . Make her to stop crying. . . . What's the matter with you? Stop it!

ADELITA: Chea wants you to go upstairs.

CANDIDO: I . . . I ain't clean.

CHEA: [*Through her tears*] We got a lot of soap.

ADELITA: You come now.

CANDIDO: [*To* CHEA] You don't cry? You promise? [*She nods eagerly*] But I don't have to stay. I got plenty places to go. To-night I see a man about a job. Me, Candido!

CHEA: I want to hear more about the West. You think a girl like me can be a cowboy? Only where would I keep the horse . . .

ADELITA: Come, we go upstairs. [*They enter the hallway of the tenement*]

SUGGESTIONS FOR THE ACTOR

1. In the stage directions mention is made of a "youngster from the tenement" who "mounts the stoop and enters the house." This "walk-on" part may easily be eliminated from the scene: Chea may shoot at an imaginary cowboy instead of at him.

2. Chea is a six-year-old. You, the actress playing Chea, may be acting the role of a child considerably younger than yourself. It is probably easier for you to play a young child than an adult, since you have experienced being a young child even though you are no longer at that stage of development. Observe six-year-olds closely. How do they walk, talk, giggle, cry, sit, stand, run, dance, jump rope, mop floors, etc.? Try performing simple physical activities such as jumping rope first as you would do them, then as a six-year-old girl might do them. As a six-year-old you may be performing some of these activities for the very first time, struggling to acquire new skills.

3. Chea and Adelita are sisters. How would you describe the relationship between these two sisters? You, the actresses playing these two roles, must *seem* like sisters as you perform the scene. As an exercise try improvising (making up as you go along) a scene not in the play. In this improvised scene perform at least one of the simple physical activities that you, the actress playing Chea, worked on before. For instance you, Adelita, may be prac-

ticing your dancing. You may be determined to perfect a step before your next lesson at the Neighborhood House, which will take
place in a little while. You, Chea, may be trying to learn the step
too. A conflict may arise if you keep interrupting Adelita to ask
her for help—or praise. Or you may decide to help Adelita with
her household chores. At times your attempts to help may really
be a hindrance.

4. Candido's uncle is really dead. Candido is lying when he
says, "My uncle he has a big car and we go all over." His uncle
was hit by a truck and died in November. He had been a thirty-
seven-year-old automobile mechanic when he died. Candido was
very proud of him.

a) For Adelita: You have a "sixth sense"—somehow you realize that Candido is lying. How do you know? Is it something
about him that gives him away—a look in his eyes, a tone of
voice, a movement of his body? Or something else entirely? What
happens to you when you "sense" a future or past event? Do you
suddenly "see" the event in your mind? Do you "see" his uncle's
tragic accident? Decide exactly what process occurs when you
"sense" an event. How does this strange awareness affect you? Do
you feel any different physically?

b) For Candido: Why do you lie? At what points in the scene
are you lying? When are you telling the truth? Did you really go
out West with your uncle when he was alive? Did you take an airplane over the Rocky Mountains? Did you really see "plenty cowboys"? Later in the play when you admit that your uncle is dead,
you assert that you really did see the Rocky Mountains when you
went out West with him. Do you really have "plenty places" to go
tonight? Do you really have a job interview?

In the scene following this one, you tell Mr. Gomez that Adelita
"knows I don't say the truth." What makes you realize that she is
not deceived?

c) For Chea: How much of Candido's story do *you* believe?
How do his words affect you? What do you want to do?

5. For Adelita: Why do you perform a pirouette at the beginning of the scene? Do you dislike Mrs. McGinty so much that you
are delighted to hear about her husband giving her a black eye?
(See "Introduction.") Are you so elated that you want to dance?
Or do you begin to dance in order to distract Chea, so that she

will stop gossiping about Mrs. McGinty? Are you showing off for
Candido's benefit? Or do you pirouette for a different reason?
You, the actress, should select the reason that best fits your inter-
pretation of the character.

It would be most helpful for all of you to read the entire play,
several times if possible.

Candido is pronounced *"kahn*-dee-do"; Chea is pronounced
"chay-ah."

From *David and Lisa* by James Reach, adapted from the book by Theodore Isaac Rubin and the screenplay by Eleanor Perry.
Act I

INTRODUCTION

Originally a story entitled *Lisa and David* by psychiatrist Theodore Isaac Rubin, then an award-winning movie, *David and Lisa* is now a fascinating play as well.

The following scene takes place in the Day Room of the Berkely School for emotionally disturbed adolescents, a residential treatment center located in Westchester, a suburban county close to New York City. The atmosphere here is friendly and informal; the staff is kindly, dedicated to helping these young people.

At the beginning of the play, David Clemens is described:

He is a tall, thin boy of sixteen. He is immaculately dressed, as he always is, in a dark suit, white shirt, dark tie. His blond hair is fault-lessly parted and combed, his black shoes faultlessly shined. His features are straight and fine, but his face has a taut, pinched quality. When he speaks, his voice is low and well modulated, but often with a tone of sarcasm or bitterness. His pronunciation is excellent—each word enunciated with clarity. There is a certain stiffness about his posture; he holds his back very straight and walks with notice-able rigidity.

David is mentally ill. Part of his illness is his fear of being touched by anyone. He actually feels that he may *die* if someone touches him. He feels compelled to perform certain ritualistic acts over and over again, such as washing his face or learning the exact time. He is also brilliant, particularly in mathematics, physics, drawing timepieces (his chief hobby) and playing chess.

His family lives in Connecticut. His mother is attractive, chic, domineering, overly possessive and overly seductive. At the conclusion of a meeting with David's psychiatrist, Dr. Alan Swinford, she stares at Alan "with a definite sexual challenge." She has little use for her husband. David is hostile toward her, terrified of her physical closeness. His father is a "successful, aggressive, no-nonsense type of man," who believes David could cure himself if he would only exert willpower.

Although David never touches anyone, when he is alone he longingly strokes a "torn, stuffed Teddy Bear, clearly a carryover from childhood."

Until recently, David had refused help from Alan, the psychiatrist. Although he has lived at this school since the beginning of the term (it is now close to Christmas), David has entered Alan's office only once to talk. He wanted to hear Alan's analysis of his recurring nightmare, which Alan interpreted as a fear of death.

David keeps pretty much to himself, showing no interest in the other patients, with one exception: Lisa.

Lisa is even sicker than David. "She is a startlingly beautiful girl of fifteen, but at times she appears to be much younger. She wears her black hair long, and she has large dark eyes." Part of her mental illness is that she assumes two different personalities: Lisa and Muriel. When she is Lisa, her mood is "pixieish and mischievous." She behaves like a little girl, hopping and jumping about, speaking only in rhyme. Her rhyming is an act she feels compelled to perform. She insists that everyone answer her in rhyme, except her psychiatrist, John. When she is her other self, Muriel, she usually acts "dreamy and remote," although not in this scene. As Muriel, she does not speak at all; she prints her thoughts on a pad, unintentionally misspelling most of the words.

The following is a description of an abrupt personality change:

Very suddenly, LISA stops her jumping around. The pixieish expression fades from her face. Her eyes, no longer crinkled up in a childish smile, are unusually large and lucid. Her movements are calm, as she walks * * * with ladylike dignity. Now, for the first time, she appears to be her actual age.

Lisa's parents are dead. "She's spent most of her life in orphanages and institutions." She has been under treatment here for three years. Although still quite ill, she has greatly improved since her arrival at the Berkely School.

Lisa had aroused David's interest the first time he met her. He will not admit to himself that he wants to be her friend. He realizes how sick she is; his attitude toward her is kindly, "almost professional." In reality, however, her attachment to someone else, her psychiatrist, fills him with jealousy.

SCENE: *The Day Room. At one table,* DAVID *is seated, looking at a science magazine. At the other table,* SIMON *and* ROBERT *are playing a game of chess. After a moment,* LISA *skips into the room and crosses directly to* DAVID.

LISA: David, David, look at me. Who do you see? Who do you see?

DAVID: Lisa I see—looking at me.

LISA: David, David, here you are. Come with me far, oh, far!

DAVID: Not now—not today—[*He fumbles for a rhyme*] I say. Some—some other day, I say. [*He tries to think of another rhyme*] Lisa—why must we rhyme? It's—it's so hard to do—and, and—it takes so much time.

LISA: Funny David, can't you see? Rhyming stops her—she then can't be.

DAVID: [*Excited by his discovery*] That's it—that's why! You stop Muriel! You don't have to be Muriel when you rhyme! [*During the above, as soon as* LISA *realizes he isn't rhyming, her face turns stormy. Now she rakes her hands through her hair and glowers at him, then she darts away.* DAVID *rises*] Lisa! Come back! I'll rhyme—this time!

LISA: [*Bitterly*] Rhyme—rhyme! Time-slime! Rhyme-slime!

     [LISA *sits at the other table. She draws a pad and crayons toward herself and begins to print.* DAVID *crosses and sits opposite her*]

DAVID: [*Penitently*] Talk to me—I'll rhyme, you'll see. [LISA *opens her mouth and throws back her head. She seems to be laughing, a deep, sarcastic but silent laugh. This combined with her wild hair gives her a menacing appearance, and* DAVID *is alarmed*] I'll walk or talk, I'll walk or talk! [LISA *holds up the pad; on it she has printed in huge letters: MURIEL.* DAVID *nods*] Okay, okay, I say, I say. You're Muriel today. [*She frowns, draws the pad back and prints on it: TAUK PLAIN STRAIT*] Fine. That makes it easier, if you don't want me to rhyme. [*He prints as he speaks*] Look, It's t-a-*l*-k, not t-a-*u*-k. You ought to learn how to spell. Spell it out loud for me. [LISA *prints a large NO*] It's all right, if you don't want to, Lisa. [LISA *immediately assumes the menacing expression. Hastily*] I mean Muriel! Frankly, I prefer the name Lisa. [LISA *rises and comes around the table, pointing her index finger at him. Terrified,* DAVID *jumps up and backs away from her. She follows him, her finger still pointing.* DAVID'S *expression is one of mixed fear and fury. He barks at her*] Don't you touch me! Now be careful— don't touch me! [ROBERT *and* SIMON *break off their chess game to watch;* ROBERT *avidly;* SIMON *with bored disgust.* LISA *pokes her finger at* DAVID *and draws it back quickly, two or three times, laughing her silent and sarcastic laugh. By this time,* DAVID *is backed as far as he can get.* LISA *continues to advance on him, threatening him with her finger*] Muriel, I warn you! Don't you touch me—don't, Muriel!

     [LISA *smiles a shy half-smile; returns to the table and sits down. Visibly unstrung.* DAVID *turns and hurries off*]

SUGGESTIONS FOR THE ACTOR

1. Both of you (David and Lisa) are mentally ill. You (the actors) may be wondering how to act "crazy." The answer to that

question is simple: Don't. Your character's behavior will certainly
seem "crazy" to anyone who does not share your character's particular delusions. The audience will undoubtedly think of you as
"sick." But your character's behavior would not be abnormal or
inappropriate *if* those delusions were real. Suppose, for example,
that you were hospitalized and that you refused to eat anything at
all. You would starve to death unless you were fed intravenously.
Crazy behavior, all right. Suppose, however, that you correctly
believed the food to be poisoned. In that case your behavior
would not be crazy at all. It would be normal and justified, appropriate to the dangerous circumstances. You, David, believe that
you may die if anyone touches you. If you, the actor, convince
yourself that this belief is correct, then your character's behavior
will no longer seem bizarre to you; anyone would react that
strongly if his life were really at stake.

If you, Lisa, really were a little girl instead of a fifteen-year-old,
then your running, jumping, giggling, silly rhyming, etc. would be
normal activities for your age. Your "crazy" behavior has a purpose similar to David's—self-preservation. We are not told much
in this play about your fears. We are given one strong clue, however, in this scene, when you, as Lisa, explain, "Rhyming stops
her—she then can't be." You are terrified of revealing something
within yourself, the part of yourself that you call Muriel. Remember that when you are Muriel, you act your real age. As Lisa,
you become a little child. You may be afraid because you consider
that part of yourself evil. In fairy tales and dreams and perhaps in
the mind of a very sick girl, evil is punishable by death. To save
your life, you must protect yourself. You never express yourself
freely because you have to suppress that part of yourself. As Lisa
you speak only in rhyme. When you are Muriel, you dare not
speak at all. Your fury at David when he refuses to "play the
game" will no longer seem crazy to you (the actress) when you
realize that he is destroying your protective disguise. He is tearing
down the barricades that you had so carefully erected in order to
hide Muriel and save yourself. You no longer make your psychiatrist "play the game," however, because you have grown to trust
him. You are confident that he will not hurt you.

We are not told what it is about Muriel that you (Lisa) fear.
You, the actress, are therefore free to invent specific reasons for

your panic, so long as they fit the given facts. In the original story by Dr. Rubin, the author suggests that Lisa fears her own uncontrollable anger.

2. Even though you (Lisa) do not speak when you become Muriel, you nevertheless express yourself clearly with your face and body. You are thinking a constant stream of words, not just the few that you print on your pad. You know exactly what David fears most. In the past you have agreed not to touch him, but now you want to get even with him. You know just how to do that.

3. If you (the actor) are having trouble believing in your character's delusions and feeling your character's panic, then try remembering and substituting a private terror of your own. Make sure that your fright is equivalent to the panic felt by the character you play. What did you *do* when you were terrified?

4. The chess players are not essential to this scene when it is performed out of context of the rest of the play. It would probably be advisable to eliminate these roles. Otherwise, the actors playing the nonspeaking roles of Simon and Robert must develop full characterizations in order to react in character to all that happens. Answering the questions on the "Actor's Check List," beginning on page 336, will help them create human beings onstage.

5. Until now you, David, have rhymed willingly enough. Why do you now object? One possibility: You have just spoken with Alan about your recurring nightmare. Perhaps you find his interpretation of your dream so disturbing that the effort of rhyming is too much for you at this moment. Another possibility: You are envious of John, Lisa's psychiatrist. She does not make *him* rhyme.

From *All the Way Home* by Tad Mosel, based on *A Death in the Family* by James Agee. Act III, Scene 1

INTRODUCTION

This Pulitzer Prize play by Tad Mosel was based on the novel *A Death in the Family,* also a Pulitzer Prize winner, by James Agee. It is about loss, but it is also about the many loving relationships that can exist within a family, with love spanning five generations. The older generations get reborn through the young.

The following scene takes place in Knoxville, Tennessee, in May of 1915. Rufus' father, Jay Follett, died two days before in an automobile accident. Jay had left home in the middle of the night because he had been told that his father was seriously ill. He had driven to his father's house, three hours away, in his old Ford. (Earlier that day the family had gone on an outing in Jay's brother's fancy new Chalmers, a car that makes sixty miles an hour.) Jay's father, as it turned out, had not been very sick after all, and Jay had headed back home the following day. On the way home, however, a small cotter pin had fallen out of the steering mechanism of his car; he had therefore lost control of the vehicle. His instantaneous death was apparently caused by a brain concussion when he was thrown against the steering wheel. He was then thrown clear of the car, which went up an eight-foot embankment.

Jay once had had a "drinking problem." He had since overcome it, but his past drinking was evidently remembered by the father of the "Third Boy" in this scene. Even Jay's widow, Mary, wonders whether Jay might have been drinking before the accident.

Rufus is a six-year-old boy. He had been close to his father, who had tenderly loved his wife and child. Jay had delighted in playing and talking with his young son. It had brought back his own lost youth. He would hoist Rufus on his shoulders and sing old songs to him. They had shared a love of railroad trains. He had been proud of Rufus' ability to read and spell. On a clear day this week he had told Rufus that "if you squint your eyes, you can see the North Pole." Rufus had been "enchanted."

Rufus is often teased by the three older boys. They make fun of his name. His father had told him to be proud of his name because it had been his great-grandfather's. Jay had told him to stand up for it, and to spell *b-r-a-v-e* and *p-r-o-u-d*. "Just keep spellin' that," he had said of the word "proud." He had also told Rufus, "One of these days you'll get those boys to shake you by the hand."

For a long time Rufus had wanted a sporty cap like the ones worn by the older boys, but his mother had made him wear conservative caps instead. When his understanding Aunt Hannah had come to visit two days ago, she had taken him shopping and allowed him to pick out a cap all by himself. By adult standards, it is loud and tasteless, "a thunderous fleecy cap in jade green, canary yellow, black and white, which sticks out inches to either side above his ears and has a great scoop of a visor beneath which his face is all but lost."

As the scene opens, Rufus wears a shirt and tie, knickers, a dark cap and jacket, and black shoes and stockings.

The older boys wear shoes or sneakers, stockings, knickers and shirts with ties or vests. They may wear sporty caps and jackets or sweaters.

AT RISE: RUFUS *in black is alone in his bedroom. He goes into his mother's room, down the stairs, into the kitchen, then into the living room. No one is around. He takes off his black cap, puts it on the sofa, then from under his jacket takes out his gaudy cap, puts it on and goes out into the street. The* BOYS *enter from down right on their way to school. The* FIRST BOY *runs past.*

RUFUS: My daddy's dead! [*The* BOY *ignores him*] My daddy's dead!

SECOND BOY: Huh! Betcha he ain't!

RUFUS: Why, he is so.

SECOND BOY: Where's your satchel at? You're just making up a lie so you can lay outa school.

RUFUS: I am not laying out, I'm just staying out, because my daddy's dead!

[*The* THIRD BOY *has joined them*]

THIRD BOY: He can lay out because his daddy got killed. [RUFUS *looks at him gratefully. And the* THIRD BOY *seems to regard him with something like respect*]

FIRST BOY: How do *you* know?

THIRD BOY: 'Cause my daddy seen it in the paper. Can't your daddy read?

RUFUS: [*Astounded*] The *news*paper—?

THIRD BOY: Sure, your daddy got his *name* in the papers. Yours too.

FIRST BOY: [*With growing respect*] *His* name's in the paper? Rufus'?

THIRD BOY: Him and his daddy both, right in the paper.

RUFUS: He was killed instintly. [*He snaps his fingers*]

THIRD BOY: What you get for drivin' a auto when you're drunk, that's what my daddy says.

RUFUS: What's drunk?

SECOND BOY: What's *drunk?* Drunk is fulla good ole whiskey. [*He staggers around in circles, weak-kneed, head lolling*] 'At's what drunk is.

RUFUS: Then he wasn't.

SECOND BOY: How do *you* know?

RUFUS: Because my daddy never walked like that.

THIRD BOY: How'd he get killed if he wasn't drunk?

RUFUS: He had a fatal accident.

SECOND BOY: How'd he *have* a fatal accident if he wasn't drunk?

RUFUS: It was kuhkushon.

SECOND BOY: Hell, you don't even know what you're talkin' about!

FIRST BOY: [*Simultaneously*] Don't even know how his own daddy got killed! [*They scoff and jeer.* RUFUS *begins to think he has lost his audience*]

THIRD BOY: My daddy says we gotta feel sorry for Rufus here 'cause he's an orphan.

RUFUS: I am?

THIRD BOY: Sure, like the Belgian kids, on'y worse, 'cause that's *war,* and my daddy says any kid that's made an orphan just 'cause his daddy gets drunk is a *pore kid.*

FIRST BOY: He says his daddy *wasn't* drunk.

SECOND BOY: Yeah.

RUFUS: Maybe he was a little.

FIRST BOY: Izzat so?

RUFUS: I remember now.

THIRD BOY: Sure he was.

SECOND BOY: Good ole whiskey.

THIRD BOY: Pore kid. My daddy says his ole Tin Lizzy run up a eight-foot embankment—

RUFUS: [*Bravely*] That's all you know about it.

FIRST BOY: [*To* THIRD] Let *him* tell it.

SECOND BOY: Yeah, *you* tell it, Rufus.

THIRD BOY: Well, come on and tell us then.

RUFUS: Well—it wasn't any old Tin Lizzy he was driving, in the first place, it was a—a Chalmers. And my daddy was going like sixty!

SECOND BOY: 'Cause he was drunk.

RUFUS: [*Nodding*] Good ole whiskey.

THIRD BOY: Pore kid.

RUFUS: [*Now completely confident*] And then the auto didn't run up any eight-foot embackemb—what you said—either, it ran up a—a pole.

THIRD BOY: *A pole?*

RUFUS: [*Jumping up on the swing*] a hundred feet high!

[*Doubts have now set in among the* THREE BOYS]

SECOND BOY: Aw, what kinduva pole is that?

RUFUS: The *north* pole. [*They stare at him blankly to see if it is an old joke, but he is too excited to notice. He points off*] Out there! If you squint your eyes you can see it! [*He squints his eyes and peers, searchingly, and the* THREE BOYS *look at one another.* ONE *makes circles with his forefinger at the side of his head,* ANOTHER *silently blubbers his lower lip,* ANOTHER *rolls his eyeballs back so that only the whites are showing*] Can you see it?

THE THREE BOYS: Oh, yeah! Sure, Rufus! We see it! So that's the North Pole! Hmmm! Always wondered where it was!

RUFUS: And my daddy's auto ran up it and fell right back on top of my daddy like— [*Suddenly he jumps from the swing*]— whomp! and that joggled his brain loose in his head and it—fell out and the hand of death came down out of the sky and scooped it up. [*Now somewhat out of breath*] And that's kuhkushon.

FOURTH BOY: [*Running on*] Hey, I'm waitin' on you.

FIRST BOY: [*Edging off*] Yeah. Sure, Rufus. Well, we gotta go. [RUFUS *quickly puts out his hand with supreme confidence. The* FIRST BOY *shakes it hurriedly*] S'long, Rufus.

SECOND BOY: [*Shaking* RUFUS' *hand*] That's a nice new cap you got, Rufus.

THIRD BOY: [*Shaking hands*] We'll be seeing yuh, Rufus.

[*They hurry off, looking back over their shoulders at him, talking among themselves, one saying "Whomp!" and clapping his hands together, another blubbering his lower lip, another staggering, whether in imitation of a drunk or an imbecile, it is hard to say.* RUFUS *looks after them, beaming with pride. The* BOYS *go.* RUFUS *is alone*]

RUFUS: P-r-o-u-d. [*Scuffling into the living room, making up a song*] B-r-a-v-e-p-r-o-u-d. [*Gets a pipe, picks up paper, sits in Morris chair*] "He is sur-sur-vived by his wi-wife, Mary." Mama has her name in the paper. "And a son—Rufus." Me! My daddy's dead. Whomp! He can't ever come home—not tomorrow or the next day or the next day or the next day or the next day or the next day or the next day— [*He is crying. He throws the pipe, newspaper and ashtray aside*] Whomp! Good ole whiskey! Whomp! Good ole whiskey! Good ole whiskey! Good ole whiskey! Good ole whiskey!

SUGGESTIONS FOR THE ACTOR

1. For the actor playing Rufus: You may be acting the part of a child much younger than yourself. Observe some six-year-olds. Then, as an exercise, perform these and other activities as a six-year-old boy might do them: walk, run, jump, sit, try to snap your fingers, shake hands (use a partner for this activity), make up a song, pretend to smoke your father's pipe, try to read a newspaper aloud, paint a picture, try to paint a wall without making a mess, storm about the room in a fury, "hitting and banging the furniture." Why are you enraged? (Invent a reason different from Rufus' in the above scene.)

2. It is hard to climb or descend imaginary stairs in a believable way. Unless you can use real steps, it would probably be best to begin the scene with your (Rufus') entrance into the living room.

Why do you put on your "gaudy cap" and go outside? Why do you call out, "My daddy's dead!" when you see the other boys?

3. For Rufus: When the boys begin to scoff and jeer after you tell them that your father's death was caused by "kuhkushon" (concussion), how do you attempt to win them over? For a while you succeed in your attempt. They believe you when you pretend that you remember seeing your daddy drunk. They believe you when you claim that your daddy drove a Chalmers, which "was going like sixty." But your imagination gets the better of you; you go too far. When you tell the boys that the pole was a hundred feet high, they begin to doubt you. When you tell them the pole was the North Pole, you lose your audience altogether. Now the boys humor you as though you were a lunatic or an idiot. You are blissfully unaware, however, of the change that has just taken place. You do not catch their sarcasm or the faces and gestures they make to each other. When they shake your hand, you think you have won a great victory. Your daddy told you, "When a man shakes you by the hand, that means you've won him over." You are p-r-o-u-d of your accomplishment.

According to the stage directions you jump up on a swing while you are feverishly inventing that wild story. You, the actor, can easily replace that physical action with another—running, jumping, turning, performing a handspring, etc.—any movement that reflects your intense inner excitement.

Do you, Rufus, really believe that you can see the North Pole if you squint? How much of your story do you believe?

4. This scene may be ended with the departure of the three boys. Unless you, the actor playing Rufus, can perform the final soliloquy (speech alone on stage) without *forcing* your emotions, do not act it at all. This monologue is difficult to act truthfully because you, Rufus, become hysterical after you read your father's obituary in the newspaper. You keep repeating the sound "whomp," which evidently represents the blow of the auto falling on your father. (In reality, the car did not even touch your father when it fell back, next to his dead body.) At the end of the soliloquy "RUFUS storms about the room, hitting and banging the furniture." This seems to be the first time that you, Rufus, break down since your father's death. In the first part of the scene you are actually *using* the tragedy as a means of gaining the sympathy and

respect of the older boys. Yet you dearly loved your father. Is this the first moment that your loss hits you full force?

Sometimes when tragedy occurs, one doesn't feel the impact right away. It often takes time to comprehend the significance of what has happened. At first one may feel nothing at all. Have you, the actor, ever experienced a tragic loss? If so, what was your initial reaction? When did you fully realize that your loved one (a person or perhaps even a beloved pet) was gone forever? Did you become hysterical? What did you want? What did you do? Try to remember concretely everything you saw, heard, smelled, touched and tasted at that time.

5. For the actors playing the three older boys: The play itself does not provide information regarding the family backgrounds, personalities, etc. of the characters you play. You will each have to imagine your own "biography." Of course you must give yourself a name. How old are you? Answer the questions on the "Actor's Check List," beginning on page 336. What is your relationship with each of the other boys in the scene? Is one of you the leader? If so, which one? What is your attitude toward Rufus? Why do the three of you torment him all the time? Improvise a scene (make it up as you perform) in which the three of you plan to tease Rufus. Imagine that this conversation takes place before the death of Rufus' father.

From *I Too Speak of the Rose* by Emilio Carballido, translated from the Spanish by William I. Oliver

INTRODUCTION

Mexican playwright Emilio Carballido combines the realistic with the fantastic in a striking manner. He presents a realistic incident in the following scene. Two children playing in a garbage dump accidentally derail a freight train. The accident later results in enormous financial losses when scavengers remove all the over-turned freight. The children are jailed.

We are then shown how different the same simple incident can appear to people with different preconceptions. The same events are seen next from the viewpoint of a Freudian professor, then a Marxist professor and finally the accident is interpreted through the mystical visions of a medium.

Here is an account of what actually happens before the children make their way along the railroad tracks to the garbage dump.

Early one morning on a school day, a young boy called Polo (his real name is Leopoldo Bravo) attempts to remove coins from a telephone booth with a wire. Toña, a young girl, stands guard. He extracts a coin. Pleased, they approach a candy vendor and "flip coins" with him for candy. The vendor lets them have some candy, but they gamble away their bus fare. Now they cannot get to school. They don't mind, however, since Toña neglected to do her homework anyway, and Polo has no shoes ("Can't buy any until next week"). They spend all but five cents of their little remaining change on food. To his amazement, Polo finds twenty cents in the phone booth when he simply lifts the telephone and replaces it on the hook.

An adult friend of theirs arrives, a young man named Maximino, who works in a garage. He warns them against tampering with pay telephones. His motorcycle is broken. Polo and Maximino discuss this mechanical difficulty "man to man." Polo belittles Toña because she is ignorant of such matters; she in turn scoffs at Maximino's old motorcycle. Maximino offers to give the children their bus fare, but Toña wants him to write an excuse for their absence instead. He asks them where they "plan to hang out all morning." The garbage dump by the railroad tracks, they tell him. Says Polo, "We may find something. You can see the train go by." Toña takes Maximino's picture from his wallet; she wants to keep it on her mirror because she has a "crush" on him. Maximino obliges Toña by writing a little note on the picture. She comes upon a photograph of Maximino's girl friend and makes fun of her, calling her "cross-eyed." Again offering them bus fare, Maximino takes his leave.

*The lights * * * come up on the dump. It is a great carpet of garbage surrounded by a few plants and branches. In the background we see the railroad tracks. It is bright daylight. The* SCAVENGERS *walk about examining the garbage, picking up papers and stray bottles. They save some and discard others. One of the* SCAVENGERS *steps on a piece of glass and hurts her foot. She exclaims softly, and goes off limping and grumbling. The man looks at the woman but goes on scavenging. He kneels down amid the garbage and discovers a shoe. He examines it but leaves it behind.* POLO *and* TOÑA *enter upstage balancing on the railroad track. The* SCAVENGER *was about to leave. He has been gathering the things he wanted to save when he sees the kids. He speaks to them.*

SCAVENGER: [*In need of a drink*] Say, uh . . . you wouldn't have five cents, would you?

POLO: No.

SCAVENGER: I need it . . . you know for a cure. I'm in a bad way, sonny.

[POLO *shakes his head. The* SCAVENGER *starts off*]

TOÑA: Oh, mister . . . Go on, Polo, give it to him! Mister, come here!

[POLO *makes a face but gives him the money*]

SCAVENGER: (*Mumbling so that he is scarcely understood*] God bless you. Bless you. [*And he goes off*] Yeah.

TOÑA: Did you give him everything?

POLO: Sure.

TOÑA: He only asked for five cents! Oh, you're so stupid!

POLO: You told me to give it to him!

TOÑA: But not everything . . . he only asked you for five cents!!

POLO: You're crazy . . . and what's worse, you're dumb!

TOÑA: That's what you say. . . . God, what a stink.

POLO: Garbage.

TOÑA: Smells of weeds, too. Real . . . real stinky weeds . . . see them over there!? And it smells of . . . oh, look at the flies! There's a dead animal somewhere, for sure! [*She breaks into song, imitating some orchestral arrangement of a dance tune*]

POLO: You crazy?

TOÑA: You know how to dance? My sister taught me this one. Look. [*She executes a step while she sings*] You know how?

POLO: Yes. [*He dances with her for a while and then he backs away letting her dance by herself*] Here's part of an engine. [*He reaches into the garbage and pulls out an unrecognizable piece of steel. He turns it about in his hands examining it*]

TOÑA: What's it for?

POLO: An engine. I'll take it to Maximino. [*He puts it down to one side*]

TOÑA: I'm going to pick some flowers. [*She begins to pick the tiny, little flowers. All of a sudden she screams*]

POLO: What's wrong?

TOÑA: I got pricked. It's got thorns. OOoogh, my, my, my! *She sucks her finger then, truculently*] Look . . . it drew blood. [*She sings and dances a new step, and picks more flowers*]

POLO: I went to see the *Masked Avenger Against the Monsters* yesterday.

TOÑA: On Sunday I went to see the *Black Shadow of the Mansion* . . . Frightened me so much I screamed that night because I was having dreams.

POLO: What did you dream of?

TOÑA: I don't know. It was ugly . . . Those are wasps. Oh, look! There's lots of them. They sting!

POLO: Only if you're afraid of them. [*He balances on the railroad track*] I hear there are guys that walk on a wire way up high and they carry a stick so's to hold their balance. They walk across the wire. You think it's true?

TOÑA: Sure. I've seen them in the movies.

POLO: Yeah, but in the movies that's all tricks.

TOÑA: I saw a woman who climbs up on a horse and stands up, you know. And then she stands on one foot like this and the horse runs around, I saw her . . . a circus.

POLO: When did you go to a circus?

TOÑA: Once . . . my father took me!

POLO: Your father's dead.

TOÑA: He took me before he died! He was pretty nice, my father. And there was a bear on a little bicycle . . .

POLO: What's so hard about riding a bicycle?

TOÑA: Well, it was damn hard for the bear. Look at the little flowers I got . . .

POLO: Not many.

TOÑA: I'll pick more later on. I don't want to be stung by a wasp. Hey . . . see that tub over there? That would be great for planting flowers! Gee, you could put a big plant inside of that one. [*It's a round zinc washtub. She goes to pick it up but she cannot lift it*] It's heavy!

POLO: I'll bet! [*He gives her a Bronx cheer*] What's the matter, can't you pick it up? [*He goes to her. He tries but cannot lift it. He tries again. It won't budge. He straddles it. He can't move it. She laughs so hard she drops her flowers. She continues laughing as she picks them up*] What the hell! What's the matter with this thing, huh? [*He is actually scared of it*]

[TOÑA *suddenly stops laughing. She too senses something unreal about the weight of the object*]

TOÑA: Can't you move it?

POLO: [*Worried*] No.

[TOÑA *exclaims and moves away from it holding the flowers to her breast*]

TOÑA: Gee, it's funny it should weigh so much!

POLO: Chicken! [*But he, too, moves away from the tub. There is a pause*] Let's find out what the hell's the matter with it.

TOÑA: You'd better leave it alone.

POLO: [*Walking beside the tub cautiously*] I wonder why it's so heavy. [*Then, understanding*] It's full of cement.

TOÑA: Yeah? I wonder why.

POLO: Must be one of those things bricklayers use or masons for . . . well I don't know . . . something. Look, it's full of cement!

TOÑA: So that's it. [*She examines it*] Yeah, it *is* full of cement. You couldn't plant any plants in that. [*She starts singing and dancing again and puts some of the flowers in her hair*] What do you think?

POLO: [*Pushing the tub with his foot*] Hey, you can roll it! Want to help me? Come on!

TOÑA: Wait a minute. [*She puts some more flowers in her hair*] All right. [*She helps him and the two of them push the tub*] Where will we take it?

POLO: To the other side of the tracks. [*They roll the tub upstage*] It's harder if we go that way.

[*They push the tub in the most difficult direction, upstage and to the left. We hear a train whistle*]

TOÑA: The train's coming! Hurry up!

[*They hurry. They are now at the very highest point. We hear the train whistle again. They look at each other*]

THE TWO OF THEM: Let's put it on the tracks!

[*The idea makes them giggle nervously and happily as they push the tub. It is heavy and there are obstacles in the way. It starts to roll back but they push. The train whistles once more, closer. They push the tub, then run off. Whistles. The train approaches, the lights dim, and we hear the racket of a derailment. Darkness. Flashes of lightning reveal the young pair as they stare with fascination. Darkness*]

NEWSBOY: [*We hear him in the dark*] Read all about the derailment! Great losses! Great losses! Disaster caused by delinquent children! The *Daily Press!* Get your *Daily Press!*

SUGGESTIONS FOR THE ACTOR

1. Any number of actors may take the roles of Scavengers. The actor playing the Scavenger with speaking lines should read the discussion on p. 298 of playing a drunk. If actors cannot be ob-

tained for these "bit" parts, you may begin the scene with Toña's question "Did you give him everything?"

2. For the performers playing Polo and Toña: In this exercise you concentrate on imagining and "using" the washtub, and on communicating with your partner.

(a) Enact this incident (derived from the scene) without speaking, as yourselves rather than Polo and Toña. You, the actress, visualize the "round zinc washtub." Walk over to it and try to lift it. Concentrate on "seeing" it and "feeling" its immense weight. You cannot budge it. Since *you* use it first, you must make clear to your partner the size of the imaginary tub, its shape and its exact location. You, the actor, must observe her actions carefully, visualize the washtub yourself, walk over to it and try to lift it. It must not change at all in size, shape or position when you attempt to lift it. You straddle it. You cannot move it either. As you both gaze at the (imaginary) object, you develop a certain attitude toward it: you both become afraid of it, sensing something "unreal" about its incredible weight. Without speaking, you communicate your feelings to each other. You both move away from the washtub. Then you, the actor, return to it, discovering that it is filled with cement. You experiment with it. You push it with your foot and find out that you can roll it. Wordlessly you communicate to your partner that you would like her to help you roll it. You, the actress, agree to help him. Together, with tremendous difficulty, you roll it a little way uphill. Suddenly you hear a train whistle. You look at each other. Either you both decide at the same instant to roll it downhill onto the tracks, or one of you gets the idea first and shares it with the other through looks, gestures and movements. You push. "It is heavy and there are obstacles in the way. It starts to roll back" but you push harder and finally succeed in rolling it all the way down the hill onto the tracks. "See" the washtub hit an approaching train, the derailment and the overturning of all the freight, sack after sack of food. React as you think you would in real life. Would you look at your friend? If so, what message would you convey?

In order for the two of you to push the washtub *together,* you must be aware of each other, and you must communicate. It is all right to make sounds, such as grunts, giggles, sighs or shouts, if they "come naturally." *Never mouth words.* Don't try to impress the audience with the tremendous weight of the tub, or the effort required to push. Don't try to give a performance.

(b) Now act this exercise again, adding words this time if talking will help you to solve your immediate problem. Don't talk just for the sake of making conversation.

(c) Now perform this same exercise as Polo and Toña, inventing your own words as you act. Again, don't talk any more than is necessary. This time respond to the accident as the characters do in the written play. Fascinated, you watch, paralyzed with fear as you begin to comprehend what you have done.

3. As Polo and Toña, act the entire scene without speaking. In other words, perform all the *physical actions* of the characters you play. Focus on everything you see, hear, smell, feel and taste. It is morning. The sun is shining brightly—on piles of garbage. Imagine the railroad track on which you balance. How wide is it? For purposes of this exercise, you get off the track and scavenge too. You walk through the garbage. Smell it! You smell "stinky weeds" and perhaps a "dead animal." "See" and "hear" the flies buzzing around you. How do you react to them? Notice various objects among the garbage; pick up some of these things, examine them (with all your senses—except for taste) and discard them. Avoid bits of broken glass. Notice the few plants and branches nearby and the little flowers. A Scavenger approaches you, Polo, for money. You shake your head. You, Toña, wordlessly communicate to Polo that you want him to give the money to the Scavenger. (Do you nudge him? In what other ways might you convey your desire?) Play the rest of the physical actions in the scene. Your character must have a reason for every movement and gesture. Perform all the physical actions which you think you will use when you act the written scene—those actions indicated in the script and/or those you add yourself.

4. Was there any part of the last exercise that gave you particular trouble? If so, work on that section as a separate exercise. You may be having trouble performing a physical action, such as Toña's dance, or finding a suitable reason for an action. You may be having difficulty remembering a sense impression, such as the smell of garbage, the sound of a train whistle or the prick of a thorn on your finger. This exercise is for your benefit only. Con-

centrate on believing in what you are doing yourself; ignore the audience, if there is one.

5. Answer the questions on the "Actor's Check List," beginning on page 336. Those of you with "bit" parts must invent the past lives of the characters you play. We know from the play itself that you, Polo and Toña, are both poor. Polo, your mother works for a "lady," perhaps as a domestic. Toña, your mother does menial work at a hospital. We know that you, Polo, are repeating fifth grade. Your teacher thinks children who fail should not be readmitted to school. She has no sympathy for you, no understanding of the problems of the poor. When you are put in jail, your mother scolds you and calls you names. She says that your father was a "drunken good-for-nothing," that she should have let him beat you, that she always spoiled you and kept you tied to her apron strings. In truth, she loves you more than your brothers; you are her favorite. We learn from the scene included here that you, Toña, had a warm relationship with your father before he died. You have a kind, loving mother, who brings your favorite candy to jail. She describes you as, "The one who helped me most. Such a good girl. Poor thing." Your sister Paca, who is probably older than you, gives your mother her good pin to bring to you. Previously, she would always get angry when you wore it. You have other sisters too, younger than Paca.

Decide where in Mexico you live. It would be helpful to learn a little about life and customs in that part of Mexico, including the customs of children. What are typical Mexican foods, games, sports, costumes, songs, dances, celebrations? Can you find any information about Mexican schools? Browse through books about Mexico in your library; study the photographs of places and people.

From *Junior Miss* by Jerome Chodorov and Joseph Fields, based on the book by Sally Benson. Act III

INTRODUCTION

This bubbly, lighthearted comedy was first produced in 1941 and has enjoyed wide popularity ever since.

The setting is "the living room of the Graves's home in Manhattan's upper 60s off Central Park." The neighborhood is upper class, but "The total effect is middle class, of people who have a fairly steady struggle to maintain their position." The Graves family consists of an attractive couple in their thirties, Harry and Grace, still in love, and their two adolescent daughters. Lois is a pretty, popular sixteen-year-old, with an air of sophisticated detachment. Judy is "13, tall for her age and heavily built. From her shoulders to her knees, she is entirely shapeless, which gives her a square broad look in spite of her height." She has muscular legs covered with scratches and a little round stomach. Judy's best friend is Fuffy, who lives on a lower floor in the same apartment building. "FUFFY is the same age and height as JUDY * * * and overflowing with animal spirits. She is blond and not quite so lumpy."

Judy and Fuffy are movie fans; in their daily lives they constantly play the roles of their favorite screen stars. They therefore misinterpret and overdramatize ordinary as well as not-so-ordinary events. Influenced by a movie entitled *Wife vs. Secretary*, Judy wrongly concludes that her father is having an affair with his boss's daughter Ellen. She also mistakenly believes that her uncle Willis is an ex-convict. He has just returned to New York after

having been away ten years for reasons nobody has explained to
Judy. Her inspiration is another movie, called *Criminal Code*. She
determines to make a match between Ellen and Uncle Willis, to
save her parents' marriage and to help Uncle Willis "go straight."
Her plan succeeds only too well. Ellen has been very much
overshadowed by her domineering father, J. B. Curtis, blustery,
insensitive and highly successful in his law practice. On New Year's
Day J.B. comes to visit, in order to announce that he plans to give
Harry Graves a junior partnership in his firm. Harry and Grace
are resting because of hangovers after a New Year's Eve party.
Judy speaks with J.B. privately, asking him to hire an ex-convict,
Uncle Willis, because he and Ellen are engaged! Nobody but Judy
and Fuffy knew that Ellen and Willis were even acquainted, much
less engaged! J.B. is furious. When Ellen and Willis arrive with
the surprise announcement that they are already married, J.B.
blames Harry for everything. In a foul mood from his bad hangover, Harry refuses to placate J.B. and he is fired.

The next evening Judy is dressing for a party, her first formal
dance. She wears a bathrobe over her underclothes. She overhears
a dismal conversation between her parents. Harry suggests that
Grace and the girls move in with their grandparents in Kansas
City for a while until he can find another job, because they have
no savings. Normally Judy and her sister, Lois, are far from sweet
to each other, but when Judy, sobbing, tells Lois the awful news,
Lois does her best to comfort Judy. Judy "embraces her lovingly."
Just then Fuffy knocks and enters. She wears a wrapper and her
hair is in curlers. She has a different shade of polish on each
fingernail, "ranging from mother-of-pearl to deep purple," so that
the girls can help her choose which color to wear to the party that
night. Her brother will escort her, and his friend is supposed to
take Judy. Lois calls the nail polish "revolting." She says it is disgusting for Fuffy to "try to act like a femme fatale," and she stalks
out of the room. "FUFFY looks after her scornfully."

FUFFY: [*Sitting on arm of sofa*] Boy, what a poison puss!

JUDY: [*Instantly*] Don't you dare call my only sister Lois a
poison puss!

FUFFY: [*Stares at her wide-eyed*] Huh?

JUDY: [*Pugnaciously*] You heard me!

FUFFY: [*Rising*] Since when has that drip become your sister?

JUDY: [*Advancing on her*] I warned you, Fuffy!

FUFFY: [*Backing away*] Okay, okay—I take it back. Say, what's the matter with you? Are you goin' screwy? Boy, you've changed since the last time I saw you!

JUDY: [*Nods profoundly, goes to chair*] Yes, Fuffy— You know, in the last fifteen minutes I've aged *fifteen years*.

FUFFY: [*Impressed*] What happened?

JUDY: I can't tell you anything except that we have suddenly become poverty-stricken.

FUFFY: [*Awed*] No kiddin'?

JUDY: [*Nods*] Yes, and what's more—I'm not going to the party.

FUFFY: You're *not?*

JUDY: [*Enjoying herself tremendously*] What's the use? It'd be a farce to pretend that I'm enjoying myself at a time like this.

FUFFY: But what happened?

JUDY: Never mind—you saw *The Grapes of Wrath,* didn't you? Well, we're practically Okies.

FUFFY: Oh, Judy! You mean you're migrating away?

JUDY: Yeah—Pop lost his job and we're going to live in Kansas City.

FUFFY: How ghastly! . . . But what about *me?* You're the only true friend I ever had. We've been through so much together!

JUDY: [*Sadly*] Yes, we've been bosom friends ever since that first day in the elevator when we first decided to be bosom friends.

FUFFY: And what about the basketball team? We'll never find another roving center like *you!*

JUDY: [*Nods and sighs, rises*] It can't be helped. The school is suffering no more than I am.

FUFFY: Oh, Judy, you just *can't* go. You're the only thing that makes my family bearable.

JUDY: But what can I do?

FUFFY: Oh, there *must* be something. . . . [*Suddenly struck with an idea*] Maybe you could get a job and take some of the strain off your father?

JUDY: A job! What kind of a job?

FUFFY: Oh, any kind of a job just to begin with. Even if it's only thirty-five or forty dollars a week.

JUDY: [*Eagerly*] Oh, that's wonderful, Fuffy! Then I could redeem myself! Oh, wouldn't that be super?

FUFFY: We'll cut school tomorrow and go 'round answering all the classified ads.

JUDY: [*Offering her hand*] What a pal!

[*They shake solemnly*]

FUFFY: [*Nobly*] I don't have to go to this party, you know. I could stay home and keep you company.

JUDY: No, Fuffy, you run along and enjoy yourself . . . and— when the phonograph is playing and they're all dancing I know there'll be one person thinking of me.

FUFFY: Who?

JUDY: Why, you, of course.

FUFFY: Oh, yes, naturally.

JUDY: I'd rather have it that way.

FUFFY: Gee, Judy, I hope when my crisis comes I can face it as bravely as you have!

SUGGESTIONS FOR THE ACTOR

1. Now is your chance to be a "ham" and still remain completely in character. As Judy and Fuffy, you both adore melodrama. Avid moviegoers, you are constantly building elaborate plots around real-life people and situations, acting the parts of imaginary heroines. You think nothing of changing roles—and movie plots—from moment to moment. In this brief scene you, Judy, assume many different melodramatic roles. You relish each one in turn: Defender of Lois, Poor Migrant (find out who the Okies were in American history and in John Steinbeck's novel *The Grapes of Wrath*), Bosom Friend, Family Breadwinner and Martyr. Decide which role you are playing at every moment of the scene.

2. Improvise this scene not shown in the play: Your first meeting in the elevator, when both of you, two strangers, *decided* right then and there to be "bosom friends." Plan your circumstances first: When is this happening (the year, the season, the month, the day of the week and time of day)? How old are you? How is each of you dressed? Where is each of you coming from? Where are you going? Why? (Is the elevator going up or down?) You might wish to include an elevator operator in the scene, whose reactions to your conversation would depend upon his or her particular circumstances and frame of mind.

3. For Fuffy Adams: The play provides you with a few hints about your family background, but not many. We know from your mother's phone calls that she "cramps your style." You resent her restrictions and refer to her as "the menace." You have a fifteen-year-old brother named Barlow, who resembles you. He plays poker, or claims he does, and even though he is escorting you to the formal party, he dislikes dancing. We know that Judy's father does not think much of your father's intelligence. You went to a "progressive" private school, where you were encouraged to express yourself freely. Hence your language is sometimes coarser than Judy's. You, the actress playing Fuffy, will have to use your own imagination in creating a detailed background for your character. (See "Actor's Check List," beginning on page 336.)

4. In the early 1940s, when this play was a Broadway hit,

"thirty-five or forty dollars a week" had far more value than that amount has now. The equivalent salary today would be more than four times that amount. The humor of Fuffy's lines, "Oh, any kind of job just to begin with. Even if it's only thirty-five or forty dollars a week," lay in the fact that a thirteen-year-old girl could not possibly earn that much money at the time. Fuffy, however, is dead serious.

You might choose to bring the scene up to date. If it were set in the present, the salary Fuffy mentioned would have to be vastly increased. The line "* * * you saw *The Grapes of Wrath,* didn't you?" might also be altered in order to indicate that you, Judy, are referring to a *revival* of that movie classic. You might say, for instance, "You saw *The Grapes of Wrath* on TV, didn't you?" or "You saw *The Grapes of Wrath* at the Museum of Modern Art, didn't you?" (The Museum of Modern Art is a Manhattan art museum where old films are shown regularly.)

From *The Effect of Gamma Rays on Man-in-the-Moon Marigolds* by Paul Zindel.
Act II

INTRODUCTION

This compelling drama by Paul Zindel takes place in an incredibly sloppy, all-purpose downstairs room made of wood, formerly a vegetable store, situated in a small town. It is now part of a house inhabited by Beatrice, a poor, frustrated, bitter widow, her two teen-age daughters, Ruth and Tillie, Nanny, a very old, helpless woman whom Beatrice gets paid to tend, and a pet rabbit in a cage. "A door to NANNY'S room leads off from this main room * * * There is a hallway and a telephone. A heavy wooden stair-case leads to a landing with a balustrade, two doors, and a short hall. BEATRICE sleeps in one room; TILLIE and RUTH share the other."

The kitchen area is near the bottom of .the staircase. Most of the front window (formerly the storefront) is covered over with newspapers.

One reason for Beatrice's frustration is that her responsibility toward Nanny ties her to the house. She has no interest in or un-derstanding of Tillie's aspirations. Tillie is an extraordinarily gifted young scientist. In Act I, Ruth "gives the impression of being slightly strange. Her hair isn't quite combed, her sweater doesn't quite fit, etc." She had undergone a nervous breakdown in the re-cent past. She suffers now from hysterical seizures.

Early in Act I, Tillie begs her mother for permission to attend school that day; her science teacher is going to perform an experiment. Beatrice refuses her permission. She needs Tillie for chores at home. While getting ready for school, Ruth tells her mother that everyone laughed at Tillie yesterday at the school science assembly when she cranked the model of an atom, because of her ridiculous appearance. "She had that old jumper on * * * and a raggy slip that showed all over and her hair looked like she was struck by lightning." Ruth also informs her mother that the school keeps a "history" of their family and its peculiarities. It says that Ruth exaggerates and tells lies and has nightmares.

In the next sequence Tillie brings home marigold seeds for her special science experiment; they have been exposed to cobalt-60. She plants them carefully in boxes. Later, Ruth has a seizure because of a nightmare. For the first time in this play Beatrice reveals a softer side to her nature. With great kindness and warmth she comforts Ruth. At the end of Act I Ruth rushes home; she is bursting with pride because Tillie is one of the finalists in the Science Fair. The principal telephones Beatrice. When the principal asks her, as Tillie's mother, to sit up on the stage at the final judging, Beatrice is terrified that both mother and daughter will be laughed at. She says to Tillie, "I'd look just like you up on the stage, ugly little you!" Tillie begins to cry. Beatrice suddenly glimpses what she has done to her child. At the end of Act I, Tillie starts toward her mother, who "opens her arms to receive her."

In Act II, we learn that Beatrice has painstakingly printed the titles on Tillie's three-panel screen. Enormously proud of her daughter, she has come to realize at last that Tillie has brought honor upon them.

Act II opens with the following scene:

The room looks somewhat cheery and there is excitement in the air. It is early evening and preparations are being made for TILLIE *to take her project to the final judging of the Science Fair.*

TILLIE *has been dressed by her mother in clothes which are clean but too girlish for her awkwardness. Her hair has*

*been curled, she sports a large bow, and her dress is a
starched flair.*

RUTH *has dressed herself up as well. She has put on too
much makeup, and her lipstick has been extended beyond
the natural line of her lips. She almost appears to be sinis-
ter.*

*A large three-panel screen stands on one of the tables.
THE EFFECT OF GAMMA RAYS ON MAN-IN-THE-
MOON MARIGOLDS is printed in large letters running
across the top of the three panels. Below this on each panel
there is a subtopic:* THE PAST; THE PRESENT; THE FUTURE.
Additional charts and data appear below the titles.

RUTH: The only competition you have to worry about is Janice
Vickery. They say she caught it near Princess Bay Boulevard
and it was still alive when she took the skin off it.

TILLIE: [*Taking some plants from* RUTH] Let me do that, please,
Ruth.

RUTH: I'm sorry I touched them, really.

TILLIE: Why don't you feed Peter?

RUTH: Because I don't feel like feeding him . . . Now I feel like
feeding him. [*She gets some lettuce from a bag*] I heard that it
screamed for three minutes after she put it in because the water
wasn't boiling yet. How much talent does it take to boil the skin
off a cat and then stick the bones together again? That's what I
want to know. Ugh. I had a dream about that, too. I figure she
did it in less than a day and she ends up as one of the top five
winners . . . and you spend months growing atomic flowers.

TILLIE: Don't you think you should finish getting ready?

RUTH: Finish? This is it!

TILLIE: Are you going to wear that sweater?

RUTH: Look, don't worry about me. I'm not getting up on any
stage, and if I did I wouldn't be caught dead with a horrible
bow like that.

TILLIE: Mother put it—

RUTH: They're going to laugh you off the stage again like when
you cranked that atom in assembly . . . I didn't mean that . . .
The one they're going to laugh at is Mama.

TILLIE: What?

RUTH: I said the one they're going to laugh at is Mama . . . Oh,
let me take that bow off.

TILLIE: It's all right.

RUTH: Look, just sit still. I don't want everybody making fun of
you.

TILLIE: What made you say that about Mama?

RUTH: Oh, I heard them talking in the Science Office yesterday.
Mr. Goodman and Miss Hanley. She's getting $12.63 to chap-
eron the thing tonight.

TILLIE: What were they saying?

RUTH: Miss Hanley was telling Mr. Goodman about Mama . . .
when she found out you were one of the five winners. And he
wanted to know if there was something wrong with Mama because she sounded crazy over the phone. And Miss Hanley said
she *was* crazy and she always has been crazy and she can't wait
to see what she looks like after all these years. Miss Hanley said
her nickname used to be *Betty the Loon.*

TILLIE: [*As* RUTH *combs her hair*] Ruth, you're hurting me.

RUTH: She was just like you and everybody thought she was a
big weirdo. There! You look much better! [*She goes back to the
rabbit*] Peter, if anybody stuck you in a pot of boiling water I'd
kill them, do you know that? . . . [*Then to* TILLIE] What do
they call boiling the skin off a cat? I call it murder, that's what I
call it. They say it was hit by a car and Janice just scooped it up
and before you could say *bingo* it was screaming in a pot of
boiling water . . .

Do you know what they're all waiting to see? Mama's feathers!
That's what Miss Hanley said. She said Mama blabs as though

she was the Queen of England and just as proper as can be, and that her idea of getting dressed up is to put on all the feathers in the world and go as a bird. Always trying to get somewhere, like a great big bird.

TILLIE: Don't tell Mama, please. It doesn't matter.

RUTH: I was up there watching her getting dressed and sure enough, she's got the feathers out.

TILLIE: You didn't tell her what Miss Hanley said?

RUTH: Are you kidding? I just told her I didn't like the feathers and I didn't think she should wear any. But I'll bet she doesn't listen to me.

TILLIE: It doesn't matter.

RUTH: It doesn't matter? Do you think I want to be laughed right out of the school tonight, with Chris Burns there, and all? Laughed right out of the school, with your electric hair and her feathers on that stage, and Miss Hanley splitting her sides?

TILLIE: Promise me you won't say anything.

RUTH: On one condition.

TILLIE: What?

RUTH: Give Peter to me.

TILLIE: [*Ignoring her*] The taxi will be here any minute and I won't have all this stuff ready. Did you see my speech?

RUTH: I mean it. Give Peter to me.

TILLIE: He belongs to all of us.

RUTH: For me. All for me. What do you care? He doesn't mean anything to you any more, now that you've got all those crazy plants.

TILLIE: Will you stop?

RUTH: If you don't give him to me I'm going to tell Mama that everybody's waiting to laugh at her.

TILLIE: Where are those typewritten cards?

RUTH: I MEAN IT! Give him to me!

TILLIE: Does he mean that much to you?

RUTH: Yes!

TILLIE: All right.

RUTH: [*After a burst of private laughter*] Betty the Loon . . .
[*She laughs again*] That's what they used to call her, you
know, Betty the Loon!

TILLIE: I don't think that's very nice.

RUTH: First they had Betty the Loon, and now they've got Tillie
the Loon . . . [*To rabbit*] You don't have to worry about me
turning you in for any old plants . . .
How much does a taxi cost from here to the school?

TILLIE: Not much.

RUTH: I wish she'd give me the money it costs for a taxi—and
for all that cardboard and paint and flowerpots and stuff. The
only time she ever made a fuss over me was when she drove me
nuts.

TILLIE: Tell her to hurry, please.

SUGGESTIONS FOR THE ACTOR

1. When you, Tillie, miss the cards which contain your all-impor-
tant speech, you undoubtedly hunt for them. Of course you do not
know where they are, but you, the actress playing Tillie, really do
know. Yet you must convince yourself that you do not know
where they will turn up, that each place you search may be the
right place. Don't anticipate not finding them in the drawers, in
any of your books, etc. Don't just go through the motions of
searching. *Really look*. Know why you are searching in each particular place. Why is it so urgent to find the typewritten speech

right now? What will be the consequences if you don't find the cards before the taxi arrives? You do find them. When? Where?

2. Here is a useful acting exercise in which you play yourself rather than a character:

It is the end of a school day. You decide on the particular circumstances, including the season, month, day of week, etc. You had just walked out of the classroom when you realized that you were missing something terribly important to you. It may be notes for an important exam tomorrow, or a big report you have been slaving over (no carbon copy at home), or a valuable piece of *borrowed* jewelry, or a lot of money. You decide; invent all the surrounding circumstances, including the terrible consequences if you don't find the article right now. You rush back into the classroom and hunt for the missing article, first in all the logical places, then even in illogical places. Your teacher is waiting not very patiently to lock up the room because she is late for an appointment. You certainly do not want to hold her up, but you must find the missing article now! Your teacher tells you she can wait only one more minute. What do you do? In another minute she says she must lock up. Do you find the article? Begin the exercise with your entrance into the classroom. Let someone else play the teacher.

3. For both actresses: Try to observe a real rabbit. What movements does it make? How does it eat? Observe the rabbit with as many of your senses as possible, very quietly, for a long period of time. How would you describe the personality of this particular rabbit? What are your feelings toward this creature? What do you think its attitude toward you might be? Recall this rabbit "with your senses" when you relate to the imaginary rabbit in the scene. (Unless, of course, you perform with a real rabbit!) If you cannot manage to observe or clearly recall a rabbit, then mentally substitute another small animal normally kept in a cage, one familiar to you.

4. Improvise another scene between the two sisters, a situation not in the play. Do not attempt this exercise until you are thoroughly familiar with the play and your character. What is the relationship between you (Ruth and Tillie)? Ruth, your feelings toward Tillie, toward the rabbit, etc. keep changing with lightning speed. Unstable as you are, however, something, either internal or

external, must trigger each change of mood. Be sure you know what it is. Tillie, how do you react to Ruth's sudden shifts of mood? Plan your circumstances before you begin (where you are, when this is, what you were each doing previously). You may choose to enact an "ordinary" afternoon after school, or perhaps the occasion of the rabbit's arrival.

From *Freedom Train: The Story of Harriet Tubman* by Dorothy Sterling

Harriet Tubman is a truly heroic figure in American history. It is hard to believe that our history books have seldom granted her a rightful place of honor beside the other "giants" of our land: Patrick Henry, Nathan Hale, etc.

Harriet Tubman was an escaped slave. She could have enjoyed her liberty in one of the "free" states or in Canada. Instead she chose to risk her life again and again; she crossed the "line" back to the slave states nineteen times, in order to guide other slaves to freedom! Known as "Moses," she helped more than three hundred of her people escape. Offers of rewards for her capture mounted from $1,000 to $5,000, then to $10,000 and finally to $40,000! Daring as she was, she was never reckless. Careful, shrewd, full of clever tricks, she was never caught, nor were any of the slaves she "conducted." Said she, "On my Underground Railroad I never ran my train off the track and I never lost a passenger."

The Underground Railroad was not an actual railroad. These were code words. The "passengers," or "freight," were the runaways; the "stations" were places of shelter such as houses and barns. The "conductors" (including Harriet Tubman) were people strongly opposed to slavery, who helped hide and feed the escaping slaves and guided them to their next hideout along the route to freedom. Often these people were white Quakers, such as Thomas Garrett and John and Ezekiel Hunn, or free Negroes.

According to this thrilling biography, which tells the astounding

story of Harriet Tubman's life, she was born on a Maryland plantation around 1821. The plantation grew corn, wheat and tobacco, using slave labor. As a young child, she learned how to
find her way about the woods from her father, how to find food
and drink, and how to find north by means of the North Star and
the moss that grows on the north side of the trees. She could neither read nor write, but this early education was to prove invalua-
ble later on.

When she was fifteen, Harriet stepped in the way of an overseer
about to catch Jim, an escaping slave. He had run away twice before, only to be returned in chains. Furious, the overseer hurled a
heavy weight at Jim, but hit Harriet instead. She nearly died. She
suffered from sudden sleeping spells for the rest of her life as a result of her brain injury—luckily she always awoke in time to
avoid capture. Her master now wanted to sell her, but because of
her sleeping spells (often pretended), no one would buy her. Her
master therefore allowed her to "hire her own time." She could
take any job so long as she paid him a share of her earnings. Mr.
Stewart, a lumberman who rented her father from their master by
the year, allowed Harriet to farm a stump-filled piece of his land
and sell the produce.

Later she fell in love with a free Negro, John Tubman, a carefree, devil-may-care individual, and married him. He moved into
her cabin in the Stewart slave quarters and she had to support
him. Then one scorching hot Sunday in summer, her master died.
Her mistress had always hated Harriet, whose manner around
Master and Mistress had always been sullen. Afraid that she
would soon be sold to the cotton planters of the Deep South, Harriet decided to run away. She confided in John, her husband, but
he opposed her plans, scoffing at her fear of being sold. They
quarreled. She left the cabin and secretly resolved to escape.

Dorothy Sterling describes Harriet at the age of fifteen: "Harriet was a woman. She was not beautiful. Her hair was short and
crinkly, her mouth large, her heavy-lidded eyes blackest black.
She was only five feet tall, and her broad, hard-muscled body was
clothed in an ill-fitting castoff dress from the Big House, or in a
coarse cotton shift. A red and yellow bandanna, wrapped tightly
around her head to protect it from the glaring Maryland sun, was
her only adornment.

"Despite her plain appearance, there was a magnetic quality about Harriet. When she ran barefoot across the fields with her head erect and her firm muscles rippling under her dark, lustrous skin, men and women stopped to admire her grace and strength."

The following selection is not a scene from a play, but part of a chapter from this fictionalized biography. It is meant to serve as a basis for an improvised scene. (See "Suggestions for the Actor," beginning on page 67.)

Long ago Jim had told Harriet about the white people called Quakers, the plain folk whose gray or black dress and gentle speech hid a burning hatred of slavery. "Quakers almost as good as colored," he'd chuckled. "They call themselves Friends and you can trust them every time."

When she was selling pies from door to door in Bucktown, Harriet noticed a tiny, blond woman whose bonnet and dress marked her as one of the "good" white people. Silently she had followed her home. Standing half hidden behind a tree, she had studied her neat brick cottage and the white picket fence which enclosed a garden of hollyhocks and delphiniums and a yard of squawking chickens.

Now, after her quarrel with John, Harriet made for the Stewart kitchen. Borrowing a market basket, she set off down the road. Across the creek, past a cornfield, and then the brick house was in sight. Despite her anger and her fear, her movements were deliberate. She had thought about this for a long time.

"Watch your step now," she whispered as she unhooked the gate. "Got to act just right."

At the door of the house she hesitated, then boldly lifted the brass knocker. The latch clicked and the door swung back. The tiny lady in gray smiled questioningly at her.

"Please, mistress. I saw your hens and I thought maybe you sell me some eggs. I have money to pay." Harriet pointed to her basket.

"I'm afraid I couldn't sell thee eggs on First Day. But thee looks hot. Won't thee come in and drink some lemonade?"

Harriet nodded. The interview was proceeding as she had hoped it would. She followed her hostess to the parlor, trying not to look frightened. This was her first experience as a guest in a white household. "Careful, careful!" she warned herself.

The lemonade was cool and sweet, and Harriet's voice was steady when she asked, "Do you know Master Garrett up in Wilmington? I hear he's a Quaker, just like yourself."

"I don't know a *Master* Garrett." The white woman smiled as she emphasized the word. "Thomas Garrett lets no man or woman call him 'Master.'"

Harriet looked up with an answering smile, but she hesitated to go on. This was so easy that it might be a trap.

Pretending not to notice her visitor's uncertainty, the Quaker continued, "I have visited Thomas Garrett many times, breaking my journey with the Hunn family. Does thee know of Ezekiel Hunn in Camden or John Hunn in Middletown?"

Breathless, Harriet shook her head.

"Both good men. Thee would like them. Were I traveling, I would follow the Choptank River north to its source, just at the border between Maryland and Delaware. The road there runs straight to Camden. North by east, it's fifteen miles to Ezekiel's. A clapboard house with green shutters and a red brick chimney. Any—" She hesitated to find the right word. "Any workingman can point it out. The railroad goes through Camden now, you know."

Harriet's eyes sparkled and her lips curved in their broadest smile. "Sure would like to meet *Mister* Hunn and *Mister* Garrett. Everyone talking about that new railroad. I've been wanting to try it for a long, long time."

The Quaker poured more lemonade into Harriet's glass. "In case you should be going, I wonder if you'd mind carrying a message for Ezekiel?"

While Harriet finished her drink, her hostess wrote a few words on a piece of paper. Gravely Harriet stowed the note in her market basket and made ready to depart.

"Let me give you a few eggs so that your trip won't have been wasted." The Quaker's blue eyes twinkled.

"This trip's not wasted." Harriet grinned back. "But in case I meet someone on the road, be a good idea to have the eggs."

At the door, the two women reached out at the same moment to shake hands. "Godspeed," the Quaker whispered, and Harriet, too moved to speak, smiled her thanks.

SUGGESTIONS FOR THE ACTOR

1. This selection is intended for use as *improvised* drama. In other words, familiarize yourself with the general story; when you play the scene, invent your own specific physical actions and words as you go along. It is unnecessary to memorize lines. The two selections in this anthology from *Freedom Train* provide you with *another approach* to acting. Other selections in this anthology, even excerpts from plays, may also be used as a basis for improvisation.

In improvised drama, otherwise known as "informal drama," you are acting for yourselves, not for an audience. Improvised-drama sessions are generally conducted in a large room rather than on a formal stage. No elaborate stage sets or costumes are required. One area of the room can serve as a thicket one moment, a clearing in the woods the next and the interior of a cabin the next; you are limited only by your own imagination. Frequently the story to be dramatized is told or read aloud first; then the group discusses it and plans the dramatization to some extent: the beginning and end of each scene, and the setting. The group also decides what changes, if any, need to be made in order to make the original story more dramatic, concrete, actable. The events must be shown, not described. The group may choose to enact only a scene or two rather than the entire story. Usually roles are not permanently cast; whoever wants to play a particular role in a particular scene gets a chance to try it. Two people, for example, may act the first "scene" of a story. Then the group as a whole will evaluate this first playing: What was particularly good and what specific improvements might be made the next time. Then two more actors perform the same scene—building on what went before, utilizing the suggestions, keeping what they liked best of the first playing and adding new creative touches of their own.

The group evaluates the second playing. Then either a third pair acts the scene, or the group proceeds to the next part of the story.

2. Even though it is unnecessary to memorize this scene from *Freedom Train,* it would be a good idea to learn the following key names and places mentioned in the story. Another possibility is to list them on a wall or blackboard within view while you are acting.

Thomas Garrett in Wilmington
Ezekiel Hunn in Camden
John Hunn in Middletown
Follow Choptank River north to its source, at the border between Maryland and Delaware—fifteen miles northeast to Camden.

3. You, Harriet, and you, the Quaker lady (give her a name!), communicate with looks, body movement and gesture, tone of voice and touch more truthfully than with words. You dare not always say what you mean. For instance, when you talk about the new railroad (there was an actual new railroad, new steam engines going to Washington), you are really referring to the Underground Railroad. You have to "feel each other out" at first. What do you, Harriet, really want of the Quaker lady? What do you pretend to want? You also want to avoid a possible trap. Might you, the Quaker lady, also fear a trap at first? The author does not mention this possibility, but might you, the Quaker lady, wonder whether Harriet could have been sent as a spy by her master? Or perhaps you hesitate to discuss escape openly for fear of scaring Harriet away. Are you afraid of being overheard? You observe each other carefully and react to all you see and hear, not only to the words themselves. Little by little, you begin to relax. Do you, Harriet, succeed in subtly communicating your real desire to the Quaker lady? If so, how do you, the Quaker lady, respond? What do you want to do for Harriet? Gradually a bond of friendship is formed between you, symbolized by your handshake at the end of the scene.

Some useful questions for group evaluation after each playing: Did the two actresses communicate with looks, gesture and movement, tone of voice and touch? What specific meanings did you, the audience, observe them communicating in these ways? How did the relationship between the two characters change during the course of the scene? Was there a growing sense of mutual trust?

3. In a relevant theatre game invented by Grace Stanistreet, described in her book *Teaching Is a Dialogue* (Garden City, New York, Adelphi University, 1974), the players communicate through tone of voice alone. Everyone sits in a circle. Player 1 (now called the "initiator") tries to communicate a specific meaning or emotion to the player on his or her right, Player 2 (now called the "responder"), through tone of voice alone, without using any real words. Only animal sounds may be used—barks or meows. If Player 2 does not grasp any meaning, Player 2 does not respond and Player 1 must try again. If Player 2 thinks he or she does understand the meaning or feeling, Player 2 barks or meows back an appropriate response. Then Player 2 (now taking the role of initiator) tries to communicate a new meaning or emotion to Player 3, and so on around the circle until each player has had a turn at both giving (initiating) and responding to a "message."

For instance, how could you communicate the message "I have a terrible pain!" with your voice, using only barks? How could you convey, through meows, the meaning "Darling, I love you!" or "Help! Murder! Police!"?

If you do not feel comfortable using animal sounds, you may change the ground rules and substitute numbers, letters of the alphabet or any other meaningless sounds.

4. Plays differ in structure from stories. A dramatic scene reveals a struggle of some kind, even if the struggle is only in someone's mind. If the scene between Harriet and the Quaker lady seems to require a stronger conflict when it is performed, try experimenting with these or other obstacles standing in the way of Harriet's receiving the help she needs so desperately.

(a) The unexpected arrival of a patroller (slave catcher), hunting for an escaped slave. Or

(b) The unexpected arrival of a neighbor, a slaveholder. Or

(c) The presence of a relative, who has been visiting here for some weeks. This relative approves of slavery.

You, the Quaker lady, might then try to get rid of this unwelcome person quickly. If you failed, then you and Harriet might try to find sly ways of communicating to each other secretly despite the visitor's presence.

From *Freedom Train: The Story of Harriet Tubman* by Dorothy Sterling

INTRODUCTION

See pages 63–69 for background and for a discussion of how to go about dramatizing a story or a portion of a story.

"Old Cudjoe" was the oldest slave on the plantation. He had been born on the slave ship sailing from Africa. The mother of the present mistress had taken a fancy to him when he was small, allowing him to learn to read and write.

After a slave uprising, slaves were forbidden to hold meetings. Before that all the slaves would gather under the oak tree every Sunday, where Old Cudjoe would tell them Bible stories. A favorite was the story of how Moses had led the enslaved Jews to freedom.

Trudging down the road, Harriet thought fleetingly of John. Should she share with him the paper in her basket and its promise for the future? "No." She shook her head. "This is for my brothers and me. John can't be trusted."

Instead of turning off at the Stewart plantation, she headed for her parents' cabin. Benjamin and William Henry and her older brother, Robert, were still excitedly discussing Master's death and the change it could mean in their lives. Fearful that Old Rit might unwittingly give away her secret, Harriet kept silent until she could speak to her brothers alone.

Outside, under the oak tree where Old Cudjoe had read the story of Moses, she told them of her plans. "Next Saturday night we start," she concluded. "That way we'll have all day Sunday before they notice we're missing. By the time that alarm goes out on Monday——" She left the sentence unfinished.

Each brother entered his protest. The hound dogs, the patrollers, the unknown paths through woods and swamps, the armed posses, and the cold loneliness of the North.

"Let's wait," Robert urged. "Let's see what Mistress does."

"Wait!" Even in a whisper, Harriet's tone could be fierce. "I'm not waiting no longer. I reasoned this out in my mind. There are two things I have a right to, liberty or death. If I can't have one, I'll have the other. I'll fight for my liberty as long as my strength lasts, and when the time comes for me to go, the Lord will let them take me."

The silence was heavy. Then William Henry nodded. "I'll go, Hat."

"I'll go." "I'll go," the other two agreed.

"Not a word to Daddy or Ma," Harriet cautioned. "Things'll be bad enough for them when we turn up missing. Mistress'll be shaking them, threatening them with her whip. But what they don't know, they can't tell. After a while, she'll have to let them be."

SUGGESTIONS FOR THE ACTOR

1. Try out various physical settings. The argument could take place inside your cabin or outdoors. You might be performing some physical task for your family on a Sunday. Indoors, for example, you might be tending to the fire or stirring batter for cornbread. Outside the cabin you might be husking corn or feeding the pig. You could be working in Master's fields (chopping down weeds around the corn with a hoe, maybe), whispering from time to time. You (the actors) would then have to change the day of the week from Sunday to another day because Sunday

was a day of rest. You could be sprawled on a pile of corn ears in the fodder house, etc.

Here is the author's description of your slave cabin:

> The windowless cabin was dark in the daytime, but a few slanting rays of sunshine found their way in through the cracks in the log walls, making a crazy pattern on the bare earth floor. From the door, hanging crookedly on its hinges, a patch of light shone on the fireplace. With its chimney of split sticks plastered with mud, the fireplace was the heart of the cabin, the source of heat and light and food. Neatly stacked on the hearth was an assortment of pots and pails. On one side was the potato hole, covered with boards, where sweet potatoes kept firm and hard all winter long. On the other were two backless, battered chairs. Straw pallets lined the log walls. These were the beds.

Slave cabins frequently smelled of smoke from the chimney, even in summer.

2. This scene will be more suspenseful, as well as more believable, if you are constantly aware of the danger of being overheard. For instance, at any moment your mother, "Old Rit," might return to the cabin. Old Rit cannot lie to save her life. Without meaning to, she might give away your secret plans if she knew them. Or, if your scene were set in the fields, the overseer might hear you at any time. If your scene were set outside the cabin, Mistress might pass by the slave quarters. What might the terrible consequences be, if you were overheard?

3. Before the first playing, the entire group might list some of the arguments for and against attempting escape. When you act, feel free to make any or all of these points, or none. You may think of new arguments as you perform. You must not simply argue, however; it is important to observe and listen to each other, and to react in character.

Remember that each side is trying its hardest to convince the other of its point of view. You (the actors playing Harriet's brothers) must not "give in" without a reason, simply to end the scene. In order to convince you, Harriet must say or do something so impressive that it *really* changes your minds.

4. This scene may be played effectively with one or two brothers, as well as with three. If more than one brother takes

part, then each brother should have a personality different from the other(s). Plan what you are each like in personality and appearance (see "Actor's Check List," beginning on page 336), and decide what your particular relationship is to each of the other characters in the scene.

Benjie is described as Harriet's favorite brother. Benjie, William Henry and Harriet were brought up together. Robert is older. He was already married and living elsewhere during Harriet's adolescence.

5. This scene will be much more interesting if there is some physical activity accompanying the argument. It may help to have some physical task to perform, such as fetching water from the spring or gathering wood for the fire. It will help to move about the acting area at times. You, the brothers, can sometimes refuse Harriet with a movement away from her as well as with words or even in place of words. You, Harriet, can sometimes beg with a touch, insist with a strong gesture, threaten with a sudden, sharp movement. Be sure, however, that the character you play always has a reason for moving. Try not to position yourselves at the same vertical (up-and-down) level all the time. Remember, you can stand, sit, kneel, even sprawl on the ground at various points in the scene, so long as the character you play has a reason for changing vertical levels at each particular moment.

Which physical settings provided the best opportunities for movement?

Monologues for Girls

From *Anne Frank: The Diary of a Young Girl* by Anne Frank, translated from the Dutch by B. M. Mooyart-Doubleday

INTRODUCTION

The destruction of millions of people is likely to leave us numb—it is more than the mind can grasp. But we can clearly imagine, and sharply feel the senseless destruction of one vibrant human being. Anne Frank was one of the millions of Jews killed by the Nazis during World War II. Before they were caught by the Nazis, Anne and her family hid in rooms above Mr. Frank's office in Amsterdam, Holland, for nearly two years. Anne recorded her thoughts and experiences during this entire period of her adolescence in a diary, which she called "Kitty." After her death, her remarkable journal was found and published. The English translation was entitled *Anne Frank: The Diary of a Young Girl.*

The Franks generously shared their hiding place and small food supply with the Van Danns, a Jewish family consisting of husband, wife and adolescent son Peter.

Some of Mr. Frank's Christian employees knew about the secret hiding place and helped these Jews at tremendous risk to their own safety. They visited the "Secret Annexe," as Anne called it, each week, bringing supplies and even books for much-needed entertainment. They tried to protect the Franks from danger. These friends included Mr. Koophuis and Elli Vossen, a twenty-three-year-old typist.

The original Dutch title of this diary, *Het Achterhuis,* literally means "the house behind." In Amsterdam's old buildings the apartments facing a garden or court were sometimes divided from those facing the street. The "Secret Annexe" was really the hidden back apartment of this old house, situated on a canal. On the ground floor were the offices, where Mr. Frank's employees worked in the daytime. On the second floor there was a door at each end of the central landing. The left-hand door led to storerooms at the front of the building. The right-hand door, hidden by a "swinging cupboard" held by a hook, opened onto a secret staircase leading to "the Frank family's bed-sitting-room," a lavatory and a small bedroom-study for Anne and her older sister. With her father's help, Anne decorated her room with movie-star photographs and picture postcards, transforming the bare walls into "one gigantic picture." The Van Danns slept on the top floor, which also served as general living room, dining room and kitchen.

Anne had a wonderful relationship with her father. Wise and understanding, he was also sufficiently young at heart to sympathize with his adolescent daughter. She went through a phase when she bitterly resented her mother for treating her like a baby. Her sister, Margot, was quiet, serious, helpful. Most of the adults wished Anne would behave more like Margot. They considered Anne too noisy, giddy, "smart-alecky." She wrote that on the outside she was "nothing but a frolicsome little goat who's broken loose." Inwardly, however, she was quite different from what showed on the outside. She longed to write well, to go on living even after her death, through her written words. In this Anne succeeded—all too soon.

Despite their constant fear, these fugitives tried to lead as normal a life as was possible under difficult circumstances. The young people kept up their studies under Mr. Frank's kindly instruction. They had to be completely quiet during the day, so as not to be discovered by workers in the offices downstairs, but at night they were able to lead what was nearly a normal existence. The event described in the following selection evidently took place in the evening, or they would not have been making noise.

In October 1942, Anne was thirteen years old.

To us, the readers, this diary entry is unintentionally, heartbreakingly ironic because we know what Anne did not know as she recorded the incident. Even though this particular fright turned out to be a false alarm, her worst fears and her wildest imaginings would come true less than two years later.

"On August 4, 1944, the *Grüne Polizei* [Green Police] made a raid on the 'Secret Annexe.' All the occupants, together with * * * Koophuis, were arrested * * *.

"In March 1945, two months before the liberation of Holland, Anne died in the concentration camp at Bergen-Belsen."

ANNE:

Tuesday, 20 October, 1942

Dear Kitty,

My hand still shakes, although it's two hours since we had the shock. I should explain that there are five fire extinguishers in the house. We knew that someone was coming to fill them, but no one had warned us when the carpenter, or whatever you call him, was coming.

The result was that we weren't making any attempt to keep quiet, until I heard hammering outside on the landing opposite our cupboard door. I thought of the carpenter at once and warned Elli, who was having a meal with us, that she shouldn't go downstairs. Daddy and I posted ourselves at the door so as to hear when the man left. After he'd been working for a quarter of an hour, he laid his hammer and tools down on top of our cupboard (as we thought) and knocked at our door. We turned absolutely white. Perhaps he had heard something after all and wanted to investigate our secret den. It seemed like it. The knocking, pulling, pushing, and wrenching went on. I nearly fainted at the thought that this utter stranger might discover our beautiful secret hiding place. And just as I thought my last hour was at hand, I heard Mr. Koophuis say, "Open the door, it's only me." We opened it immediately. The hook that holds the cupboard, which can be undone by people who know the secret, had got jammed. That was why no one had been able to warn us about the carpenter. The man had now gone downstairs and Koophuis wanted to fetch Elli, but couldn't open the cupboard again. It was a great relief to me, I can tell you. In my imagination the man who I thought was trying to get in had been growing and growing in size until in the end he appeared to be a giant and the greatest fascist that ever walked the earth.

SUGGESTIONS FOR THE ACTOR

1. If you wish to *act* this monologue rather than simply read aloud from the diary, you, the actress, need to invent a logical reason for Anne to speak these words at this moment. Perhaps you (Anne) have just finished describing the incident in your diary; you wish to make sure that you have not omitted anything important.

If you have in mind a different reason for Anne to read aloud, a reason that makes sense to you, try your own idea instead.

You also need to decide where you (Anne) are as you read. It is evening. Are you at the little table in your own room? On your bed? On the floor? In a different room? Visualize the room before you begin to act and set up whatever actual "props" you need, including, of course, a diary (cardboard-covered notebook).

2. This selection involves a sudden, dramatic shift in emotions, from terror to relief. As an exercise try to recall some episodes in your own life, in which you underwent a similar change in mood. For example, have you ever imagined that you were being followed by a "mugger," only to learn that the supposed criminal was really only an ordinary person, going about his or her own business? When you were younger, did you ever get lost at the beach, in the woods, in a crowd? What did you want to do? What action did you take? Do you remember how you finally spotted a member of your family in the distance? Do not struggle to recapture the emotions you once felt. Instead concentrate on recalling everything you saw, heard, smelled, felt and tasted at that time. Then get up "onstage" and reenact the experience. If you were silent during the actual event, you may wish to perform soundlessly now. If you talked to yourself at the time, as people often do under stress, then feel free to speak your thoughts aloud now too. Perhaps you were silent except for the last moment, when you

gave a cry of relief, or when you shouted to attract the attention of the relative or friend you had found at last. In other words, you may either express yourself aloud or act silently, or both, whichever feels more natural to you in these circumstances. Try several "change-of-mood" exercises: Recall actual situations in which your emotions changed from fear to relief. *You must not anticipate the endings.* In real life you did not know that the episodes would end happily. Don't plan ahead as you act. Let each moment just happen to you, one moment at a time. When you play Anne, you relive the experience as you describe it. You must not expect Mr. Koophuis (pronunciation similar to "Cope-house") until you hear his voice. At that point you are greatly relieved. Remember, you do not think of your life as a tragedy; you do not know how that will end either.

3. When you mention Mr. Koophuis and Elli, visualize kindly people that you (the actress) know, but when you speak of "the greatest fascist that ever walked the earth," imagine any terrifying creature, real or unreal. A menacing figure from a particularly vivid nightmare might be a sufficiently horrifying image.

4. You, Anne, do not treat your diary as an inanimate object. You gave your diary a girl's name, Kitty, because you make believe that "she" is your friend and confidante. "Kitty" never gets annoyed with you, as others do. In describing your diary, you once quoted an old saying: "Paper is more patient than man." For all your clowning, you are inwardly lonely, longing for a close friend. Kitty was the very first and most precious belonging you packed when you prepared to go into hiding.

5. To capture Anne's continual feeling of confinement, try to recall a time in your own life when you were confined or forced to remain quiet although you were aching to run and shout. Have you ever been forced to remain in bed or to sit quietly indoors while recuperating from an illness? Imagine your frustration if that confinement had lasted for months. As an exercise at home, make believe that *you* are living in hiding from the Nazis, as Anne was. Imagine your circumstances—where you are, when this is, why you are in hiding. For one entire morning or afternoon, try to make no noise at all. You may pursue such quiet activities as reading, studying, drawing or solving a puzzle, but take care not to talk, or walk with shoes on, or turn on water. Don't do any-

thing that may be heard by people on another floor or in the next apartment. What will happen to you if someone hears you? Imagine what it must be like to live this way all day, every day, until evening.

From *The Member of the Wedding* by Carson McCullers.
Act I

INTRODUCTION

Frankie Addams is "a gangling girl of twelve with blonde hair cut like a boy's * * *. She is a dreamy, restless girl, and periods of energetic activity alternate wth a rapt attention to her inward world of fantasy. She is thin and awkward and very much aware of being too tall."

This is the delicate, often humorous, tender story of Frankie's emergence into adolescence. The transformation is a painful one. All sorts of strange new feelings, sometimes contradictory, come crowding in upon her, feelings that she herself does not even understand.

She lives in a small southern town (in 1945) with her father, an old-fashioned, absentminded widower. He loves Frankie in his own way, but is too preoccupied with his business, a jewelry store, to pay much attention to her. Frankie's mother died the day Frankie was born. She spends her days with the housekeeper, Berenice, a "stout motherly Negro woman" who is devoted to her and to her seven-year-old cousin, John Henry. Her small cousin, a "delicate, active boy," wears gold-rimmed spectacles which make him look wise beyond his years. He lives next door but likes to spend his days in the Addams kitchen, talking and playing cards with Frankie and Berenice.

The scene from which this monologue was adapted takes place

near evening, on a Friday in August. Today has probably been the most important day of Frankie's life, so far. Her older brother, Jarvis, a soldier, brought home his fiancée, Janice, to meet the family. Their visit was brief because Jarvis had to return to his army barracks a hundred miles away in Winter Hill, but they are returning Sunday for a home wedding.

Frankie's emotional response to the couple overwhelms her. She adores them both; she is thrilled and yet also somehow deeply disturbed by their visit.

A group of girls a few years older than Frankie hold club meetings and parties nearby on Friday nights. Frankie usually watches them from her yard; she is not a member of the club. The girls held an election this afternoon. Frankie had hoped to be chosen as a new member, but to her great disappointment, they elected someone else instead. Frankie had befriended a girl her own age before the summer, but her one friend moved away to Florida. Frankie has no desire to form a club of her own with the little neighborhood children as Berenice suggests in a futile attempt to comfort her. Says Frankie, "I don't want to be the president of all those little young left-over people." She takes out her misery on John Henry, whom she sends home.

She suddenly begins to sob. Referring to the engaged couple, she cried, "* * * They went away and left me." Berenice teases her: "Frankie's got a crush on the *wedding!*" Frankie vows to leave home right after the wedding, although she has no idea where she will go.

Berenice's gentleman friend and her brother call for her. She leaves Frankie alone in the house; Mr. Addams is expected home soon.

"FRANKIE, feeling excluded, goes out into the yard." It is growing dark. The kitchen light "is throwing a yellow rectangle in the yard." She calls John Henry over to spend the night. Her father returns shortly after John Henry's arrival. She now ignores John Henry completely; she is lost in her own thoughts.

Frankie wears shorts. John Henry is dressed in a white linen suit.

In the yard is an arbor of scuppernong grapes. "A sheet, used as a stage curtain, hangs raggedly at one side of the arbor."

In the past Frankie often wrote and acted in plays out in the arbor, all kinds of plays except for love stories because she "never believed in love until now."

It is so quiet here that Frankie predicts stormy weather ahead.

FRANKIE: Don't bother me, John Henry. I'm thinking.
* * *
About the wedding. About my brother and the bride. Everything's been so sudden today. I never believed before about the fact that the earth turns at the rate of about a thousand miles a day. I didn't understand why it was that if you jumped up in the air you wouldn't land in Selma or Fairview or somewhere else instead of the same back yard. But now it seems to me I feel the world going around very fast. [FRANKIE *begins turning around in circles with arms outstretched* * * *] I feel it turning and it makes me dizzy. * * * [*Suddenly stopping her turning*] I just now thought of something.
* * *
I know where I'm going.

[*There are sounds of children playing in the distance*]

I tell you I know where I'm going. It's like I've known it all my life. Tomorrow I will tell everybody.
* * *
[*Dreamily*] After the wedding I'm going with them to Winter Hill. I'm going off with them after the wedding.
* * *
Just now I realized something. The trouble with me is that for a long time I have been just an "I" person. All other people can say "we." When Berenice says "we" she means her lodge and church and colored people. Soldiers can say "we" and mean the army. All people belong to a "we" except me.
* * *
Not to belong to a "we" makes you too lonesome. Until this afternoon I didn't have a "we," but now after seeing Janice and Jarvis I suddenly realize something.
* * *
I know that the bride and my brother are the "we" of me. So I'm going with them, and joining with the wedding. This coming Sunday when my brother and the bride leave this town, I'm

going with the two of them to Winter Hill. And after that to
whatever place that they will ever go. [*There is a pause*] I love
the two of them so much and we belong to be together. I love
the two of them so much because they are the *we* of me.

SUGGESTIONS FOR THE ACTOR

1. As a preparatory exercise, you, the actress, should imagine in
concrete detail everything that happened to you, Frankie, from the
time you woke up this morning until this moment. Be specific. If
you took a walk, where did you go? Why? What did you see?
Whom did you meet? What did you talk about? Be sure to include
any activities shown earlier in the play, but you will have to invent
many activities yourself.

2. You, Frankie, are at first talking to your small cousin, John
Henry, but you quickly lose conscious awareness of his presence.
He might just as well be one of the little bugs in the yard that you
automatically brush away with your hand, your mind on something else altogether. You, the actress, should visualize a small
boy, perhaps your own brother or cousin, when you first begin to
speak. After that put him out of your mind except perhaps for a
split second or two when you may see him without really focusing
on him.

3. Imagine the setting. "See" the darkening sky, the kitchen
light hitting the yard, an elm tree in semidarkness, the grape arbor
with the ragged sheet as curtain. (Imagine your outdoor performances here, when you tried so hard to create an acting troupe out
of the little neighborhood children.) How oddly quiet it is, except
for the occasional buzzing of insects. Imagine the "smell of
mashed grapes and dust." "Feel" the grass, and maybe even some
mashed grapes, beneath your feet. Imagine the never-to-be-forgot-
ten celebration right here this afternoon, in honor of Jarvis and
Janice.

4. Most human beings have felt lonely at one time or another.
Most of us have felt the need to belong, to be a "member" of
something. Remember a time in your own life when you felt left

out, and longed to be part of a particular group. Then, instead of trying to force out of yourself the emotions you once felt, allow your feelings to come back automatically by recalling all the sights, sounds, smells, tastes and textures which you associate with that experience of loneliness. What actions did you perform to get what you wanted so badly?

5. What do you, Frankie, want most? What *inner action* do you perform during this monologue in order to get what you want? Making a decision is an example of an "inner action," as I am using the acting term, because it is something you do mentally rather than physically, and you do it for a *purpose*. What momentous decision do you make now? At what precise moment do you make it? You make it because of a sudden realization. What is it that you realize concerning the special relationship between you and the engaged couple? Exactly when do you come to this realization?

6. This monologue allows for tremendous variety of physical movement because of the sudden, dramatic changes in your (Frankie's) moods. When you think you feel the earth spinning, you are wildly exhilarated, nearly hysterical. Your mind is spinning because of all that's happened today. Your body movements would be big, fast, wild, reflecting your inner turbulence. What is your inner state when you reach the most crucial decision of your life? How would your body reflect this shift in mood? What is your state of mind when the thought dawns on you that Jarvis, Janice and you "belong" together? How would your body express your inner thoughts now?

From *Growing Up Puerto Rican,* edited by Paulette Cooper. "Raquel: The Foster Child"

INTRODUCTION

Paulette Cooper has interviewed young Puerto Ricans of many different social backgrounds. Most of them were taken from their homes in Puerto Rico to the ghetto slums of a North American city. Ms. Cooper allows them to tell their own stories in their own words—their problems with family, school, drugs, sex, etc., their hopes, their despair, their failures and sometimes their successes.

Raquel's story is one of the saddest. Her parents were born in Puerto Rico, but she and her brother were born here. Her mother deserted the family when Raquel was a little girl. Unable to support both children, Raquel's father put her into foster homes.

Now, after the events described in this selection, Raquel continues to be unhappy in the "home." Her father never visits her. Her brother is a "junkie." He comes to her only for the money to buy drugs, since she has a part-time job in a store. She has few friends. Her brother's frequent visits disturb her so much that she cannot do well in school. She still dreams of finding her loving foster family some day; she has made hundreds of phone calls to people with the same last name as theirs, both in this country and in Puerto Rico.

RAQUEL: Until I was about twelve, I was sent to many foster homes. I don't remember very much of those years and I don't want to. Some of those people mistreated me, none of them loved me, and they took me only for the money. The city pays a certain amount of money to people who take foster children, and some people take the money but don't do anything for the children with that money. None of mine, except one, meant anything to me, and I suppose I meant even less to them. They weren't homes to me, just houses and they were simply a place to sleep. I don't like to talk about it.

But one of the places, the last one I stayed in, was different. It was a Puerto Rican family and they really loved me. The strange thing is they had their own children too, but they treated me just like one of their own. I don't know whether they collected the city money for me, but they certainly spent more than their allotment on me. If they bought clothes for their own children, they would buy me clothes as well and just as expensive. If my foster mother or father wanted to bring their children a present, there was always a present for me. They were also physically affectionate which was something I wasn't used to with my own father. They would kiss me and tell me they loved me and that I was just like their own child to them. Sometimes I would even call them "Mommy" and "Daddy."

But then one day the city took me away. I suppose they thought it best, since there was a home they could put me into where I could stay until I was twenty-one. I guess they decided that one permanent cold place was better than a lot of foster homes. My foster parents didn't want to give me up but they had to. Maybe with their own children they couldn't afford to keep me and pay everything for me if the city didn't help. Maybe they just couldn't fight the red tape—you know, when the city decides it's going to do something there isn't much you can do about it. I think part of it also was that they wanted to go back to Puerto Rico—they had often told me they would take me also, and the city probably wouldn't let them take me out of the country. I don't know; but I know they were as unhappy as I was when I was taken away to the home.

They came and visited at first, but visiting days were even worse than the days they didn't come. The whole family would come to see me and those days were so beautiful. But when they left I knew they were going to their home where I should be also. I would cry for days after they left and when they came back they would tell me that they had cried also. They said they were still working on getting me back but there was always "red tape," and they couldn't. After a while, I became so upset after they left that they didn't come back. It wasn't their decision. The Mother Superior told me that she had told them not to come back—in fact, she wouldn't let them back when they tried to come and see me. She felt it upset me too much and that I had to learn to adjust to my new home—if you could call it that. At first I didn't know why they hadn't returned and I felt very badly about that—I thought they weren't coming any more because they had decided they didn't love me any more, or maybe they got a new foster child. And then one day the Mother Superior told me why. I started screaming and saying that I would run away and find them. But that wasn't so easy. For one thing, we were watched pretty closely, and since they knew I wanted to run away, I was watched even more closely than the other children. Also, I had no money so it would have been hard for me to get very far, and the home was quite far from where the family lived. That was another problem: I didn't know where that was—I knew it was a long ride from there to the home, but I wasn't sure exactly what neighborhood I had lived in and what their address was. I was only about eleven at the time, and had led a sheltered life with them. So I had no way to find them. It was a common name and I knew there were thousands of people in the city with that name. So I gave up.

SUGGESTIONS FOR THE ACTOR

1. To whom are you (Raquel) talking? One possibility: You might be telling Paulette Cooper, the editor of *Growing Up Puerto Rican,* the story of your life. (She interviewed you, as well as six-

teen other young Puerto Ricans, using a tape recorder.) What is your impression of her? In your life so far, you haven't encountered many sympathetic adults, interested in your problems. Is it a relief to tell your troubles to someone? You, the actress, might try addressing your monologue to an actual girl or woman, someone sympathetic-looking, seated in the audience. Pretend that she is Paulette Cooper.

2. You, Raquel, probably remember more about the years when you were sent from one unloving foster home to another than you care to admit, even to yourself. You want to avoid those painful memories. It might help you, the actress, to recall at least one painful memory, some episode in your own life similar to what Raquel might have experienced. For instance, did you ever receive a harsh or unjust punishment? Do you wish that you could "block out" this unpleasant memory?

3. Imagine every member of the loving Puerto Rican family. How many children are in the family? What are their names and ages? Picture each one, recalling actual children whom you know and love "in real life." Imagine the personalities of all the children in this family, their relationships to each other and to you. Imagine the affectionate mother and father too; visualize real people, perhaps your own parents. Imagine the home where you were happy.

Visualize your (Raquel's) real father too. He never gave you the love you needed. Since he could not afford to keep two children, he kept the boy, your brother. Imagine a cold, undemonstrative man, someone you (the actress) know.

Imagine the Mother Superior too. You, Raquel, dislike her intensely because she refused to allow the family you love to visit. In reality, she may have been trying her best to help you adjust to your new "home"; it was not her idea to take you away from your loving home. Whatever she is really like inside, however, she strikes you as indifferent and unsympathetic. Therefore, visualize a cool, unsympathetic woman whom you, the actress, know and dislike. Imagine your present surroundings. What are your feelings toward these physical surroundings?

3. Your (Raquel's) over-all desire throughout the monologue is for love. You also have smaller, more immediate wants at various points. At first you want to avoid painful memories. Then you

want to comfort yourself by reliving, immersing yourself in the memory of the happiest experience of your life. After that, as you mentally relive the terrible separation you describe, you long to stay with your loving foster family. When the Puerto Rican family stops visiting you in the new "home," you desperately want them to come back. Finally you want to run away to them. Do you do anything, or consider doing anything, in order to get what you want?

From *My Lord, What a Morning*
by Marian Anderson.
"Philadelphia Childhood"

INTRODUCTION

In *My Lord, What a Morning* the great singer Marian Anderson tells the story of her life.

She was a happy child, born in Philadelphia to loving, conscientious black parents. Her father was poor, hardworking—he sold coal and ice, and took many other jobs as well. Marian's mother had been a schoolteacher in Virginia. When Marian was a little girl, her mother stayed home and took care of her as well as her two younger sisters, Alyce and Ethel. Occasionally, as the need arose, Mrs. Anderson did not hesitate to do outside work such as cleaning or laundering. When Marian was ten years old, her father died. After that Marian's mother worked hard to support her family; she took whatever jobs she could find.

Marian's father had been active in the Union Baptist Church. From the time she was six years old, Marian sang in the junior choir, then in the senior choir. The choirmaster was the first person to recognize her talent. Eventually she was called upon to sing in other places and was paid progressively higher fees. Her first voice teachers, impressed with her rare gift, trained her without charge. Later her friends and her church managed to raise a considerable sum of money so that she could receive the best formal training available.

After achieving world renown as a magnificent concert performer, Marian Anderson became the first black to sing as a regular member of the Metropolitan Opera company.

MARIAN: When I was about eight years old Father got us a piano. He bought it from his brother, who had had it in his home, where no one used it. When it arrived at our house what excitement and joy! We ran our fingers over it, listening delightedly to the notes of the scale. Father, I remember, permitted me to sit on his knee. I tried playing a scale with five fingers, slipping the thumb under the hand to get all eight notes without a break, the way I had seen people play in school and church. When Father put his hand on the piano, I tried to guide his fingers to play a scale. Because he was understanding, he hit two notes with one finger, and his scale did not come out as well as mine.

I did not have music lessons; there was not enough money for a teacher. However, we did acquire from somewhere a card, marked with the notes, that one could set up directly back of the keys. With the help of this, we learned some simple melodies. But it did not occur to me that I might be able to learn to play the piano properly. I was walking along the street one day, carrying a basket of laundry that I was delivering for my mother, when I heard the sound of a piano. I set down my basket, went up the steps, and looked into the window. I knew it was wrong to peep, but I could not resist the temptation. I saw a woman seated at a piano, playing ever so beautifully. Her skin was dark, like mine. I realized that if she could, I could.

As Mother has said so often, "Remember, wherever you are and whatever you do, someone always sees you." I remembered that woman, who never knew the effect she had on me, when I tried years later to study the piano. I loved music, but I had been taking it for granted that it must be for others.

SUGGESTIONS FOR THE ACTOR

1. Were you (the actress) ever thrilled by a musical instrument or by the sound of music? If so, then recall that experience as you work on Marian's reaction to the new piano. If you never responded ecstatically to music or to a musical instrument, then, in preparing your role, recall something, some place or even someone that did thrill you as a child. For instance, did you ever receive a special gift that filled you with joy and excitement? How did it look? Sound? Feel? Smell? Did you taste it (or anything else) at the time? Try to recall in detail everything you experienced then with your five senses. What did you do? What did Marian do when she first saw the new piano?

2. When you, as Marian, refer to your father, picture a loving, understanding man, someone close to you (the actress) in real life. You may wish to think of your own father. When you were a little girl, did he ever intentionally let you win at a game? How did you react to "beating" him? You, as Marian, may react the same way when your father intentionally strikes two notes at once so that your scale will sound better than his.

You (the actress) may wish to picture your own mother and "hear" the sound of her voice when you, as Marian, quote one of your mother's favorite sayings: "Remember, wherever you are and whatever you do, someone always sees you."

3. As an exercise, act without words the following situation for yourself, not for an audience: You, as Marian, are walking along the street, carrying laundry to deliver for your mother. Visualize the laundry basket; remember how it feels to carry a basket filled with laundry. How heavy is it? Suddenly you hear the sound of a piano. Concentrate on recalling the sound of piano music which you (the actress) have heard before. Picture the house from which the sound is coming. Picture a window on the ground floor. You love music so much that you are tempted to look into the window. But you know that it is wrong to peep through windows. You have conflicting desires. You are dying to know who is playing that lovely music, but you also want to do the right thing; your parents would not want you to be a "peeping Tom." Your curiosity wins out; you set down the basket and peep through the win-

dow. Imagine the room and the piano. To your surprise you see a
black woman playing beautifully. (Born in 1908, Marian was a
child in an era very different from today. Accomplished black pi-
anists were less common than they are now.) Visualize a dark-
skinned woman whom you (the actress) have seen in real life.
When you (Marian) see the pianist's dark skin, how do you
react? What is your chain of thoughts? What do you want to do?
What effect does she have on you years later?

Throughout the exercise focus on really "hearing" the music.
Don't *pretend* to hear it. Don't try to *show* in any way that you
are listening to music; just try to recall the sound. This attempt is
strictly for your own benefit, not for an audience. In the same way
concentrate on really "seeing" the street, the laundry basket, the
house, the window, the room within and the black woman playing
the piano. "Feel" the weight of the laundry. You might try carrying a real basket of laundry before performing the exercise. Is it a
hot summer afternoon? A cold morning in winter? Decide on the
season, day of the week and time of day. Try to "feel" the sun or
wind, etc. on your body.

From *Dance to the Piper* by Agnes de Mille.
"Pavlova"

INTRODUCTION

She was to become a famous dancer and ballet choreographer. She would be praised the world over for such rousing folk ballets as *Rodeo* and her pioneering ballet sequences in such Broadway musicals as *Oklahoma!* (at a time when the dances in the average Broadway show were little more than chorus-girl routines). As Agnes de Mille describes her childhood in her delightful autobiography *Dance to the Piper,* she could not practice ballet for the long hours each day which she considers necessary to become technically perfect, because her parents forbade her to do so. Therefore, as an adult she would make the most of her great strengths when she danced and choreographed: pantomime, revealing character through movement, humor, lyric grace and a tremendous feel for American folk music and folk dance. In some of her ballets and dance sequences she would incorporate the movements, the gestures and rhythms of the American West—the walk of the cowboy, the high-spirited barn dances, even the typical squinting from the brilliant Western sun.

On the afternoon she describes in the following selection, she was still a child growing up in the American West—in California, where her father was one of the first screenwriters and directors in the early days of the movie industry. He worked for her uncle, the fabulous director and producer of screen spectacles, Cecil B. de Mille. Agnes' father was an intellectual, a former Broadway playwright who did not think much of dancing as a profession. He cer-

tainly had no desire for his daughter to become a dancer. From
the day, however, that Agnes and her younger sister, Margaret,
were taken to see the incomparable Russian ballerina Anna
Pavlova, Agnes knew that dancing meant more to her than anything else in the world.

AGNES: Anna Pavlova! My life stops as I write that name.
Across the daily preoccupation of lessons, lunch boxes, tooth
brushings and quarrelings with Margaret flashed this bright, un-
worldly experience and burned in a single afternoon a path over
which I could never retrace my steps. I had witnessed the power
of beauty, and in some chamber of my heart I lost forever my
irresponsibility. I was as clearly marked as though she had
looked me in the face and called my name. For generations my
father's family had loved and served the theater. All my life I
had seen actors and actresses and had heard theater jargon at
the dinner table and business talk of box-office grosses. I had
thrilled at Father's projects and watched fascinated his picturesque occupations. I took a proprietary pride in the profitable
and hasty growth of "The Industry." But nothing in his world or
my uncle's prepared me for theater as I saw it that Saturday
afternoon.

* * *

As her little bird body revealed itself on the scene, either im-
mobile in trembling mystery or tense in the incredible arc which
was her lift, her instep stretched ahead in an arch never before
seen, the tiny bones of her hands in ceaseless vibration, her face
radiant, diamonds glittering under her dark hair, her little waist
encased in silk, the great tutu balancing, quickening and flashing over her beating, flashing, quivering legs, every man and
woman sat forward, every pulse quickened. She never appeared
to rest static, some part of her trembled, vibrated, beat like a
heart.

* * *

She jumped, and we broke bonds with reality. We flew. We
hung over the earth, spread in the air as we do in dreams, our

hands turning in the air as in water—the strong forthright taut plunging leg balanced on the poised arc of the foot, the other leg stretched to the horizon like the wing of a bird. We lay balancing, quivering, turning, and all things were possible, even to us, the ordinary people.

* * *

I sat with the blood beating in my throat. As I walked into the bright glare of the afternoon, my head ached and I could scarcely swallow. I didn't wish to cry. I certainly couldn't speak. I sat in a daze in the car oblivious to the grown-ups' ceaseless prattle. At home I climbed the stairs slowly to my bedroom and, shutting myself in, placed both hands on the brass rail at the foot of my bed, then rising laboriously to the tips of my white buttoned shoes I stumped the width of the bed and back again. My toes throbbed with pain, my knees shook, my legs quivered with weakness. I repeated the exercise. The blessed, relieving tears stuck at last on my lashes. Only by hurting my feet could I ease the pain in my throat.

SUGGESTIONS FOR THE ACTOR

1. This selection is really divided into three parts. First, you as Agnes are living in the present, writing about your childhood, starting to remember the first time you saw the thrilling Anna Pavlova dance. It was one of the most important afternoons in your life. Her dancing inspired you to give up your "irresponsibility," the carefree days of your childhood, forever. She inspired you to dedicate yourself to the dance from that moment on. Secondly, you actually relive the experience. Once again you "see" (in your mind) Pavlova on that stage. You visualize clearly her appearance, her movements, her gestures. Just as clearly you recall, and experience once more, the miraculous effect she had on you and the rest of the audience. You felt that you too were jumping, turning, even flying—it seemed as though all things had become possible. Lastly, you experience anew the rest of that afternoon once her performance had ended—walking outside into

"the bright glare of the afternoon," the sharp contrast between the casual conversation of the grown-ups and the powerful emotions you felt, the resulting headache, throat ache, and later the pain in the tips of your toes as you tried to dance on them again and again in order to bring on relieving tears at last. Give yourself enough time to make these three big changes, called "transitions."

2. When you speak the first words, "Anna Pavlova!", you must see someone in your mind's eye. Have you ever admired anyone to the point of "hero worship"? If so, visualize that person. If not, you might try to recall instead a movie or play, dance, etc. that had a profound emotional effect on you. Visualize an actress or dancer, or any other performer who moved you deeply, perhaps to the point of tears.

When you describe Anna Pavlova dancing on stage, you should visualize a ballerina's performance. Have you ever seen a ballet? Try to remember it in detail. If you have never seen one, make an effort to do so, in a theatre, in the movies or on TV. Public television networks in particular often show ballet and other forms of dance.

3. Why was Agnes in pain after the performance? As you prepare to act your role, remember an experience in your own life when you were close to tears but were unable or unwilling to cry. Did you experience physical discomfort? if so, try to recall the exact pain. Concentrate on remembering in detail everything that you saw, heard, smelled, tasted and felt at that time. If you felt pain in your throat, if you found it hard to swallow, if your head ached, remember these pains with your body. If you felt other kinds of pain, remember those discomforts. Were you able to cry finally? What made you cry? What happened to the pain when the tears came? If you felt no pain during this entire experience, then try to remember with your body other headaches, throat aches and difficulties in swallowing that you felt under different circumstances. Be precise. Exactly where did it hurt? How bad was it? Was it a sharp pain or dull ache? What did you do to try to relieve the pain? What did Agnes do? Did you succeed, as Agnes did?

From *The Effect of Gamma Rays on Man-in-the-Moon Marigolds* by Paul Zindel.
Act II

INTRODUCTION

See pages 55–60 for background.

Janice Vickery is one of the five finalists in the Science Fair. She stands on the stage of the high school auditorium, delivering her speech. The other contenders and their parents are seated on the stage. It is evening.

Ruth told Tillie that Janice Vickery had caught the cat "near Princess Bay Boulevard and it was still alive when she took the skin off it." Ruth said she had heard that "it screamed for three minutes after she put it in because the water wasn't boiling yet." (See the scene on pages 56–60.) Ruth frequently exaggerates and tells lies. She first told her mother that Janice tore the skin off the cat with an orange knife. Then she changed her story: "She didn't tear it. She boiled it off."

JANICE VICKERY *is standing in the spotlight holding the skeleton of a cat mounted on a small platform. Her face and voice are smug.*

JANICE: *The Past:* I got the cat from the A.S.P.C.A. immediately after it had been killed by a high-altitude pressure system. That explains why some of the rib bones are missing, because that method sucks the air out of the animal's lungs and ruptures all cavities. They say it prevents cruelty to animals but I think it's horrible. [*She laughs*] Then I boiled the cat in a sodium hydroxide solution until most of the skin pulled right off, but I had to scrape some of the grizzle off the joints with a knife. You have no idea how difficult it is to get right down to the bones. [*A little gong sounds*]

I have to go on to *The Present,* now—but I did want to tell you how long it took me to put the thing together. I mean, as it is now, it's extremely useful for students of anatomy, even with the missing rib bones, and it can be used to show basic anatomical aspects of many, many animals that are in the family as felines. I suppose that's about the only present uses I can think for it, but it is nice to remember as an accomplishment, and it looks good on college applications to show you did something else in school besides dating. [*She laughs, and a second gong sounds*]

The Future: The only future plans I have for Tabby—my little brother asked the A.S.P.C.A. what its name was when he went to pick it up and they said it was called Tabby, but I think they were kidding him— [*She laughs again*] I mean as far as future plans, I'm going to donate it to the science department, of course, and next year, if there's another Science Fair perhaps I'll do the same thing with a dog. [*A third gong sounds*]

Thank you very much for your attention, and I hope I win!

SUGGESTIONS FOR THE ACTOR

1. You, the actress, must decide whether you, Janice, are telling the truth. Are you lying now or was Ruth lying when she said that you "caught the cat near Princess Bay Boulevard"?

2. If you, the actress, decide that you, Janice, killed the cat yourself in order to obtain its skeleton, then you, as Janice, must somehow justify your action in your own mind. Few sane people consciously think of themselves as villains. Most people rationalize, justifying their own behavior to themselves. Certainly a villain in a play must come across to the audience as despicable. But you, as Janice, would not consider yourself evil even if you did boil a live cat. How would you justify this cruel act? You might tell yourself that the cat was nearly dead anyway from the auto-

mobile accident, and that you were putting it out of its misery. You might tell yourself that no college would turn down a Science Fair winner. Your future is far more important than the life of a stray cat. You might even drum up the flimsy excuse that the cat population is much too large anyway. What other rationalizations can you think of? You, the actress, would have to select the rationalization that best fits your interpretation of the part.

3. Study photographs of cat skeletons in zoology books, science encyclopedias or other sources. As you hold the imaginary skeleton of the cat, you must "see" and "feel" it. How long is it? How wide? How high? How heavy? Handle the skeleton with care; you don't want it to fall apart.

4. Vividly imagine the acts you, Janice, describe: boiling a cat, pulling off the skin afterward and then scraping "some of the grizzle off with a knife." Was the cat really dead when you immersed it in the chemical solution? (Lye, oven cleaner and Drano are composed of sodium hydroxide.) What was your (Janice's) attitude toward the cat as you committed these acts? You could not have been terribly squeamish. Did you secretly enjoy the procedure? Or was it simply a chore to you, no more, no less than, say, boiling and peeling potatoes? Or were you greatly annoyed at all the trouble required "to get right down to the bones"?

5. The audience should find you, Janice, smug and obnoxious, but you, the actress, should not concentrate on portraying these qualities. After all, the character you play would not be thinking, "How smug and obnoxious I am!" You, Janice, might be thinking, "I'm the only one who can possibly win! That Tillie Hunsdorfer is my only real competition, and she's bound to make a fool of herself again. She looked so ridiculous in assembly when she cranked the model atom that we just couldn't help laughing. . . ." If you concentrate on such thoughts, you will automatically look and sound smug to the audience. Unlike Tillie, you have no true love of science. You love to *win,* and you are none too finicky about the means. Your laughter will probably strike the audience as particularly obnoxious. What are you thinking each time you laugh? Your first laugh reveals the insincerity of your words: Even though you call the A.S.P.C.A.'s "high-altitude pressure system" of killing animals "horrible," you laugh. Why?

6. The play itself does not deal with your (Janice Vickery's)

past life, but you, the actress, must invent the background, the physical and psychological traits of the character. Answer the questions on the "Actor's Check List," beginning on page 336.

7. If possible, have someone sound a gong or ring a bell during your monologue, at the moments indicated in the text.

8. Read Tillie's speech on pages 106–7. How different the two presentations are, even though the format is the same! What do the differences reveal about the two personalities? It would be interesting for the audience to compare the two speeches also; both monologues could be performed at the same session, Tillie's following yours.

From *The Effect of Gamma Rays on Man-in-the-Moon Marigolds* by Paul Zindel.
Act II

INTRODUCTION

See pages 55–62 for background.

Your (Tillie's) mother was all dressed up to take the taxi to school with you this evening for the final judging of the Science Fair. You told her she looked beautiful. She was feeling proud for the first time in her life. But when your sister, Ruth, learns that she cannot go too, that she has to stay home to take care of old Nanny, she maliciously bids Mama, "Good night, Betty the Loon." "Betty the Loon" had been your mother's hated nickname in high school. Realizing that Ruth must have heard it from staff members who had known her in those days, terrified of being laughed at again, your mother decides not to go after all. Heartbroken, she sends Ruth with you in the taxi to help carry your display.

In the play itself you (Tillie) speak the lines through "MANKIND WILL THANK GOD FOR THE STRANGE AND BEAUTIFUL ENERGY FROM THE ATOM" from the stage of your high school auditorium. The conclusion of your speech, as a Science Fair contestant, is not heard until the end of the play, when a tape recording of your voice provides a dramatic contrast to the sordid scene at home.

That a mind and character like yours somehow emerged from your home, your family, is nothing short of a miracle. You yourself are like one of your double-bloom marigolds, or one of those glorious mutations you speak of, which may be produced by atomic energy someday. Your sister, Ruth, may be compared to a mutation also, the "dwarf plants" whose normal development was stunted because they were grown from the "seeds closest to the gamma source."

Time: Evening. Place: Your high school auditorium. The other finalists and their parents are seated on the stage where you are standing.

TILLIE: [*Deathly afraid, and referring to her cards*] *The Past:* The seeds were exposed to various degrees . . . of gamma rays from radiation sources in Oak Ridge . . .

Mr. Goodman helped me pay for the seeds . . . Their growth was plotted against . . . time. [*She loses her voice for a moment and then the first gong sounds*]

The Present: The seeds which received little radiation have grown to plants which are normal in appearance. The seeds which received moderate radiation gave rise to mutations such as double blooms, giant stems, and variegated leaves. The seeds closest to the gamma source were killed or yielded dwarf plants. [*The second gong rings*]

The Future: After radiation is better understood, a day will come when the power from exploding atoms will change the whole world we know. [*With inspiration*] Some of the mutations will be good ones—wonderful things beyond our dreams—and I believe, I believe this with all my heart. THE DAY WILL COME WHEN MANKIND WILL THANK GOD FOR THE STRANGE AND BEAUTIFUL ENERGY FROM THE ATOM.

* * *

The Conclusion: My experiment has shown some of the strange effects radiation can produce . . . and how dangerous it can be if not handled correctly.

Mr. Goodman said I should tell in this conclusion what my future plans are and how this experiment has helped me make them.

For one thing, the effect of gamma rays on man-in-the-moon marigolds has made me curious about the sun and the stars, for the universe itself must be like a world of great atoms—and I want to know more about it. But most important, I suppose, my experiment has made me feel important—every atom in me, in everybody, has come from the sun—from places beyond our dreams. The atoms of our hands, the atoms of our hearts . . .

SUGGESTIONS FOR THE ACTOR

1. If you (the actress) are nervous about performing this mono-logue, *use* your fear to advantage; it fits the part. You, as Tillie, have to refer to your typewritten cards because of terrible stage fright. Most people would be tense in a similar situation, but you (Tillie) are unusually shy, even under ordinary circumstances. At the beginning of the play Mr. Goodman, your science teacher, called your mother at home and told her that you say hardly a word in class. To add to your present anxiety, you must have been badly upset in the taxi on the way here. Your sister (Ruth) climbed in and told you that Mama wasn't coming after all. Did she tell you *why* Mama changed her mind—because Ruth had said, "Good night, Betty the Loon"? You (the actress) must decide whether you (Tillie) understands Mama's reason for refusing to come at the last minute.

It would be useful to improvise, with a partner, the conversation between you and Ruth in the taxi earlier this evening. That scene is not depicted in the play itself. You (Tillie) understand your mother and your sister pretty well. If Ruth doesn't "spell it all out" for you, do you *guess* the truth about what happened between them while you were waiting in the taxi for Mama?

2. Real props are probably unnecessary except for the cards with your typed speech, but you must clearly visualize your entire display: the three-panel screen with "the Past," "The Present" and "The Future," and the pots of marigolds, Specifically, how have you (Tillie) demonstrated your experiment on the three-panel screen? Have you made graphs or charts comparing the growth of plants from the three categories of seeds? You say that

their growth was "plotted against * * * time." Where and how is the passage of time indicated on the screen? What divisions of time have you used—months, weeks, days?

You may wish to point to particular items of your (imaginary) display at appropriate moments throughout your speech.

3. Visualize Mr. Goodman, your science teacher, when you speak of him. Picture a kind, perceptive man you (the actress) know in real life, someone who cares about you. What is your (Tillie's) attitude toward Mr. Goodman? He has recognized your extraordinary potential, perhaps genius, as well as your extraordinary problems at home, and he has tried to help you in every way he could. He telephoned your mother because he was concerned about your emotional well-being; he gave you your pet rabbit; he supplied seeds for your experiment. After your mother had kept you home from school on the day of an important science experiment, he set up the "cloud chamber" again, just for you.

4. The speech format is the same for all the final contestants: All of you must begin with "The Past." When the gong rings, you all proceed to "The Present." At the next sound of the gong you discuss "The Future." You all must end with "The Conclusion." Read Janice Vickery's speech on pages 101–2. The differences between the two speeches, both organized within the same framework, reveal a great deal about the differences between your two characters.

If possible, have someone sound a gong or ring a bell at the moments indicated in the text.

5. At the beginning of your (Tillie's) speech you are self-conscious, afraid. Gradually you become involved in a problem outside yourself: informing the audience. Then, when you contemplate the ways atomic energy may one day help mankind, you become inspired. If thoughts about future uses of science fail to inspire you, the actress, then in preparing your role, substitute a dream of your own, perhaps your own private vision of a better world for your children. At the conclusion of your (Tillie's) speech you again become conscious of yourself, but you are no longer afraid. Now you are filled with a sense of self-worth because of your awareness that you, and all creatures, are composed of marvelous atoms.

From *This Property Is Condemned*
by Tennessee Williams

INTRODUCTION

This tiny gem of a one-act play by Tennessee Williams has only two characters: Willie, a young girl who does most of the talking, and Tom, a young boy who listens to her, not always believing what she tells him. A portion of their conversation has been converted into the monologue below.

The scene, according to the playwright, is

A railroad embankment on the outskirts of a small Mississippi town on one of those milky white winter mornings peculiar to that part of the country. The air is moist and chill. Behind the low embankment of the tracks is a large yellow frame house which has a look of tragic vacancy. Some of the upper windows are boarded, a portion of the roof has fallen away. The land is utterly flat. * * * The sky is a great milky whiteness: crows occasionally make a sound of roughly torn cloth.

The girl Willie is

* * * thin as a beanpole and dressed in outrageous cast-off finery. She wears a long blue velvet party dress with a filthy cream lace collar and sparkling rhinestone beads. On her feet are battered silver kid slippers with large ornamental buckles. Her wrists and her fingers are resplendent with dimestore jewelry. She has applied rouge to her childish face in artless crimson daubs and her lips are made up in a preposterous Cupid's bow. She is about thirteen and there is something ineluctably childlike and innocent in her appearance despite the makeup. She laughs frequently and wildly and with a sort of precocious, tragic abandon.

She holds an old, beat-up doll with a messy blond wig.

Willie had walked here along the railroad tracks—all the way from a distant water tank—balancing herself with outstretched arms, clutching the doll and a banana, rescued from a garbage pail. She had reached this spot, the farthest she had ever gone along the tracks, when she finally fell off. We learn during the course of the play that Willie is living all alone in her family's condemned old house, hiding from the social worker assigned to her case. She eats what scraps of food she can find. She tells Tom that she does not go to school because she "quituated" two year ago, in 5A. Some time ago her mother had run off with a railroad brakeman. Her father had then taken up drinking and had later disappeared. Her older sister, Alva, had died of tuberculosis—Willie calls it "lung affection." Their house had been a brothel for railroad men; Alva had been "The Main Attraction."

The outside world, the social agencies, would no doubt consider Willie's home environment sordid. But Willie does not see it that way. In her innocence, she finds beauty, glamour and romance in the life Alva had led. She idolizes her dead sister and wants to be just like her.

Frank Waters is a young boy who has evidently rejected Willie even though she had once exhibited herself in front of him. Wanting to impress him, through Tom, she invents one of her stories about her popularity with railroad men, then becomes carried away by her own imagination.

A few notes explaining references in this monologue to remarks made earlier in the play: When Alva had been alive there really had been "musical instruments going all the time" in their house. The freight superintendent had been Alva's most important "beau." Willie inherited all of Alva's clothes, except for her solid gold beads, which Alva had been wearing when she died. Willie claims that she also inherited all of Alva's "beaux." When Willie says, "maybe not like death in the movies, with violins playing—," she is thinking specifically of the tragic romance *Camille,* which she had seen at a local movie house the previous spring. The tragic heroine, Camille, had also died of tuberculosis, but unlike Alva's grim death, Camille's death had been beautiful.

WILLIE: * * * The sky sure is white. Ain't it? White as a clean piece of paper. In Five A we used to draw pictures. Miss Preston would give us a piece of white foolscap an' tell us to draw what we pleased. * * *

I remember I drawn her a picture one time of my old man getting conked with a bottle. She thought it was good, Miss Preston, she said, "Look here. Here's a picture of Charlie Chaplin with his hat on the side of his head!" I said, "Aw, naw, that's not Charlie Chaplin, that's my father, an' that's not his hat, it's a bottle!" * * *

Oh, well. You can't make a school-teacher laugh. * * *

Will you give Frank Waters a message? * * *

Tell him the freight sup'rintendent has bought me a pair of kid slippers. Patent. The same as the old ones of Alva's. I'm going to dances with them at Moon Lake Casino. All night I'll be dancing an' come home drunk in the morning. We'll have serenades with all kinds of musical instruments. Trumpets an' trombones. An' Hawaiian steel guitars. Yeh! Yeh! [*She rises excitedly*] The sky will be white like this. * * *

[*She smiles vaguely and turns slowly toward him*] White—as a clean—piece of paper . . . [*Then excitedly*] I'll draw—pictures on it! * * *

Me dancing! With the freight sup'rintendent! In a pair of patent kid shoes! Yeh! Yeh! With French heels on them as high as telegraph poles! * * *

I'll—wear a corsage! * * *

[That's] flowers to pin on your dress at a formal affair! Rosebuds! Violets! And lilies-of-the-valley! When you come home it's withered but you stick 'em in a bowl to freshen 'em up. * * *

That's what Alva done * * * I'm going back now * * * [To] the water-tank * * * An' start all over again. Maybe I'll break some kind of continuous record. Alva did once. At a dance marathon in Mobile. Across the state line. Alabama. You can tell Frank Waters everything I've told you. I don't have time for inexperienced people. I'm going out now with popular railroad men, men with good salaries, too. Don't you believe me? * * *

Well, if I wanted to I could prove it. But you wouldn't be worth convincing. [*She smooths out Crazy Doll's hair*] I'm going to live for a long, long time like my sister. An' when my lungs get affected, I'm going to die like she did—maybe not like in the movies, with violins playing—but with my pearl earrings on an' my solid gold beads from Memphis. . . . * * *

[*Examining Crazy Doll very critically*] An' then I guess— * * * [*Gaily but with a slight catch*] Somebody else will inherit all of my beaux! The sky sure is white. * * * White as a clean piece of paper. I'm going back now. * * *

So long. [*She starts back along the railroad track, weaving grotesquely to keep her balance. She disappears*]

SUGGESTIONS FOR THE ACTOR

1. Visualize the white sky, a few bare winter trees, some telephone poles, the abandoned house and the flat land below the embankment of railroad tracks. "Hear" the occasional cawing of crows. "Smell" the rotten banana or banana peel. Are you still eating the banana when you begin to speak? If so, then either "taste" the imaginary banana or eat a real banana. "Feel" the moist, chill air.

2. It would be easier to speak your monologue to a real boy whom you thought of as Tom, than to try to imagine Tom and all his reactions. You might wish to select a member of the audience and address him. Another possibility would be for an onstage actor to play the nonspeaking role of Tom, reacting to everything you tell him, sometimes disbelieving you. The actor would have to work on Tom's characterization even though he has no lines. Tom is slightly older than you (Willie). He wears corduroy pants, a shirt and a sweater; he carries a kite. He had hoped to fly his kite, but the morning is windless.

3. Throughout the monologue what are all your (Willie's) thought associations that lead you from one subject to another? For example, at the beginning of the monologue you associate the

white sky with a clean piece of paper. Then what does a clean piece of paper remind you of?

4. Your (Willie's) mood during the first part of this monologue would probably be peaceful and relaxed as you contemplated the sky, then amused as you remembered Miss Preston. You would be relaxed physically as well as emotionally; you might be sitting or even lying down on the ground, maybe finishing your banana. Then as your daydream about dancing like Alva began to absorb you, your whole body would change, tense, along with the change in your emotions. You would probably rise at some point, much too keyed up to sit or lie down any longer. In fact, you would probably be too excited to stand still. Your excitement would grow and grow to a fever pitch. What might you do physically at that point? When would your emotional fever begin to subside? Your daydream about dying would certainly differ in mood from your daydream about dancing and drinking. Alva's death was horrible, not at all romantic. Her lovers had all deserted her. No music was permitted by the hospital. Do you *want* to die like her, or do you just assume that you *will* die like her? Why do you examine Crazy Doll "very critically" just before you speak of someone else inheriting all *your* beaux? Do you want that to happen? What thoughts and feelings are you covering up? At the end of the monologue, when you say, "The sky sure is white," in what way is your mood different from what it was the first time you made that same observation? Why is your mood different now? What do you want to do? Why do you leave at this moment?

5. Do you, the actress, ever daydream? Did you daydream when you were younger? Have you ever been emotionally "carried away" by your thoughts or daydreams? As you were thinking excitedly, did you move, perhaps without meaning to? If you were walking down the street, did you begin to walk faster or skip or even break into a run? Exactly what were you imagining? Try to remember everything you did physically while you were so engrossed. Can you use some of these actions as you portray Willie? Which ones?

6. Give Crazy Doll a distinct personality. What is your (Willie's) attitude toward your beat-up old doll? As an acting exercise, perform some typical physical action as Willie (such as hunt-

ing for scraps of food or walking back along the tracks to the water tank), talking aloud to Crazy Doll the whole time. Do you, Willie, ever answer yourself in a different voice, pretending to be Crazy Doll?

From *My Sister, My Sister* by Ray Aranha.
Act I

INTRODUCTION

This psychological drama is experimental in form. The heart-breaking story is not unfolded in the usual, chronological order of events. We are inside the mind of a mentally ill, sixteen-year-old black girl, Sue Belle. We, the audience, see and hear what is really happening to her at the present moment; we also see and hear her memories of the past and her fantasies, which she confuses with present reality. Sometimes all three—the present, the past and her delusions—are interwoven in Sue Belle's brain as well as onstage. "With Sue Belle's sickness, what is not real is so close to what is real that they cannot be divorced."

The following monologue is one of Sue Belle's memories of the past. The adolescent Sue Belle remembers herself as a six-year-old child. The actress need not necessarily change completely into a six-year-old as she speaks. In the beginning the change from adolescent to young child is an emotional change, taking place inside Sue Belle; any outward changes in voice or body would come as a result of these inner changes.

As the play opens, sixteen-year-old Sue Belle is alone in her room on a rainy night. No one else lives in the house any more— her mother is dead; her father deserted the family long ago; her sister ran away. Deeply disturbed by her confused, jumbled thoughts, Sue Belle awaits the arrival of Eddie, her future husband.

She relives a childhood conversation with her mother, whose

whole life was dedicated to her fundamentalist religion. Little Sue Belle has been frightened by Mama's frequent warnings of hell fire and eternal damnation; her mama now tries to reassure and comfort her. At the same time Mama tells her that the devil hides himself in all the colors that men are. Sue Belle asks whether the devil is ever a blue color. Her mama answers, "Well, if there was blue people, he would be, but there ain't." She gives Sue Belle a big box of crayons and a large sheet of drawing paper, gifts from a white woman, Miss Beatrice, who often gives presents to their family. Sue Belle is delighted.

Sue Belle's sister Evalina, an adolescent at this point in the play, sneaks into the house in the evening, not wanting her parents to know that she has been out so late. Evalina tries to study in the bedroom, but Sue Belle makes noise playing with her dolls and disturbs her. Sue Belle likes Evalina even though her big sister mistreats her. She tries to be Evalina's friend, her "soul sister," but Evalina says she is much too young. Evalina scoffs at Sue Belle for calling her dolls her "babies" when she doesn't even know where babies come from. Evalina leaves the bedroom to take a bath.

Evalina hates and envies Sue Belle because their adored daddy no longer pays much attention to his firstborn child; he plays with cute little Sue Belle instead. Evalina desperately needs her father, but he has little time for her. She has rejected her mother's religion. Her mother thinks of Evalina as evil and gives all her love to Sue Belle, who is deeply influenced by her mother's beliefs.

Daddy drinks too much. He bitterly resents his wife's all-consuming religion. The former closeness between this couple is gone; he feels shut out by her constant preaching. He tells his wife that in her mind, sin is always "black sin"; evil is "black evil." How can their children love themselves when they are being trained to despise their blackness? he argues.

The play is set in the South in the late 1950s. Sue Belle's house is "a two-storied wooden building, aging and rotting from disrepair, dark and somber." In the bedroom shared by the two sisters "there is a small stool, a small phonograph, a small closet and a night table on which is a lamp of Jesus kneeling in the Garden of Gethsemane. A window sill holds fifteen dolls of various shapes and sizes." Petal is Sue Belle's newest doll, a special present from Daddy.

The child Sue Belle fantasizes about Jesus visiting her. In her vivid imagination he is always frowning, as in the pictures of him which she has seen. After Evalina leaves the bedroom to take a bath, "SUE BELLE sits quietly; presently JESUS enters * * * bedroom doorway and stands watching her."

SUE BELLE (Child): Hey, Jesus. Evelina mad at me again. I don't know why. You wanna see something? [*Moving to crayons and drawing paper*] See what Miss Beatrice give me. She's really nice. You'd like her. [*A pause*] What's the matter? Don't you wanna see these colors? There's a lot of 'em. [*A pause*] You still feelin' sad? Ain't you neva gonna be happy? Mama told me how You had two little boys and one 'em killed the other wit' a slingshot. [*A pause*] How come he done that, Jesus? I mean, You made the sun and everything. Couldn't You make that rock miss? * * * You know, Evelina don't like You. She don't like me neither. I don't know why. But I don't think she'd kill me. I mean, you gotta be real bad to do somethin' like that. I don't mean to make You mad by sayin' You little boy is bad . . . but maybe if one of Yo' boys got in trouble, You shoulda whupped him like Mama do me . . . then they woulda minded You and not get killed. [*A pause*] You know what? I wish You wouldn't be so sad. You make me sad. Hey, I know what! Why don't we play some real good music and You jus' sit and I'll draw Yo' pitcher. [*JESUS crosses to bed and sits*] That'll make You feel good. I draw real good. My daddy told me I do. [*Moving to records and phonograph*] What You wanna hear? Evelina ain't got no church music. [*A pause*] And what color you want to be? Red or purple? I know. Blue. Blue. Cause Yo' yard in the sky is blue. And Petal got on a blue dress. And the devil is all colors but blue. And Evelina got a real good song called, "Blue . . . Blue . . . Blue Moon." [*Putting on record "Blue Moon"*] There. [*Returning and settling down to color and draw*] Now let's see. [*She draws a slow round circle*] Heah is Yo' face. [*Rising and examining it*] No. It look kinda lop-sided, don't it? You got a real nice face. I'm gonna be careful. [*She retraces it, making the circle rounder*] There. Now. Eyes. *Two round circles for eyes*] Mouth. [*A straight line for mouth*] No. [*Holding it up in view of audience*] Now it don't look right, do it? I know why. That's 'cause You still frownin'. Don't You never laugh, Jesus? Ain't You neva gonna be happy? Well, I'm gonna make You happy in ma pitcher. [*Curving up straight line for smile*] Now. [*Holding it up in view of audience*] That's real nice. Now I'm gonna put in . . . [*Quick swirly lines*] Yo' hair on Yo' face. [*Straight line down for body*] Stomach. [*Upside down "V" for legs, straight lines for arms and very long, long lines for fingers*] Fingers. [*A pause*] I forgot . . . I forgot . . . Mama said You suffered awful on the Cross. I gotta put that in. Right here. [*Huge out of proportion nails, almost as long as the arms, going into the hands with large circles for blood. She rises, pleased with herself, and hangs it on the wall*] You like it? Huh? Look at it, Jesus. You like it? How come You won't neva smile, Jesus?

SUGGESTIONS FOR THE ACTOR

1. Why do you, the child Sue Belle, have this fantasy or day-dream right now? Evalina just said to you, "How kin I even try to like you? You jus' too stupid." She then left you, to take a bath. You must be feeling rejected by her. Do you seek comfort from Jesus? Can you, the actress, think of another possible reason for this fantasy? Use whichever psychological reason you prefer.

2. You, the actress, must decide whether
      (a) you, the child Sue Belle, are *making believe* that Jesus is in the room with you,
                                    or
      (b) you, the child Sue Belle, *really* believe He is there.

The play is deliberately vague regarding the figure of Jesus. The audience is not sure whether the child Sue Belle is actually hallucinating or just deeply involved in "make believe." But you, the actress, must be sure.

In the play the role of Jesus is portrayed by a white actor. Jesus looks exactly as He is "usually pictured." It might be distracting for you, however, to use a real actor, unless he closely resembled pictures of Jesus. It might be better to study paintings, sculptures, etc. depicting Jesus so that you might visualize Him clearly as you performed.

3. Your mother's fanatic preaching, her constant warning of eternal punishment have brought unhappiness to your home. Perhaps you (Sue Belle) somehow associate the frowning Jesus with that kind of religion. Maybe you urgently want Him to be happy so that you and your family may be happy too. What actions do you perform throughout the monologue to make Jesus smile?

4. What is your (Sue Belle's) chain of thoughts during your frequent pauses? During some of your pauses, you may be waiting for some happy response from Jesus. While waiting, you are undoubtedly thinking all the time.

5. When you ask Jesus what color he wants to be, you come up with an answer yourself. Don't anticipate what your answer will be—don't plan ahead. You, Sue Belle, should decide on the color at this very moment, after considering other possibilities. You figure out various reasons for choosing the color blue, discovering one reason at a time. You have not prepared a "laundry list" of reasons; you cannot glibly spout one reason after another. You have to stop and think. Also, you have to struggle to recall the full title of Evalina's record. Eventually the name comes to you.

6. You, the actress, must visualize not only Jesus, but also the people you mention—Miss Beatrice, Evalina and your mama.

Decide on Miss Beatrice's relationship to your (Sue Belle's) family; the play does not provide that information. Is she your mother's employer? A neighbor? Visualize a kindly white woman, someone you (the actress) know in real life.

Evalina "is dressed in the teen vogue of the fifties but with a clumsy attempt at sexuality, perhaps in jeans or tight shorts."

Do you (the actress) have an older sister? Did she ever mistreat you even though you admired her and wanted to be her friend? If so, picture your own sister when you speak of Evalina. If not, try to think of any girl who treated you badly although you liked her.

Your (Sue Belle's) mother loves you, but she has no use for your sister. Her attitude toward Evalina probably makes you uneasy. For one thing, it makes your sister hate you all the more. Also it might occur to you that your mama could turn against you too, if you ever acted "real bad."

When you speak of Mama, think of a strong black woman, a harsh disciplinarian, but someone who loves you dearly and whom you love in return. If your (the actress') own mother fits that description, then visualize her.

Monologues for Boys

From *You're a Good Man, Charlie Brown* by Clark Gesner, based on the comic strip *Peanuts* by Charles M. Schulz.
Act I

INTRODUCTION

You're a Good Man, Charlie Brown is a "musical entertainment" consisting of songs and sketches based on the comic strip *Peanuts*. There was no script when the original production went into rehearsal. In fact, the play script, or "book," was not written until after the show opened. The invention of the sketches was a joint creative effort by everyone involved in getting the comic strip *Peanuts* onstage—actors, writer, director, technical people, etc. The words were later set down by Clark Gesner, who composed the music and lyrics.

If there remains a child in these United States who did not know and love Charles M. Schulz' comic-strip characters Snoopy, Lucy, Linus, Schroeder, Patty and of course Charlie Brown himself, that youngster must be a rare specimen.

"Charlie Brown has never pitched a winning baseball game, has never been able to keep a kite in the air, has lost ten thousand checker games in a row, and has never successfully punted a football. Charlie Brown can do just about anything—the wrong way. That's what makes him so lovable."

A jangling school bell sounds. "CHARLIE BROWN is left alone at center stage, seated, clutching a paper bag." He sits on a recently painted wooden bench.

124 THE YOUNG ACTORS' WORKBOOK

CHARLIE BROWN: I think lunchtime is about the worst time of the day for me. Always having to sit here alone. Of course, sometimes mornings aren't so pleasant, either—waking up and wondering if anyone would really miss me if I never got out of bed. Then there's the night, too—lying there and thinking about all the stupid things I've done during the day. And all those hours in between—when I do all those stupid things. Well, lunchtime is *among* the worst times of the day for me.

Well, I guess I'd better see what I've got. [*He opens the bag, unwraps a sandwich, and looks inside*] Peanut butter. [*He bites and chews*] Some psychiatrists say that people who eat peanut butter sandwiches are lonely. I guess they're right. And if you're really lonely, the peanut butter sticks to the roof of your mouth. [*He munches quietly, idly fingering the bench*] Boy, the PTA sure did a good job of painting these benches. [*He looks off to one side*] There's that cute little redheaded girl eating her lunch over there. I wonder what she'd do if I went over and asked her if I could sit and have lunch with her. She'd probably laugh right in my face. It's hard on a face when it gets laughed in. There's an empty place next to her on the bench. There's no reason why I couldn't just go over and sit there. I could do that right now. All I have to do is stand up. [*He stands*] I'm standing up. [*He sits*] I'm sitting down. I'm a coward. I'm so much of a coward she wouldn't even think of looking at me. She hardly ever *does* look at me. In fact, I can't remember her ever looking at me. Why shouldn't she look at me? Is there any reason in the world why she shouldn't look at me? Is she so great and am I so small that she couldn't spare one little moment just to . . . [*He freezes*] She's looking at me. [*In terror he looks one way, then another*] She's *looking* at me.

[*His head looks all around, frantically trying to find something else to notice. His teeth clench. Tension builds. Then, with one motion, he pops the paper bag over his head*]

SUGGESTIONS FOR THE ACTOR

1. What are some of the "stupid things" you, Charlie Brown, did yesterday and this morning? What stupid or silly things, em-

barrassing to remember, have you, the actor, ever said or done? Think of them when you, as Charlie Brown, refer to "all those stupid things" you've "done during the day."

2. During this soliloquy you eat a peanut butter sandwich. The eating must be believable to you, the actor, so that it will be believable to the audience. You can use a real peanut butter sandwich or you can pretend to eat. If you decide to eat an imaginary sandwich, practice at home with a real peanut butter sandwich. Notice what it looks like, smells like, sounds like, feels like in your hands and in your mouth, how it tastes, how you chew and how you swallow it. Does the peanut butter *really* stick to the roof of your mouth? Notice also how much space the sandwich takes in your hands, and how you use not only your hands but other parts of your body when you remove it from the paper bag, unwrap it and eat it. Observe the paper bag with all your senses too, as well as the "Baggie" in which the sandwich is wrapped. Later try to remember all these observations as exactly as possible when you pretend to eat. This work is called "sense memory."

3. It is essential for an actor to stress the key words in his part. An inexperienced actor may have some difficulty, however, in choosing the important words in this selection because words and ideas are often repeated. He may have particular difficulty in stressing each *new* idea.

To solve this problem, reread the monologue, selecting each word that represents a new idea. These words need to be emphasized when you speak. Which words refer to ideas that you, Charlie Brown, have already expressed? These words should *not* be emphasized unless there is a special reason for doing so. If an actor stresses an idea that is not new, and fails to stress the new thought, it will be difficult for the audience to understand the meaning.

Take, for example, the sequence, "I'm a coward. I'm so much of a coward she wouldn't even think of looking at me. She hardly ever *does* look at me [italics in play script]. In fact I can't remember her ever looking at me. Is there any reason in the world why she shouldn't look at me?" In the second sentence is the word "coward" a new thought? If it is not a new thought, then it should not be emphasized. In which sentence does the word "look" or "looking" represent a new idea? In which sentences is it an old idea, one that should no longer be stressed?

4. Visualize the "cute little redheaded girl" over there on that bench, with the empty place next to her. What is she doing whenever you look in her direction? Picture someone you know slightly in real life, a pretty girl whom you admire from afar. Your mental image need not necessarily have red hair.

5. You, Charlie Brown, are being pulled in two different directions by your conflicting desires. You want to make friends with the little redheaded girl, but you also want to avoid rejection. These opposite feelings do not come simultaneously, however; first you are pulled one way, then the other, like the rope in a tug-of-war. First you want to join her; then you imagine how you would feel if she laughed at you. Again you have an impulse to join her; this time you even go so far as to stand up. What horrible thoughts push you right back down again? In still another moment of daring, you (mentally) defy her to look at you. All of a sudden you realize with utter terror that she really *is* looking at you! Your courage keeps springing up and flopping down like a seesaw, or a jack-in-the-box.

You, the actor, should not *anticipate;* you should not expect what is going to happen. You, Charlie Brown, never know in advance what thoughts and feelings are going to hit you next. For instance, when you first stand up, you fully expect to walk over to the redheaded girl. For that moment you believe completely that this time you are going to "make it." If you stand up with a show of confidence and determination, your subsequent change of heart will be much funnier than if you rise halfheartedly in the first place. Fear overcomes you, however, and you crumple, body and soul, like jack-back-in-the-box.

From *The Adventures of Tom Sawyer* by Samuel Langhorne Clemens

INTRODUCTION

Perhaps the best loved of all American novels for young people, *Tom Sawyer* was written in 1876 by one of our greatest humorous writers, Samuel Clemens. You may know him better by his pen name, or pseudonym, Mark Twain. This story takes place in a small Missouri village, St. Petersburg, around the 1830s or 1840s. The hero, Tom, is a young boy with a normal sense of mischief, a hunger for excitement and a wild imagination fed by swash-buckling adventure tales. But despite all his dreams of becoming a pirate, highway robber or some other romantic villain, Tom is a civilized creature, reared by his respectable aunt Polly. On the other hand his friend Huckleberry Finn is not the least bit civilized, not if he can help it. Huck is the son of the town drunk-ard, an outcast who doesn't bother Huck much, except when he flies into one of his drunken rages. On those occasions Huck fears for his life.

Early in *Tom Sawyer,* Huck is described as follows:

Huckleberry was cordially hated and dreaded by all the mothers of the town, because he was idle and lawless and vulgar and bad—and because all their children admired him so, and delighted in his for-bidden society, and wished they dared to be like him. Tom was like the rest of the respectable boys, in that he envied Huckleberry his gaudy outcast condition, and was under strict orders not to play with him. So he played with him every time he got a chance.

Huckleberry was always dressed in the cast-off clothes of full-grown men, and they were * * * fluttering with rags. His hat was a vast ruin with a wide crescent lopped out of its brim; his coat, when he wore one, hung nearly to his heels and had the rearward buttons far down the back; * * * one suspender supported his trousers; the seat of the trousers bagged low and contained nothing; the fringed legs dragged in the dirt when not rolled up.

Huckleberry came and went, at his own free will. He slept on doorsteps in fine weather and in empty hogsheads in wet; he did not have to go to school or to church, or call any being master or obey anybody; he could go fishing or swimming when and where he chose, and stay as long as it suited him; nobody forbade him to fight; he could sit up as late as he pleased; he was always the first boy that went barefoot in the spring and the last to resume leather in the fall; he never had to wash, nor put on clean clothes; he could swear wonderfully. In a word, everything that goes to make life precious, that boy had. So thought every harassed, hampered, respectable boy in St. Petersburg.

But Huck's condition changes drastically. He saves a kindly, extremely religious woman known as the Widow Douglas from being cut up by a vengeful criminal called Injun Joe. In gratitude she takes Huckleberry into her home, intending to bring him up as her own son. Huck and Tom find an enormous box of gold coins hidden in a cave by Injun Joe and another scoundrel. Each boy now owns six thousand dollars, an unheard-of sum in those days. The money is invested for them, and they collect the interest. Each now has a huge income—"a dollar for every week-day in the year and half of the Sundays." Huck soon discovers, however, that wealth and respectability are not all they are "cracked up to be." He stays with the Widow for three miserable weeks and then one day disappears.

Tom finds him three mornings later among some old empty barrels behind an abandoned building, once a slaughterhouse.

Huck had slept there; he had just breakfasted upon some stolen odds and ends of food, and was lying off, now, in comfort, with his pipe. He was unkempt, uncombed, and clad in the same old ruin of rags that had made him picturesque in the days when he was free and happy.

Tom tells him how upset and worried everyone is, especially the good Widow, and urges Huckleberry to go home. The following selection is Huck's reply.

HUCKLEBERRY: Don't talk about it, Tom. I've tried it, and it don't work, Tom. It ain't for me; I ain't used to it. The widder's good to me, and friendly; but I can't stand them ways. She makes me git up just at the same time every morning; she makes me wash, they comb me all to thunder; she won't let me sleep in the woodshed; I got to wear them blamed clothes that just smothers me, Tom; they don't seem to let any air git through 'em, somehow; and they're so rotten nice that I can't set down, nor lay down, nor roll around anywher's; I hain't slid on a cellar-door for—well, it 'pears to be years; I got to go to church and sweat and sweat—I hate them ornery sermons! I can't ketch a fly in there, I can't chaw. I got to wear shoes all Sunday. The widder eats by a bell; she goes to bed by a bell; she gits up by a bell—everything's so awful reg'lar a body can't stand it. * * *

It's awful to be tied up so. And grub comes too easy—I don't take no interest in vittles, that way. I got to ask to go a-fishing; I got to ask to go in a-swimming—dern'd if I hain't got to ask to do everything. * * * The widder wouldn't let me smoke; she wouldn't let me yell, she wouldn't let me gape, nor stretch, nor scratch, before folks—[*Then with a spasm of special irritation and injury*] And dad fetch it, she prayed all the time! I never *see* such a woman! I *had* to shove, Tom—I just had to. And besides, that school's going to open, and I'd 'a' had to go to it— well, I wouldn't stand *that,* Tom. Looky here, Tom, being rich ain't what it's cracked up to be. It's just worry and worry, and sweat and sweat, and a-wishing you was dead all the time. Now these clothes suits me, and this bar'l suits me, and I ain't ever going to shake 'em any more. Tom, I wouldn't ever got into all this trouble if it hadn't 'a' been for that money; now you just take my sheer of it along with your'n and gimme a ten-center sometimes—not many times, becuz I don't give a dern for a thing 'thout it's tollable hard to git—and you go and beg off for me with the widder.

SUGGESTIONS FOR THE ACTOR

1. The author took pains to reproduce the regional dialect with accuracy. Some of these expressions may be unfamiliar to you. One meaning of "ornery" was "of inferior quality." In the exclamation "I hate them ornery sermons!", "ornery" meant "low-down," "contemptible." Using modern slang, you, the actor, might say, "I hate those rotten sermons!" or "I hate those lousy sermons!" "I can't chaw" meant "I can't chew tobacco." "Dad fetch it" was a mild oath or curse, similar to "Darn it!" "I ain't ever going to shake 'em any more" meant "I'm never going to give them up any more." "Sheer" meant "share." A "ten-center" was a dime. I don't give a dern for a thing 'thout it's tollable hard to git" meant "I don't give a darn for a thing unless it's fairly hard to get" ("tollable" meant "tolerably"). "You go and beg off for me with the widder" meant "You go to the Widow Douglas and get her to release me from my commitment to live with her."

As an exercise, act this selection in your own words, using present-day slang.

2. At the beginning of this monologue you, Huck, are inwardly torn. You do not wish to make the Widow Douglas unhappy; she has been extremely good to you. But what can you do? You cannot stand any more "civilizing"; you are just not cut out to be a gentleman. At first all you want of Tom is that he give up his struggle to bring you back home. You are feeling guilty enough already; you want him to stop torturing you with his dramatic descriptions of the Widow's distress. Then you want to bring him around to your point of view. You want to convince him that the respectable life is unbearable, but try as you will, you cannot convince him. As far as he is concerned, he and all his other friends have to lead that kind of life. They manage all right. Why can't you? Finally you want to persuade Tom to take your share of the money and to speak to the Widow for you.

It would be helpful for you, the actor, to address your monologue to a real boy whom you think of as Tom, either someone in the audience or an actor onstage playing the part of Tom. Really try your best to convince him. Observe his reactions. When one approach doesn't work, try a new tack.

3. Have you, the actor, ever wanted to "chuck" everything, give it all up to be free of routine, duty, responsibility? Surely everyone feels that way sometimes, young and old alike. (Do you feel that way every time your alarm clock wakes you out of a deep sleep?) Recall an occasion in your life when that desire was particularly strong. What duties, chores, routines did you want to escape? What activities did you long to pursue instead? Have you, the actor, ever felt that in some ways your life was too *easy?* You, Huck, feel that way. Civilized existence lacks the excitement, the adventure of the primitive, natural life. You miss the daily struggle to survive. Food tastes better when you have to fish or hunt for it (or steal it) yourself; you don't "give a dern for a thing" unless it's hard to get.

4. This monologue is filled with both pleasant and unpleasant memories of physical feelings, sensations, including memories of how it felt to move in various ways. How frustrated you (Huck) were when you were forbidden to roll on the grass, slide on a cellar door, stretch, etc. Try to remember all these desired physical sensations with your body as you speak the words. Remember the unpleasant feelings with your body also, those sensations which you associate with respectability, such as "sweating" because you were overdressed, or being combed too vigorously and too often. What other uncomfortable sensations do you (Huck) recall?

From *Manchild in the Promised Land*
by Claude Brown

INTRODUCTION

Claude Brown, author of the amazing autobiography *Manchild in the Promised Land,* was educated in the black ghetto streets of Harlem. As a small boy he learned all about "playing hookey," stealing, making homemade guns and other such activities from older, street-wise friends. When afraid of how his father might beat him for punishment, he went "catting": He stayed away from home for weeks at a time. The police sometimes picked him up and took him to various children's centers, from which he often ran away. He was expelled from one school after another until he landed in Children's Court. The judge told his mother that if he was still in New York State by the following September, he would be sent away. His parents sent him South after that to live with his grandparents for a year.

He describes his grandfather as "evil." He almost killed Claude once, with a gun, for fooling around with the minister's daughter. His grandfather "had the devil in him, and everybody knew it."

Claude's early life went from bad to worse, including years in reform schools. But eventually, miraculously, he decided to pursue a different kind of education. As a young man he was graduated from college, Howard University, attended law school and wrote this outstanding book, published in 1965. Claude Brown would probably attribute the strength of character that this astounding turnabout demonstrates to the same streets of Harlem that nearly destroyed him. He writes, "despite everything that Harlem did to our generation, I think it gave something to a few. It gave them a strength that couldn't be obtained anywhere else."

One person believed in Claude all along. That person was Ernst Papanek, director of Wiltwyck, the reform school to which Claude was sent at the age of eleven. When Papanek first arrived at Wiltwyck as the new director, Claude and the other boys did not know what to make of this "odd bird." He spoke with an accent. He would not allow the boys to be hit by staff members. He was always kind and yet somehow managed to maintain discipline. He never lied. Papanek remained Claude's friend long after Claude had left Wiltwyck. Even though Claude remained a juvenile delinquent throughout his youth, Papanek recognized his potential and never stopped encouraging him.

CLAUDE: People used to say I was going to be just like Grandpa, since I had the devil in me too. I never paid attention to what people said about being like Grandpa until one day. That day, my cousin McKinley Wilson and me were out in the yard seeing who could pick up the biggest and heaviest sack of corn. While I was straining to pick up a sack, I heard Grandma scream and felt a stinging feeling on my neck that made me drop the sack, jump up and down, and grab my neck. When I turned around to see what had happened to me, I saw Grandma standing there with a switch in her hand. She was screaming and hollering a whole lot of things at me, but all I could make out was that she was going to kill me if I ever did that again. I didn't know what to think except that maybe she was going crazy. She had never said anything when I messed with the wasps' nests and got stung and cried and kept on messing with them. I couldn't understand why she had hit me, and Grandma didn't talk much. I knew she had mistreated me, and I had to do something about it, so I started walking, walking back to New York.

When Grandma caught up with me on the highway, she had a bigger switch, and she was real mad. After she finished beating me for running away, she said she had hit me because she didn't want me to be walking like Grandpa. I asked her if Grandpa had gotten his stroke from lifting corn.

She said, "It wasn't no stroke that makes Grandpa walk the way he do. The stroke just stiffened up his right side. But you see the way he gotta swing his left leg way out every time he take a step?"

I said, "Yeah, I seen him do that."

Grandma said that Grandpa walked that way because he was toting corn one day. I didn't understand, but I kept on listening. Then Grandma started telling me about the things I saw Grandpa cut out of the pig to keep the bacon from getting rank when they killed the pig. And she told me that right above the things that make the bacon rank are the chitterlings and that chitterlings press against a thin window in pigs and boys and men. I never knew I had chitterlings in me until that day. Grandma said if somebody lifted something too heavy for him, the chitterlings would press right through that window and the man would have a hard time walking and doing a lot of other things for the rest of his life. She said one time Grandpa was in the woods making liquor, and his dog started barking. Grandpa picked up his still and started running with it. The still was too heavy—the window broke, and now Grandpa had to walk real slow. She was saying that she didn't mean to hit me. She just didn't want me to break my window.

We walked back home up the highway. Grandma had her arm around my shoulder, and I had my arm around her waist. That was the only time I ever touched Grandma—and the only time I recall wanting her to touch me and liking her touch. When I saw the house coming at us up the road, I was kind of sad. I looked at Grandma's wrinkled face and liked it. I knew I had fallen in love with that mean old wrinkled lady who, I used to think, had a mouth like a monkey. I had fallen in love with a mean old lady because she hit me across the neck for trying to lift a sack of corn.

SUGGESTIONS FOR THE ACTOR

1. As you tell this story, to what extent will you use movement and gesture? Whatever you decide, you should mentally relive each moment as you remember it. This does not necessarily mean, however, that you must perform each physical action which you mention. Once you are able to imagine the situation, you will be in a position to decide how much to *do* with your body. Do only what seems natural to you in the telling. For instance, you may wish to grab your neck when you remember being hit by the switch, but you may not want to go so far as to jump up and down.

2. In order to imagine the events you describe, try first to picture the physical scene. Have you ever been to the South? If not, try to remember any simple wooden house in the country. Imagine the yard, filled with sacks of corn. If you do remember a southern house and yard, so much the better. You may want to decide from which direction Grandma comes and place her there (mentally) as you tell your story. You may or may not want part of your acting area to represent the yard, part of it to be the highway, the house, etc. That is your decision to make. In any case, you should visualize all these places as you speak of them.

"See" the people you describe too. Think of people you know. Visualize any friend or child relative when you mention McKinley Wilson. Picture a wrinkled old lady when you speak of Grandma. You may want to use two different images for Grandma—someone you fear in real life to represent Grandma when she hits you with the switch, and an old woman you love when you describe walking home with Grandma, your arms around each other. Imagine a mean old man with a funny walk when you speak of Grandpa.

3. *What you want* (as the character Claude) changes many times during the course of this monologue. Your emotions change too, but concentrate on what you want at each moment and what you do to get what you want. Let your emotions take care of themselves. Of course, you (Claude) are really telling this story as an adult, remembering what you wanted as a child in the South.

As you begin to relive these events in your mind, however, you feel these same desires all over again.

For example, at first you want to pick up a bigger, heavier sack of corn than McKinley Wilson's, just as you did when the contest actually took place. At that time what did you do? You probably looked at all the sacks, selected the one that looked biggest and strained to lift it. As mentioned before, you (the actor) may want to perform only some of these physical actions and not others as you tell the story. For instance, you may wish to reenact your selection of the biggest sack, but you may not want to lift an imaginary sack. Whether you perform the lifting or not, try to remember with your arms, legs, stomach, etc. how it feels to lift a heavy sack. It may be helpful to lift an actual heavy sack (but not too heavy—remember Grandpa!) just as an exercise, to observe how it feels.

Then you (Claude) feel once again the shock of the switch on your neck. (Try to remember a sharp, stinging sensation.) Instinctively you want to relieve the pain in some way. As a child, what did you *do* to relieve the pain? What do you do now?

Next, you want to get away from that crazy old mean woman who hit you for no reason. What did you do then? What do you do now?

Analyze the rest of the monologue in this way, deciding at each point what you (Claude) want, what you did about it as a child and what you do now as you describe and relive the experience.

At the end, when you see Grandma's house in front of you, you wish that this rare moment didn't have to end so soon. Remember the pleasant feeling of a loving grandma's, or mother's, arm around your (the actor's) shoulder. Imagine how it feels to put your arm around the tiny waist of a shriveled little old woman whom you love.

From *Manchild in the Promised Land*
by Claude Brown

See the "Introduction" to *Manchild in the Promised Land,* beginning on page 132.

CLAUDE: I started going down to the Wiltwyck office on 125th Street to talk to Mr. Papanek. First I went down there to see my social worker, Mr. Moore, and he wasn't in. I spoke to Papanek. He was a real nice cat. Nobody could hate him but we'd never been but so tight—not while I was up at Wiltwyck. I was too busy trying to get my own way to see what a nice cat he really was. He wasn't a pushover kind of cat. He was just a nice cat, a nice cat that you had to respect. When most people say "nice," they mean someone you can run over or get your way with, but he wasn't nice that way. The cat was nice in his mind. The way he looked at life and people was beautiful.

It was about this time that I discovered Papanek's secret. It was really very simple. He had the ability to see everybody as they really are—just people, no more and no less. Also he saw children as people, little young people with individuality, not as some separate group of beings called children, dominated by the so-called adult world. * * *

Most of the time, I never told him what was really bothering me, but we would talk about something. And regardless of what we talked about, it always made me feel better. I usually didn't tell Papanek what was really bothering me; I didn't think he could understand. He had come up in someplace called Austria, and I figured there wasn't a colored person in the whole country. So what could he know about coming up in Harlem?

I was growing up now, and people were going to expect things from me. * * *

Sooner or later you had to use drugs, and sooner or later you had to shoot somebody or do something crazy like that. And I didn't want to. I used to carry a knife, but I knew I couldn't kill anybody with a knife. I couldn't cut . . . the sight of blood used to do something to me. Dad used to carry a knife. Maybe that was why I was so scared of him. Every time I looked at that big scar on his neck where somebody had tried to cut his throat, it scared me. I never wanted a scar like that. But there was no place to go, and it seemed like all life was just closing in on me and squashing me to death.

Sometimes I used to get headaches thinking about it. I used to get sick. I couldn't get up. And sometimes I'd just jump up out of the bed and run out and say, "C'mon, man, let's go steal somethin'!" I'd get Turk, I'd get Tito, I'd get anybody who was around. I'd say, "C'mon, man, let's go pull a score." It seemed like the only way I could get away.

Sometimes I'd just play hookey from school and go down to the Wiltwyck office and see Papanek. And when he saw that I was feeling kind of bad about something, he used to tell me little stories.

Once I told him, "I don't think I'm gonna stay on the street, Papanek, not for much longer. I don't think I'll see Christmas on the streets."

I knew he really believed me, but he was trying to act like he didn't. He said, acting jovial, "Claude, oh, you're just being too pessimistic about it. If any boy from Wiltwyck can stay on the streets, if any boy is ready to come home and to get along in New York City in the school system and in the society of New York, it's Claude Brown."

He kept looking at me, and I got the feeling all the while that he was trying to see if I believed it and was going to gauge his belief by just how much of it I seemed to be believing. It made me smile at him, and I felt self-conscious about smiling at him, because at one time I'd thought he was funny or crazy, but I didn't feel that way about him any more. I couldn't afford to; he was all I had then.

He was the first person I ever wanted to do anything for. I wanted to stay out there so that Papanek would be right. I wanted to do this for him. I wanted to stay in the streets.

He would tell me things like, "Claude, you're being pessimistic, and this is one way to lose out on anything. Did I ever tell you about two frogs who were sitting up on a milk vat and fell in?"

I said, "No, you never told me."

He went on looking jovial and said, "Well, there were two frogs sitting on a milk vat one time. The frogs fell into the milk vat. It was very deep. They kept swimming and swimming around, and they couldn't get out. They couldn't climb out because they were too far down. One frog said, 'Oh, I can't make it, and I'm going to give up.' And the other frog kept swimming and swimming. His arms became more and more tired, and it was harder and harder and harder for him to swim. Then he couldn't do another stroke. He couldn't throw one more arm into the milk. He kept trying and trying; it seemed as if the milk was getting hard and heavy. He kept trying; he knows that he's going to die, but as long as he's got this little bit of life in him, he's going to keep on swimming. On his last stroke, it seemed as though he had to pull a whole ocean back, but he did it and found himself sitting on top of a vat of butter."

I'll always remember that story.

SUGGESTIONS FOR THE ACTOR

1. You, Claude, want to be accepted by your friends. You know that to be accepted, you have to live dangerously, recklessly, maybe get killed. You need these friends because you have nobody else, nowhere else to turn. Yet at the same time you have a powerful will to survive. Therefore, there is a tremendous conflict within you. Both desires are so strong that neither one can conquer the other. As a result of this war raging inside you, you

suffer from headaches and other physical symptoms. You (the actor) decide what these symptoms are. Nausea? Stomach cramps? Choose a physical symptom that you have actually experienced. Try to remember exactly how it felt. What do you (Claude) *do* to ease the pain? At times you attempt to escape from physical and mental suffering by stealing. What a vicious cycle! Your conflict leads to pain, which in turn leads to stealing. Stealing will eventually create further conflict for you, and so on, around the circle.

2. You (Claude) have other contradictory wishes. On the one hand, you want to give up trying to "make it" in society (you call society "the streets"). You would like to go back to Wiltwyck, Papanek's reform school, where you felt safe. In *Manchild in the Promised Land,* Claude Brown describes himself at the age of thirteen as "a butterfly trying to go back into the cocoon." But on the other hand you (Claude) have an intense desire to please Papanek. You want to prove to him, and to yourself, that his faith in you is justified. Which of these two opposing desires gains the upper hand by the end of this monologue?

3. This conflict within you is symbolized by the two frogs. One frog gives up and drowns. The other struggles desperately to survive even though he does not expect to "make it." This story is not just a fable to you, Claude; it represents your life. As you recall Papanek's words, you probably imagine that *you* are each of these two frogs. Do you (the actor) swim? Have you ever had an experience in water when you feared drowning? What did you *do*? As you (Claude) retell the last half of the story, you act as the exhausted but still struggling frog. It may help to use arm movements—your (the frog's) frantic strokes—which become more and more difficult to perform as you become more and more tired and as the milk gets harder and harder.

It would be useful to work on this portion of the monologue without words first. Imagine that you are drowning in an enormous vat of milk, the size of an entire room. Try the exercise as yourself first; then make believe that you are a frog. Struggle with all your might to stay above the liquid. Concentrate on imagining the consistency of the milk. How does it feel as you move in it? The more you thrash about, the harder it becomes. How difficult it is to make those last few strokes. You can hardly raise your arms.

Finally, with your last stroke, which requires almost superhuman (or super-froglike) effort, the liquid becomes a solid! You have churned butter—and you land on top! What are you thinking as you realize that you are not going to die after all? What do you want to do?

4. As a preparatory exercise, perform a scene: your visit with Papanek. You are Claude. You need someone to play Papanek. You can invent your own words as you act. You two communicate not only with words, but perhaps more importantly with looks and gestures. You observe Papanek carefully to judge whether he really believes what he is saying. He observes you just as carefully to see whether you believe his encouraging words. If *you* believe what he tells you, then maybe *he* will believe it too. Do you believe him? What do you each want of the other? What are you, Claude, thinking as Papanek tells you the story of the two frogs? In real life when you actively listen to a story, you do not simply hear words; you react to what you hear with a whole chain of silent thoughts. When you listen onstage, you should react to what you hear by thinking a series of thoughts appropriate to the character you play.

From *The Teddy Bear Habit*
by James Lincoln Collier

INTRODUCTION

The hero of this novel, twelve-year-old George Stable, lives in the Greenwich Village section of New York City with his artist father. His father is an "action painter": He flips paint onto a canvas with a spoon. For a living his father draws and writes for Smash Comics—"Amorphoman" and "Garbageman," among other superheroes. Artist or not, George's father is "square" when it comes to his son's upbringing. Because George's mother is dead, he acts as mother and father to George. He wants his son to study classical music. Since George has a good singing voice, his father pays for George's voice lessons with Mr. Smythe-Jones, whose heavy English accent and stuffy manner remind George of an English duke. Unknown to his father, who would never approve, George is also learning to play rock-and-roll on the guitar. His guitar teacher, a "beatnik" music-store owner whom George finds somewhat "scary," will attempt to use George to help carry out a criminal scheme during the course of this comic mystery-adventure.

Accompanied by his voice teacher, Mr. Smythe-Jones, George is now trying out for a part in a Broadway show—a musical-comedy version of *Winnie-the-Pooh*. For security, George has brought his teddy bear along in a paper bag. Not wanting to admit that he needs a teddy bear for comfort, he told Mr. Smythe-Jones that his paper bag contains gym clothes and sneakers, needed later for basketball practice at the Y.

They are waiting in line in an alley behind the theatre, along with about two hundred youngsters accompanied by adults. The line goes along the side of the building to a little flight of steps leading up to the stage door.

George is now second in line. The boy in front of him, wearing a pair of green suede shoes, with a face "a color to match," is called. George's stomach clenches and unclenches. He had eaten a chocolate coconut bar earlier. Now the coconut has "swollen up like a balloon" and is "trying to get out" of his throat. Mr. Smythe-Jones wants to hold George's paper bag but George refuses to give it up. The boy with the green shoes disappears through the door leading to the audition.

Under pressure, George has always panicked and "goofed up." For example, once in a spelling bee he had been doing extremely well until he realized that there was only one other contestant left. Then he "went hot and prickly" and misspelled an easy word. He thinks of himself as "a loser."

GEORGE: I was next.

I stood at the bottom of the little flight of steps wishing that instead of a stage door at the top, there was a gallows. Hanging would have been less painful and a whole lot quicker. I wished I was one of those fellows who had stolen the Hermes Sapphire from the museum. They were bound to get caught and go to jail, where they wouldn't ever have to do any auditions. Of course there was the chance that the theater would catch fire in the next two minutes. Or maybe an atomic bomb would go off in Times Square, two blocks away, and I would be instantly demolished.

I was clutching at straws and I knew it; so I clutched my paper bag tighter and waited.

Of course there were no sneakers in it. There was no towel and no gym shorts, either. What I had in the bag was a worn-out, beat-up, patched old teddy bear with one of its glass eyes missing and the threads that made up its mouth mostly rubbed away. It was a little smaller than a football, and I had owned it all my life. Really, all of my life. Pop bought it for me the day I was born. Of course I didn't actually get it until I came home from the hospital, but I actually owned it from the first day of my life. It was as old as I was, older, even, because it must have been made sometime before I was born.

The truth is that I don't own it. It owns me. The thing is, I discovered a long time ago that I wasn't so much of a loser when I had the teddy bear around. It's magical. For example, that time I goofed up in the spelling bee. If I'd had the teddy there where I could have gotten a look at him, I wouldn't have goofed. I would have gotten nervous maybe, but I probably would have gotten the answer right. I don't understand it. I just feel stronger and more confident when he's around. I can't explain it. He's nothing but some cloth and a lot of old cotton batting. There shouldn't be any magic in that. But there is. Of course a lot of the time the teddy doesn't do me any good. I can't take the teddy into a basketball game with me. And I can't smuggle him into school when I have to say a poem I've memorized. But, for example, I had to be one of the wise men in the Christmas pageant last year and sing a song, and all that jazz. I hid the teddy in this box of frankincense I was supposed to be carrying. I did my song perfectly; I was a big hit.

Or there was the time when I had to go up on the stage in assembly and make a speech about how much Mrs. Creepy had done for the school, and how much we were going to miss her, and a lot of other lies that my English teacher wrote out for me. I wrapped the teddy up in some newspaper, and during rehearsal I left him on a table offstage where I could see him when I looked around. I know it's a terrible thing for a kid as big as me to go around carrying a teddy bear. It's a weakness, and it's embarrassing to me all the time. I would hate for people to find out about it. But there's nothing I can do. You know how it is with people who want to stop smoking cigarettes but can't. They have a tobacco habit. Well, I have a teddy-bear habit.

Suddenly the stage door slammed open again and I went into a state of shock. The next thing I knew I was standing among a mess of dusty ropes and heavy electrical wires, looking out toward the stage. The kid with the green shoes was finishing his song. His face wasn't very green any more. He was singing good and loud, and I could tell how happy he was feeling that he'd made it to the end.

He finished. Somewhere out front a man's voice said, "Thank you," which is what they say when you've flunked. It didn't bother Green Shoes a bit; he was just happy to have it over with. He jumped off the stage, grinning, and went out the front of the theater, and I hated him for being so happy when I was just about to be electrocuted and drowned and beheaded and tortured to death.

SUGGESTIONS FOR THE ACTOR

1. Have you ever experienced stage fright? The occasion might have been a public performance of some kind, probably just before the performance. You might have experienced a similar fear in other high-pressure situations—being called on to speak in class, for instance, when you were unprepared, or perhaps even when you were well prepared, if you were extremely shy at that time. Fear before an important examination might resemble stage fright. Exactly what did you fear? How did the fear affect you physically—your stomach, your knees, your breathing? Try to remember all the physical sensations that accompanied your fright. What did you want to do? If you had possessed a magic lamp at that moment, what would you have wished for? Did you try to deal with your fear? What actions did you take to conquer fear? How did you, as George, handle your fear?

2. After you (George) say, "Or maybe an atomic bomb would go off in Times Square, two blocks away, and I would be instantly demolished," what thoughts go through your mind before you realize that wishing for a catastrophe was not a useful way of dealing with your fear? Give yourself sufficient time to think the thoughts that lead you (George) to say, "I was clutching at straws and I knew it."

3. You, George, now describe your teddy bear as "nothing but some cloth and a lot of old cotton batting." Nevertheless he is still terribly important to you. It seems likely that when you were a lit-

tle boy, you thought of your teddy bear almost as a person, with distinct personality characteristics. What were those personality traits? What was your relationship to your teddy bear at that time?

4. As an exercise, make believe that you are George at the age of, say, six or seven. Conduct a conversation with your teddy bear. Use a real teddy bear or another toy animal. Tell him your troubles. You, the actor, will have to use your own imagination to invent these troubles, or you may recall problems of your own childhood, problems which you, as the character George, might also have experienced as a young child. The novel does not describe your (George's) early childhood at all; we know only that your mother died when you were still a baby.

From *Growing Up Puerto Rican,*
edited by Paulette Cooper.
"Tony: The Hair-Raiser"

INTRODUCTION

See page 88 for a description of the book *Growing up Puerto Rican,* from which this selection is excerpted.

Tony is now a dropout from school. He has had serious problems ever since his arrival in the United States. He loved his grandparents and missed them terribly. One day his family received a telegram notifying them of his grandfather's death. His father and mother always fought a lot and were finally divorced. His father had a dangerous temper. Tony at various times sniffed glue, smoked "pot" and tried LSD, but he has since given up experimenting with drugs. He belonged to a tough gang of fighters called the "Hair-Raisers." Tony often wonders whether he once killed a boy in a street fight, when he threw a rock at his head. He now wishes he were back in "regular" school. He would like to learn a skill and then return to Puerto Rico with his family "and live in a house again."

TONY: My name is Tony. I was sad when I was told I had to come to America. My parents had come to America right after I was born and I lived with my grandparents in Puerto Rico until I was six. But then my parents sent for us from America, and my grandfather said, "Your mother wants you to come, so you've got to."

When we came here, we saw so many things we had never seen before. I had never been in a plane before. And that day was the first time I had worn shoes, but they were too tight because they belonged to someone with smaller feet. And my feet hurt so bad. . . . And on the plane these big kids grabbed me and my brother and made us get inside the bathroom. And once we went inside they locked us in from the outside. We were frightened until my brother saw that there was a lock inside so we were able to get out. But we felt bad, and wondered what we were getting into and what kind of people would be there.

I remember when I came to New York I saw that the door to the building was open, and I asked my mother about it. But she showed me it was the doorway to the whole building and lots of other people lived there too. We just lived in one room, the four of us, and it was so crowded, and we all slept in the same bed. But I didn't mind because we had a TV. We never had a TV in Puerto Rico, and I didn't know what it was until my brother said, "Look, look, a TV!" And we put it on. Then I saw people talking there and having so much fun, and they had a big house like we had in Puerto Rico. So I went around to the back of the box to see if I could go into the house with them—but there was nothing there, and my brother and parents, they laughed at me.

SUGGESTIONS FOR THE ACTOR

1. To whom are you, Tony, speaking? Perhaps you are addressing Paulette Cooper, who interviewed seventeen young Puerto Ricans when she compiled this book. Is it easy for you (Tony) to talk about yourself, or do you have to overcome some initial shyness, awkwardness? Do you "warm up" to the subject after you begin?

2. Can you (the actor) recall any painful separation in your own past equivalent to your separation, as the character Tony,

from your grandparents? (Remember, they had brought you up until you were six years old.) If so, try to recall everything you saw, heard, smelled, touched and tasted at the time of that terrible separation. If you cannot recall so terrible a separation, try to remember any separation, permanent or temporary, that upset you when you were small. What did you do then? What did Tony do?

3. Try to recall experiences in your (the actor's) own life equivalent to Tony's various experiences on the airplane; in other words, events that aroused in you, the actor, feelings similar to the feelings of the character you play. The airplane itself must have filled you (Tony) with wonder—its vast size, compared to the apparent size of airplanes you had seen far off in the sky; the loud whirring of the motors; the sight and other physical sensations of the takeoff and landing; the amazing sight of clouds beneath you. Have you, the actor, ever traveled by airplane? If not, try to recall another experience that filled you with a similar sense of wonder when you were a little boy.

Have you (the actor) ever worn shoes that hurt you? Can you recall exactly where they hurt? Can you recall the pain? Remember that pain as you (Tony) speak of the tight shoes. You, as Tony, must have felt even more uncomfortable because you had never worn any shoes at all until that day.

Have you ever been locked or "stuck" in a small space such as a closet or bathroom? Were you frightened? If so, try to remember everything that happened to you physically while you were frightened. For instance, did you feel hot all of a sudden? Did you perspire? What actions did you perform to get out? Would you, as Tony, recall performing any of those actions? You (Tony) must have felt outraged too in this situation, because those "big kids" had locked you in the bathroom intentionally. This experience must have made you distrustful, fearful of the future.

4. You, as Tony, were fascinated by the TV set because the pleasant life you saw on the screen reminded you of Puerto Rico. People lived in big houses on the screen instead of in one overcrowded room; they laughed and enjoyed themselves. How you longed to join them! For you, the TV had fantastic, magical properties. You wanted to jump into this magic box and live with these happy people instead of with your own parents, who fought

all the time. It must have been a rude shock when you saw nothing at the back of the box. Then, "adding insult to injury," your brother and parents laughed at you! When they laughed, what did you want to do?

Have you (the actor) ever longed to escape from a depressing situation into a happier one? What did you do to escape? Did you succeed in escaping, either mentally or physically? An absorbing interest may help one to escape mentally from dismal surroundings. Some people seek escape through drugs or alcohol, but in the long run they become more depressed than ever.

When you, the actor, were very young, did you believe that people really lived in the TV set? If so, what was your reaction when you learned the truth? How did your reaction then compare to your reaction as the character Tony?

From *The Dark at the Top of the Stairs*
by William Inge.
Act II

INTRODUCTION

This perceptive, compassionate play by William Inge takes place in the "home of Rubin Flood, his wife and two children, in a small Oklahoma town close to Oklahoma City. The time is the early 1920s."

Reenie Flood, the sixteen-year-old daughter, is a painfully shy adolescent. She has been "fixed up" with a "blind date," who will escort her to a lavish birthday party given by a newly rich family, the Ralstons, at the local country club. Her date for the occasion is Sammy Goldenbaum. The date has been arranged by Sammy's friend Punky and by Punky's girl friend Flirt, who is Reenie's friend. Both Sammy and Punky are cadets at a nearby military academy.

Before the party, which is to be a formal dance with an orchestra, Flirt, Punky and Sammy call for Reenie at the Flood home. The boys "make a colorful entrance. Both are dressed in uniforms of lustrous blue, which fit them like smooth upholstery," but in striking contrast to Sammy, Punky lacks all grace or charm. Flirt introduces the boys to the Flood family.

SAMMY GOLDENBAUM steps forth correctly, his plumed headgear in his hand. He is a darkly beautiful young man of seventeen, with lustrous black hair, black eyes and a captivating smile. Yet, something about him seems a little foreign, at least in comparison with the Midwestern company in which he now finds himself. He could be a Persian prince, strayed from his native kingdom. But he has become adept over the years in adapting himself, and he shows an eagerness to make friends and to be liked.

Reenie is still upstairs. Her father is out of town. Sammy meets Sonny Flood, Reenie's ten-year-old brother, Morris and Lottie Lacey, Reenie's aunt and uncle from Oklahoma City, and Cora Flood, Reenie's mother.

Sammy is an object of some curiosity to the family. He is Jewish (on his father's side), and there are hardly any Jews living in this part of the country. Also, his mother is a Hollywood movie actress, although not a star. His father, also an actor, had been killed in an automobile accident before Sammy was born.

While waiting for Reenie, Sammy tries hard to please everyone. He asks Reenie's aunt to dance. He plays games with Sonny. Sammy "has a way" with children; he loves them and "always seems to know just how kids feel." When Reenie appears, sweet-looking in a lovely gown, he is pleasantly surprised and he tells her so. He had expected her to be like Flirt, who is a flapper, vivacious but rather shallow and "fast." He then admits to Reenie, "You know, I've never been to many parties, have you?" She replies, "Not many," whereupon he begins the monologue which follows this introduction. He speaks with a slight stammer.

The family, including Reenie, like Sammy enormously. The two ladies find him handsome, considerate, charming and gay. Only one person, Morris Lacey, is discerning enough to realize how unhappy Sammy really is. After the young people leave, Morris tells his wife that "sometimes the people who act the happiest are really the saddest."

Later that night at the party the hostess, Mrs. Ralston, a coarse, ignorant woman despite her newly acquired wealth, will loudly insult Sammy right in the middle of the dance floor. She will yell drunkenly that no Jews are allowed at this club. A stranger here, Sammy will have no way of knowing that Mrs. Ralston has the reputation of being a stupid "blabbermouth." To him, she will sound like "the voice of the world." Unable to locate Reenie when he desperately needs comforting, he will flee from the party and commit suicide.

The Flood living room is comfortable, with an air of hospitality "despite the moodiness of shadowy corners." The furnishings are old-fashioned, "more-or-less" Victorian in style (nineteenth-century English).

It is a Friday evening in early spring.

SAMMY: I always worry that maybe people aren't going to like me, when I go to a party. Isn't that crazy? Do you ever get kind of a sick feeling in the pit of your stomach when you dread things? Gee, I wouldn't want to miss a party for anything. But every time I go to one, I have to reason with myself to keep from feeling that the whole world's against me. See, I've spent almost my whole life in military academies. My mother doesn't have a place for me, where she lives. She . . . she just doesn't know what else to do with me. But you mustn't misunderstand about my mother. She's really a very lovely person. I guess every boy thinks his mother is very beautiful, but my mother really is. She tells me in every letter she writes how sorry she is that we can't be together more, but she has to think of her work. One time we were together, though. She met me in San Francisco once, and we were together for two whole days. She let me take her to dinner and to a show and to dance. Just like we were sweethearts. It was the most wonderful time I ever had. And then I had to go back to the old military academy. Every time I walk into the barracks, I get kind of a depressed feeling. It's got hard stone walls. Pictures of generals hanging all over . . . oh, they're very fine gentlemen, but they all look so kind of hard-boiled and stern . . . you know what I mean. [CORA *and* LOTTIE *stand together, listening to* SAMMY's *speech with motherly expressions.* FLIRT *is bored.* PUNKY *is half asleep, and now he gives a sudden, audible yawn that startles everyone*] Well, gee! I guess I've bored you enough, telling you about myself.

SUGGESTIONS FOR THE ACTOR

1. Most sensitive readers would find your (Sammy's) words piti-
ful, even heartbreaking. Yet Cora and Lottie do not regard you as
unhappy. They may not be brilliant, but they are far from dim-
witted. Why do they fail to perceive your misery? The answer
must lie in *your manner* as you speak these words. You probably
do not realize how pathetic your story is. You have always lived
this way; you have no basis for comparison. No one has ever
loved you. You might even smile a lot as you talk. Why might you
smile? Do people smile only when they are happy? Can you recall
any other occasions when you, the actor, smiled or when you ob-
served others smiling? Might you (Sammy) smile to please
others? Might smiling be a nervous habit? Could it be a way of
making light of your own feelings, apologizing for them, as when
you say, "Isn't that crazy?"

2. Your moods, your desires change a number of times during
this monologue. At first you (Sammy) are suffering from dread,
"a sick feeling in the pit of your stomach." (Can you, the actor,
recall how dread ever affected *you* physically?) Perhaps you hope
that your fears will dissolve if you talk about them, share them
with a sympathetic listener. Does talking help? Later you fear that
you have made Reenie and her family think ill of your mother;
you want to convince them that she is really a lovely person even
though she has no room for you in her life. As you talk about her,
you lose yourself in the cherished memory of those two days in
San Francisco. For the moment you forget your present surroundings; you relive that glorious experience. Your mood shifts again
as you remember how you had to return to your gloomy barracks
afterward. You relive the emotional "letdown"; you recall the
hard, cold walls decorated with pictures of hard, cold generals.
Suddenly you hear Punky yawn. You become embarrassed, afraid
you must have talked too long about yourself. You cannot bear to
offend anybody.

3. When you say, "My Mother doesn't have a place for me,
where she lives. She . . . she just doesn't know what to do with
me," why do you hesitate after the word "She"? Are you stam-
mering? If so, is there any particular reason why you stammer at

this moment? What are you thinking? Is the thought too painful to express aloud? Or are you seeking a way to express your thought without making your mother seem heartless?

4. You, the actor, must decide precisely when to stammer. Do not stutter constantly. Your (Sammy's) stammer is *slight;* an occasional hesitation is sufficient. Even if one were playing the part of a severe stutterer, one would not ordinarily stutter all the time onstage; to do so would almost certainly annoy and distract the audience. Do you (Sammy) stammer when you try to produce certain sounds? If so, which sounds? Or do you stammer on certain words because the thought behind those words upsets you? Often in life even severe stutterers improve remarkably when they are relaxed, among friends. Their stuttering increases in tense, anxiety-provoking situations.

From *Narrative of the Life of Frederick Douglass, an American Slave, Written by Himself,* edited by Benjamin Quarles

INTRODUCTION

Frederick Douglass was born a slave on a Maryland plantation around 1817 (slaves rarely knew their exact date of birth). His mother, Harriet Bailey, was a slave; he never knew the identity of his father, although he gathered that his father was white. When still an infant, he was separated from his mother; she was "hired out" to a farmer. He was placed in the care of his grandmother, who lived on the outskirts of the plantation. She had been put there to rear the children of the younger slave women because she was too old to work in the fields.

When he first left his grandmother's cabin to live on Colonel Lloyd's vast plantation, he was terrified to witness the whippings of slaves. He himself was not whipped much. He was too young to work in the fields and had only a small number of chores to perform each day. He suffered mainly from hunger and cold, as he was not given sufficient food or clothing. All he had to wear were two linen shirts; he slept on the cold, damp clay floor without blankets.

When he was seven or eight he was sent to Baltimore to live with his master's relatives, Mr. and Mrs. Hugh Auld and their little son Thomas; it was Frederick's duty to take care of the child. Frederick was much better off in the city; he had enough to wear and plenty to eat. His new mistress, Sophia Auld, was kindhearted in the beginning; she had never owned a slave before and she treated him as a human being. But, according to Frederick Douglass' autobiography, the power of owning another person eventually corrupted her good nature. At first, she willingly taught Frederick to read a little, until her husband convinced her that slaves become dissatisfied with their lot if they are allowed to possess such "dangerous" knowledge. By then, however, it was too late. The seeds of dissatisfaction had already been sown. Frederick mastered reading and learned from books to think of himself as a person, not a piece of someone else's property. He struggled for years to learn how to write so that he would someday be able to write his own pass—forge his master's name to a permit allowing him to travel north. This forged pass would then be his passport to freedom. Little did he dream that he would one day become a celebrated author, whose writings would influence Europeans as well as Americans to condemn the institution of slavery.

He lived with "Master Hugh's family" for about seven years. After that he had other masters, some cruel, others relatively kind. But even under the best of them, Frederick was determined to become his own master. After one unsuccessful attempt to run away, he managed to escape to New York in 1838. From there he went to New Bedford, Massachusetts, where he lived as a free man with his wife. It was there that he assumed the name "Douglass."

In 1841, he attended an Abolitionist meeting in Nantucket and was moved to speak. He proved to be a dynamic speaker. The editor of this autobiography describes him: "There was a dramatic quality in his very appearance—his imposing figure, his deep-set, flashing eyes and well-formed nose, and the mass of hair crowning his head." In addition, he possessed a powerful voice, immense emotional vitality and an outstanding intellect. From then on he became a leading orator of the Abolition movement. One of the most effective pieces of anti-slavery propaganda ever written was his truthful autobiography, first printed in 1845. With the publication of this "best seller," Frederick Douglass became an international figure and a leader of his people until his death in 1895. In his last years he became U. S. Minister to Haiti. A reformer all his life, he actively supported the cause of women's rights as well as emancipation of the slaves and then civil rights for Negroes.

At the time of the events described in this selection, Frederick was living in Baltimore with "Master Hugh's family," where he remained from about age eight to age fifteen. He must have begun the arduous task of learning to write years before he left the Aulds.

FREDERICK: I went one day down on the wharf of Mr. Waters; and seeing two Irishmen unloading a scow of stone, I went, unasked, and helped them. When we had finished, one of them came to me and asked me if I were a slave. I told him I was. He asked, "Are ye a slave for life?" I told him that I was. The good Irishman seemed to be deeply affected by the statement. He said to the other that it was a pity so fine a little fellow as myself should be a slave for life. He said it was a shame to hold me. They both advised me to run away to the north; that I should find friends there, and that I should be free. I pretended not to be interested in what they said, and treated them as if I did not understand them; for I feared they might be treacherous. White men have been known to encourage slaves to escape, and then, to get the reward, catch them and return them to their masters. I was afraid that these seemingly good men might use me so, but I nevertheless remembered their advice, and from that time I resolved to run away. I looked forward to a time at which it would be safe for me to escape. I was too young to think of doing so immediately; besides, I wished to learn how to write, as I might have occasion to write my own pass. I consoled myself with the hope that I should one day find a good chance. Meanwhile, I would learn to write.

The idea as to how I might learn to write was suggested to me by being in Durgin and Bailey's ship-yard, and frequently seeing the ship carpenters, after hewing, and getting a piece of timber ready for use, write on the timber the name of that part of the ship for which it was intended. * * * A piece for the larboard side forward, would be marked thus—"L.F." When a piece was for starboard side forward, it would be marked thus— "S.F." For larboard aft, it would be marked thus—"L.A." For starboard aft, it would be marked thus—"S.A." I soon learned the names of these letters, and for what they were intended when placed upon a piece of timber in the ship-yard. I immediately commenced copying them, and in a short time was able to make the four letters named. After that, when I met with any boy who I knew could write, I would tell him I could write as well as he. The next word would be, "I don't believe you. Let me see you try it." I would then make the letters which I had been so fortunate as to learn, and ask him to beat that. In this way I got a good many lessons in writing, which it is quite possible I should never have gotten in any other way. During this time, my copybook was the board fence, brick wall, and pavement; my pen and ink was a lump of chalk. With these, I learned mainly how to write. I then commenced and continued copying the Italics in Webster's Spelling Book, until I could make them all without looking on the book. By this time, my little Master Thomas had gone to school, and learned how to write, and had written over a number of copy-books. These had been brought home, and shown to some of our near neighbors, and then laid aside. My mistress used to go to class meeting at the Wilk Street meeting-house every Monday afternoon, and leave me to take care of the house. When left thus, I used to spend the time in writing in the spaces left in Master Thomas's copy-book, copying what he had written. I continued to do this until I could write a hand very similar to that of Master Thomas. Thus, after a long, tedious effort for years, I finally succeeded in learning how to write.

SUGGESTIONS FOR THE ACTOR

1. Decide where you (Frederick) are as you relate these incidents, when this is, your present age and circumstances, and to whom you are speaking or writing. Why are you revealing these facts now? If you are writing, why do you speak aloud? You, the actor, must find a logical reason for doing so.

2. As you recount these past events, you mentally picture the wharf, the street and Master Hugh's house. What do you want to do at each moment of the monologue, and what actions do you

perform to get what you want? Your first action is to help the two Irishmen, even though you had not been asked to do so. Why do you assist them? You, the actor, will have to invent a reason for helping.

When the two Irishmen advise you to run away to the North, how do you react? What do you want to do? This is one of the most important moments of your life. On the one hand, you make a crucial resolution. What is it? On the other hand, you want to avoid a trap. What do you fear? What do you do or say to avoid this possible trap?

You want desperately to learn how to write, so that you may forge a pass someday. In this way you may deceive patrollers on the lookout for runaway slaves. What series of actions do you perform to learn writing?

3. When you speak of the two Irishmen, visualize two pleasant, sympathetic men, individuals you (the actor) have met but don't know well enough to trust. Try to imagine their voices too. If you can manage it, you might ask, "Are you a slave for life?" with the hint of an Irish brogue.

Picture one of the boys to whom you (Frederick) boast that you can write as well as he. You (the actor) should imagine a boy you really know. Imitate his voice and manner when you quote his doubting reply: "I don't believe you. Let me see you try it."

Also visualize real people when you refer to your mistress and little Master Thomas, who is much younger than you. When you speak of your mistress, you, the actor, should think of a scolding woman, someone you try to avoid whenever possible. Your (Frederick's) mistress had formerly been sweet and kind to you but she changed. Master Thomas goes to school, but you are forbidden to do so because you are only a slave. In fact, it is illegal for slaves to read. Do you envy your young master? What kind of child is he? How does he behave toward you? What are your various feelings toward him? How do you behave toward him? You, the actor, must invent answers to all these questions, using your own imagination.

4. Your (Frederick's) description of the laborious steps you took to teach yourself writing is a factual account. You are filled with a strong, growing sense of excitement, however, as you recall these details, building up to the last line: "I finally succeeded in

learning how to write." Your ability to write may literally set you free someday. You also realize that by mastering the skills of reading and writing you are developing your mind, which had been starved by your master. You fervently believe that this knowledge will enable you to rise above the brutishness that slavery inevitably produces.

PART II
DRAMATIC SELECTIONS
FOR YOUNG ADULTS

Scenes for Young Adults

From *Liliom* by Ferenc Molnar, English text by Benjamin F. Glazer.
Scene 1

INTRODUCTION

Written in 1909, translated into English and first presented in this country in 1921, Hungarian playwright Ferenc Molnar's fantasy is by now considered an international theatre classic. You may be familiar with the beautiful musical version of *Liliom* by Rodgers and Hammerstein, *Carousel* (1945). Molnar's play is subtitled *A Legend in Seven Scenes and a Prologue.*

The Prologue takes place in "An amusement park on the outskirts of Budapest on a late afternoon in Spring." Liliom is the merry-go-round barker, a rough, attractive ne'er-do-well. (His real name is Andreas Zavocki.) He treats the girls with playful familiarity, and they love it. Some of their escorts resent his behavior, but they are afraid of Liliom; he gives them "ugly," "menacing" looks. When Julie Zeller and Marie approach, he "favors them with particular notice as they pass into the merry-go-round." They are young, innocent, still in their teens; they work as maids in a private home. When Liliom begins his harangue, he draws the crowd away from all the other booths.

As the sky starts to darken, a lamplighter begins lighting the gas lamps.

Scene 1 is set in "A lonely place in the park, half hidden by trees and shrubbery. Under a flowering acacia tree stands a painted wooden bench. From the distance, faintly, comes the tumult of the amusement park. It is the sunset of the same day."

Julie and Marie are followed here by Mrs. Muskat, a widow, owner of the carousel. Coarsely she hurls insults at Julie, calling her "a shabby kitchen maid" and a "shameless hussy." She is in a fury because Liliom put his arm around Julie's waist in the carousel. She wants to keep Liliom for herself, and evidently senses the special attraction between Liliom and Julie. Mrs. Muskat informs Julie that if she ever tries to ride the carousel again, she will be thrown out—by Liliom. Liliom enters the park, "surrounded by four giggling servant girls," whom he scares off. Julie asks Liliom whether he would really throw her out. He replies that he would, but only if there was a reason. When he learns Mrs. Muskat's reason, however, he tells Julie to come back as often as she likes. He calls Mrs. Muskat an "old witch." Mrs. Muskat discharges him, but she is more than willing to relent until Liliom threatens to give her "the prettiest slap in the jaw you ever had in your life." Then she fires him in earnest and leaves.

Afterward Liliom warns the girls not to pity him. He brags that he doesn't need Mrs. Muskat anyway. What he needs right now is a glass of beer. He sternly demands to know whether they have money with them, but they haven't enough. "MARIE begins to weep softly." Liliom then tells the girls to remain in the park while he returns to the carousel for his belongings. He offers to take them to the Hungarian beer garden; he will pay. Liliom exits. "MARIE and JULIE stand silent, watching him until he has gone."

MARIE: Are you sorry for him?

JULIE: Are you?

MARIE: Yes, a little. Why are you looking after him in that funny way?

JULIE: [Sits down] Nothing—except I'm sorry he lost his job.

MARIE: [With a touch of pride] It was on our account he lost his job. Because he's fallen in love with you.

JULIE: He hasn't at all.

MARIE: [Confidently] Oh, yes! he is in love with you. [Hesitantly, romantically] There is someone in love with me, too.

JULIE: There is? Who?

MARIE: I—I never mentioned it before, because you hadn't a lover of your own—but now you have—and I'm free to speak. [*Very grandiloquently*] My heart has found its mate.

JULIE: You're only making it up.

MARIE: No, it's true—my heart's true love ——

JULIE: Who? Who is he?

MARIE: A soldier.

JULIE: What kind of a soldier?

MARIE: I don't know. Just a soldier. Are there different kinds?

JULIE: Many different kinds. There are hussars, artillerymen, engineers, infantry—that's the kind that walks—and ——

MARIE: How can you tell which is which?

JULIE: By their uniforms.

MARIE: [*After trying to puzzle it out*] The conductors on the streetcars—are they soldiers?

JULIE: Certainly not. They're conductors.

MARIE: Well, they have uniforms.

JULIE: But they don't carry swords or guns.

MARIE: Oh! [*Thinks it over again; then*] Well, policemen—are they?

JULIE: [*With a touch of exasperation*] Are they what?

MARIE: Soldiers.

JULIE: Certainly not. They're just policemen.

MARIE: [*Triumphantly*] But they have uniforms—and they carry weapons, too.

JULIE: You're just as dumb as you can be. You don't go by their uniforms.

MARIE: But you said ——

JULIE: No, I didn't. A letter-carrier wears a uniform, too, but that doesn't make him a soldier.

MARIE: But if he carried a gun or a sword, would he be ——

JULIE: No, he'd still be a letter-carrier. You can't go by guns or swords, either.

MARIE: Well, if you don't go by the uniforms or the weapons, what *do* you go by?

JULIE: By —— [*Tries to put it into words; fails; then breaks off suddenly*] Oh, you'll get to know when you've lived in the city long enough. You're nothing but a country girl. When you've lived in the city a year, like I have, you'll know all about it.

MARIE: [*Half angrily*] Well, how *do* you know when *you* see a real soldier?

JULIE: By one thing.

MARIE: What?

JULIE: One thing —— [*She pauses.* MARIE *starts to cry*] Oh, what are you crying about?

MARIE: Because you're making fun of me. . . . You're a city girl, and I'm just fresh from the country . . . and how am I expected to know a soldier when I see one? . . . You, you ought to tell me, instead of making fun of me ——

JULIE: All right. Listen then, cry baby. There's only one way to tell a soldier: by his salute! That's the only way.

MARIE: [*Joyfully; with a sigh of relief*] Ah—that's good.

JULIE: What?

MARIE: I say—it's all right then—because Wolf—Wolf —— [JULIE *laughs derisively*] Wolf—that's his name. [*She weeps again*]

JULIE: Crying again? What now?

MARIE: You're making fun of me again.

JULIE: I'm not. But when you say, "Wolf—Wolf—" like that, I have to laugh, don't I? [*Archly*] What's his name again?

MARIE: I won't tell you.

JULIE: All right. If you won't say it, then he's no soldier.

MARIE: I'll say it.

JULIE: Go on.

MARIE: No, I won't. [*She weeps again*]

JULIE: Then he's not a soldier. I guess he's a letter-carrier ——

MARIE: No—no—I'd rather say it.

JULIE: Well, then.

MARIE: [*Giggling*] But you mustn't look at me. You look the other way, and I'll say it. [JULIE *looks away.* MARIE *can hardly restrain her own laughter*] Wolf! [*She laughs*] That's his real name. Wolf, Wolf, Soldier—Wolf!

JULIE: What kind of a uniform does he wear?

MARIE: Red.

JULIE: Red trousers?

MARIE: No.

JULIE: Red coat?

MARIE: No.

JULIE: What then?

MARIE: [*Triumphantly*] His cap!

JULIE: [*After a long pause*] He's just a porter, you dunce. Red cap . . . that's a porter—and he doesn't carry a gun or a sword, either.

MARIE: [*Triumphantly*] But he salutes. You said yourself that was the only way to tell a soldier ——

JULIE: He doesn't salute at all. He only greets people ——

MARIE: He salutes me. . . . And if his name *is* Wolf, that doesn't prove he ain't a soldier—he salutes, and he wears a red cap and he stands on guard all day long outside a big building ——

JULIE: What does he do there?

MARIE: [*Seriously*] He spits.

JULIE: [*With contempt*] He's nothing—nothing but a common porter.

MARIE: What's Liliom?

JULIE: [*Indignantly*] Why speak of him? What has he to do with me?

MARIE: The same as Wolf has to do with me. If you can talk to me like that about Wolf, I can talk to you about Liliom.

JULIE: He's nothing to me. He put his arm around me in the carousel. I couldn't tell him not to put his arm around me after he had done it, could I?

MARIE: I suppose you didn't like him to do it?

JULIE: No.

MARIE: Then why are you waiting for him? Why don't you go home?

JULIE: Why—eh—he *said* we were to wait for him.

   [LILIOM *enters. There is a long silence*]

LILIOM: Are you still here? What are you waiting for?

MARIE: You told us to wait.

LILIOM: Must you always interfere? No one is talking to you.

MARIE: You asked us—why we ——

LILIOM: Will you keep your mouth shut? What do you suppose I want with two of you? I meant that one of you was to wait. The other can go home.

MARIE: All right.

JULIE: All right. [*Neither starts to go*]

LILIOM: One of you goes home. [*To* MARIE] Where do you work?

MARIE: At the Breier's, Damjanovitsch Street, Number 20.

LILIOM: And you?

JULIE: I work there, too.

LILIOM: Well, one of you goes home. Which of you wants to stay? [*There is no answer*] Come on, speak up, which of you stays?

MARIE: [*Officiously*] She'll lose her job if she stays.

LILIOM: Who will?

MARIE: Julie. She has to be back by seven o'clock.

LILIOM: Is that true? Will they discharge you if you're not back on time?

JULIE: Yes.

LILIOM: Well, wasn't I discharged?

JULIE: Yes—you were discharged, too.

MARIE: Julie, shall I go?

JULIE: I—can't tell you what to do.

MARIE: All right—stay if you like.

LILIOM: You'll be discharged if you do?

MARIE: Shall I go, Julie?

JULIE: [*Embarrassed*] Why do you keep asking me that?

MARIE: You know best what to do.

JULIE: [*Profoundly moved; slowly*] It's all right, Marie, you can go home.

MARIE: [*Exits reluctantly, but comes back, and says uncertainly*] Good night. [*She waits a moment to see if* JULIE *will follow her.* JULIE *does not move.* MARIE *exits. Meantime it has grown quite dark*]

SUGGESTIONS FOR THE ACTOR

1. The setting is romantic. The only real prop you need for the scene is a bench, but you must imagine the rest of the park—an entrance, a path, dense shrubbery, trees, lovely white blossoms on the tree behind the bench, etc. Acacia blossoms are occasionally blown down from the tree by the wind. (In your mind, substitute any flowering tree you wish.) "See" the sunset, the darkening sky. What do you "smell"? "Hear" the distant noise of the amusement park and the faint, tinkling music of the carousel.

2. For Julie and Marie: What is the relationship between you? You both work as maids in the Breier home. You, Marie, have recently arrived in the big city (Budapest). Although Julie is at times annoyed, even exasperated with you during this scene, she must be fond of you—your friendship lasts a lifetime. Are you, Julie, often exasperated with Marie, or are you now less patient than usual because you are tense, excited, nervously awaiting Liliom's return?

The two of you have strikingly different personalities. You, Marie, are an extrovert. You usually say what is on your mind. You are often comical without intending to be. You cry easily, laugh easily; your feelings are right there on the surface. You refrained from telling Julie about Wolf until now only because you did not want her to envy your happiness. Later in the play you put on silly, self-important airs after you and your husband become wealthy, but you are still good-hearted.

You, Julie, have far more depth of character than Marie. You are an introvert. You hide your deepest feelings from everyone, even from those you love. Marie speaks grandly of her "Passionate" and "Ideal Love." In this scene she melodramatically exclaims, "My heart has found its mate." But you, Julie, are truly swept away by overwhelming passion. Yet you never express your emotion, not even to Liliom after you marry him. You love him madly despite the terrible way he treats you; sometimes he even beats you. After attempting to commit a terrible crime, he kills himself as he is about to be captured. Marie thinks you are better off without him. She hopes you will now be sensible and marry a respectable carpenter, a widower who admires you. She cannot conceive of the depth of your love for Liliom. Politely but firmly you refuse the carpenter's offer. Alone, you struggle to earn a meager living for yourself and your young daughter.

As a preparatory exercise you two actresses should perform an "étude" (improvisation in character): as Julie and Marie, make up, improvise your own words and physical actions as you show an incident occurring before the events of the play. For example, you might act a scene in which you both perform household tasks for your employer while planning how to spend your next "day off." Perhaps you would disagree at first.

3. You, Julie, are no doubt masking your thoughts and feelings during much of your "small talk" with Marie about soldiers' uniforms and the like. At times your spoken words may be quite different from your hidden thoughts. You, the actress, should think your (Julie's) "subtext" (the thoughts beneath your spoken words) as well as your "inner monologue" (your thoughts during pauses or while Marie is talking) whenever you work on the scene. But do not attempt to memorize your inner thoughts; they need not be exactly the same at each playing.

4. For Liliom: You cover up your deepest feelings also. Sometimes you act roughly because you are ashamed to show your great tenderness, or, later in the play, because you cannot bear to see Julie's suffering.

You pretend that losing your job doesn't worry you. In this scene you pretend that you don't care which of the two girls stays, but you are secretly falling in love with Julie.

You, the actor, should think your (Liliom's) "subtext" and "inner monologue" (see above No. 3) as you prepare the role. Feel free to change or add to your character's inner thoughts as you perform.

5. Each of you should decide what the character you play wants at every moment of the scene. For example, during one section of the scene you, Marie, want to find out how to recognize a real soldier. When your immediate objective changes, a new "beat" begins. During another "beat," you, Julie, want to deny your feelings toward Liliom, while Marie wants to make you admit them. At the end of the scene she finally does force you to

commit yourself; she insists that you tell her whether she should leave you alone with Liliom. At that point you, Marie, really want Julie to leave with you, although you are afraid to come right out and say so. You, Liliom, want to be alone with Julie, but you are also afraid to speak your mind. Why are *you* afraid?

What is the *main* objective of each character in the scene?

6. If you have the time for a small research project, try to learn something about daily life in Budapest, Hungary, during the early part of the twentieth century. Books containing photographs of the city would be especially helpful. What did the "common people" wear?

7. The portion of this scene before Liliom's entrance may be played as a separate scene for two actresses.

From *One Sunday Afternoon* by James Hagan.
Act I, Scene 2

INTRODUCTION

There have been three movie versions of this tender stage comedy: a Paramount production in 1933, starring Gary Cooper, Frances Fuller and Faye Wray, a Warner Brothers production in 1941 entitled *The Strawberry Blonde,* starring James Cagney, Olivia de Havilland and Rita Hayworth, and a Warner Brothers musical version in 1948, starring Dennis Morgan, Dorothy Malone and Janis Paige. The original play by James Hagan begins with a Prologue, Scene 1, set in the present. The last scene, the Epilogue, also takes place today, but the rest of the play takes place "many years ago." Amy and Virginia, the young girls of Scene 2, which follows, are middle-aged in the Prologue and Epilogue. Amy is married to Biff Grimes, her secret childhood love of Scene 2, now a middle-aged dentist in a small Midwestern town. Amy is prim and old-fashioned, but she is also loving and sweet-natured. Biff Grimes had married Amy Lind "on the rebound." As a young fellow he had fallen in love with Virginia Brush, but his "friend" Hugo Barnstead had outfoxed him and secretly married Virginia. In the Epilogue we discover that Virginia is now rich (Hugo is president of a bank), dressed in fancy clothes, coarse, still a flirt, and without a conscience. When Hugo arrives in town, he comes to Biff's dental office to have a tooth pulled. Hugo breathes in too much anesthetic, a powerful gas. When Biff starts to bring Hugo back to consciousness, Virginia urges him to let Hugo alone—to die. She is tired of his endless complaints about his teeth!

In the following scene, however, the differences in character between Amy and Virginia are not yet so obvious, or so extreme.
They are still two innocent young girls, bubbling over with antici-
pation.

> *A lane in Avery's Park. Saturday afternoon. Spring.*
> *There is a rustic bench right of center with bushes and a*
> *street lamp back of it. There is a tree in the center at the*
> *back with bushes and woods beyond. The entrances are*
> *down right below the bench, up right beyond the bushes*
> *and left.*
> AMY LIND *seated at left end of bench and* VIRGINIA BRUSH
> *at right, are discovered sitting on a park bench. They are*
> *two young girls dressed in blue, flat straw hats and gloves.*
> VIRGINIA *is the older of the two.*
> *They are in an excited state of mind and are looking off*
> *right through the bushes.*

VIRGINIA: [*Laughing*] I'm telling you I did see him.

AMY: Where?

VIRGINIA: Coming in the Oak Street entrance.

AMY: [*Trying to look off right*] Where is he now?

VIRGINIA: How do I know—he went over towards Mason's
walk.

AMY: Was he alone?

VIRGINIA: I think so—that is, I didn't see anybody with him.

AMY: [*Disappointed*] Oh!

VIRGINIA: Now, that doesn't mean that he hasn't got his friend
along.

AMY: [*Nervously*] Did—did you tell him you would meet him
over here?

VIRGINIA: Of course I did.

AMY: Oh, Virginia—that's being forward.

VIRGINIA: That's not being forward. I guess if a girl tells a boy she will meet him in Avery's Park, that's not being forward.

AMY: What did you say his name was?

VIRGINIA: I told you, Hugo Barnstead. Isn't that a swell name for a man—Hugo. Wait 'til you see him.

AMY: How did you happen to meet him?

VIRGINIA: [*Fixing her dress*] Well—I was in the drugstore getting a Belladonna plaster for Ma—when in he comes. I knew he was looking at me 'cause he rapped on the counter and coughed twice. Then he smiled—so I smiled. Then he winked—

AMY: [*Horrified*] Oh, Virginia!

VIRGINIA: Yes, he did—just like this— [*She winks*]

AMY: Weren't you horror-stricken?

VIRGINIA: For a second I was. I saw he was awfully good-looking, so I winked back.

AMY: Virginia!

VIRGINIA: There wasn't anybody looking. Shucks, if a boy is good-looking, what's the harm in a little wink. It didn't hurt him.

AMY: I know, but—

VIRGINIA: Amy, a girl has to be up-to-date nowadays. You can't be old-fashioned any more. How are you going to get a beau if you don't wink at him?

AMY: It's brazen. Well?

VIRGINIA: Well—he waited outside for me and we walked down Meadow Street together. Oh, he was just swell. He had vanilla on him—smelt nice—he said, "What's your name?" I didn't tell him—that would be brazen. So I said, "What's yours?" He said, "Hugo Barnstead." Then he said, "Can I meet you next Saturday afternoon." I said, "I don't see why you couldn't." Then he said, "I've got a friend. Have you got one?" I said, "Yes" thinking of you, of course. "Good," he said. "This friend of mine is awfully swell-looking—tall and handsome."

AMY: [*Giggling*] Oh, golly—

VIRGINIA: Couldn't be any sweller-looking than Hugo. Hugo's the swellest-looking thing in the world.

AMY: [*Timidly*] Virginia—I'm afraid.

VIRGINIA: Of what?

AMY: Well, I never met a boy like this—that is, without proper introduction. Why, if my mother knew—

VIRGINIA: [*Offended*] What about *my* mother—

AMY: I know—but *my* mother is worse than *your* mother, Virginia. Why—if she knew I was over here in Avery's Park flirting with the boys—

VIRGINIA: You aren't flirting.

AMY: We're over here, aren't we?

VIRGINIA: You can't call that flirting—shucks, talking to a couple of harmless boys isn't flirting.

AMY: Well, you know what my mother is. You know what would happen to me if she found out?

VIRGINIA: What?

AMY: Church—twice, next Sunday.

VIRGINIA: Oh, Amy—

AMY: Yes, that's what my ma says. Going to church twice is what takes sin away—and purifies you.

VIRGINIA: You don't have to tell her you were over here, do you?

AMY: Of course not, but Ma loves to snoop.

VIRGINIA: [*Giving her a look of disgust*] Amy, you're the biggest 'fraid cat I know of.

AMY: Yes, but—

VIRGINIA: Now there are no buts—you'll have to meet this boy whether you like it or not. You are helping me out, aren't you?

AMY: Of course I am.

VIRGINIA: Well—

AMY: Well, all right. Just this once. Do you suppose he is a nice-looking fellow?

VIRGINIA: [*Looking off right—rises and crosses a little to center*] Of course he is.

AMY: Do you think he will like my new dress?

VIRGINIA: I know he will.

AMY: And do you think he will like me?

VIRGINIA: He'll fall in love with you the minute he sees you—

AMY: Now, Virginia, you stop that. Don't you talk like that.

VIRGINIA: [*Looking off right*] Well, he might. You can't tell. And *you* might fall in love with him.

AMY: Why, Virginia, I'd die!

VIRGINIA: If you fell in love with a man?

AMY: I'd fall down and die right on this spot.

VIRGINIA: That's because you're weak, Amy.

AMY: No, I'm not—but I just couldn't stand it.

VIRGINIA: I'd like to fall in love. I want to see what it feels like.

AMY: I'd die right on this spot—

VIRGINIA: [*Taking her hand*] Tell the truth, Amy—weren't you ever in love with a boy?

AMY: [*Bashful-like*] Virginia!

VIRGINIA: [*Sits on arm of the bench above* AMY] You can tell me —I won't tell anybody.

AMY: [*Pause*] Honest?

VIRGINIA: Cross my heart.

AMY: I thought I was once—I don't know. Maybe it was love, I don't know, but—

VIRGINIA: Well—

AMY: Well, when I was very young—of course, that's a long time ago, understand— [VIRGINIA *nods*] It was in school. There was a boy. I don't know—he never looked at me and I never— [*She looks at* VIRGINIA *wistfully*] Virginia, did you ever have a feeling in your heart— Something that you feel is going to happen and it doesn't—that's the way my heart was— [*She touches her heart*] It wasn't love, I know that— [*Pause*] He never even noticed me. I could have been a stick-in-the-mud as far as he was concerned. Virginia, this boy always seemed lonely somehow. Everybody had it in for him, even the teachers—they called him bully—but I know he wasn't. I saw him do a lot of good things—when the big boys picked on the smaller ones, he helped the little fellows out. I know he had a lot of good in him—good, that nobody else could see—that's why my heart—

VIRGINIA: Who was this boy?

AMY: [*Sheepishly*] You wouldn't know him—

VIRGINIA: I might.

AMY: [*Pause*] Biff Grimes!

VIRGINIA: [*Rises; backs away*] Biff Grimes! You mean that big bully that hangs around Goldstein's Drug Store?

AMY: Yes—

VIRGINIA: My mother has told me about him.

AMY: So has *my* mother but I don't care.

VIRGINIA: Why, Amy, he's terrible. The reputation—why, Amy, I'd be ashamed to mention his name. I heard that he drinks and smokes cigarettes.

AMY: [*Alibiing herself*] Of course, that was a long time ago. Shucks, I'm all over it now. He doesn't even know I'm alive— [VIRGINIA *looks up right*] Can—can you see them yet?

VIRGINIA: Yes—there they are.

AMY: [*Looks*] Oh, Lord! Virginia, do you think I had better go home?

VIRGINIA: They're looking the other way—

AMY: I'm glad—

VIRGINIA: Now, they're turning around—

AMY: What does the other fellow look like? Tell me, quick.

VIRGINIA: I can't make out his face but he's tall and he's got a nice pair of shoulders. [*Pause*] Now they see us— Hugo has got on a new suit and a red necktie. My, he does look swell—

AMY: And—and the other fellow?

VIRGINIA: Oh, my heavens!!

AMY: Must be terrible.

VIRGINIA: Amy, do you know who it is?

AMY: How would I know? I'm not looking that way.

VIRGINIA: It's Biff Grimes—

AMY: [*Rises*] Biff Grimes!

VIRGINIA: Yes, that's who it is, Biff Grimes—

AMY: [*Rises*] Oh, Virginia—I can't stay here.

VIRGINIA: Well, you can't go now.

AMY: Why? [AMY *sits*]

VIRGINIA: 'Cause they have seen us— [*Crosses to the lamp post. Looks off right. Returns and sits*] yes, here they come, walking this way.

AMY: [*Frightened*] What'll I do, Virginia?

VIRGINIA: Do? Do nothing. Sit where you are—

AMY: Don't you feel frightened?

VIRGINIA: My heart is jumping a little.

AMY: Mine is just kerplunking all over.

VIRGINIA: Now, listen—we won't say a word to them. Just let them pass. Of course, if they say something—we'll say something.

AMY: And if they don't say anything—we won't say anything.

VIRGINIA: No—just drop your eyes.

AMY: Drop my eyes?

VIRGINIA: Yes—that will show them we are good girls and they can't trifle with us.

AMY: All right—let me know when they get here. [*They fix their dresses, clasp their hands together, and sit.* BIFF *and* HUGO *are heard off right*]

VIRGINIA: [*Whispers—closing her eyes*] Here they are. [*She deliberately drops her handkerchief in front of her*]

AMY: [*Closing her eyes*] "Our Father which art in Heaven—"

SUGGESTIONS FOR THE ACTOR

1. Remember a park that you once visited on a fine spring day. Try to recall particular sights, sounds, smells, even tastes and textures that you associate with the experience. Did you drink from a water fountain? Eat a popsicle? Sit on a hard wooden bench? Did you have to watch out for splinters? Did you walk on grass? How did that feel as compared to walking on pavement or on a dirt path? Was the sun on your face or on your back? Its position of course depended on the time of day. Remember exactly how it felt on your body.

2. Both of you plan your "set" together. The only actual properties (objects onstage) you will need are several chairs pushed together to represent a park bench. You can imagine all the rest, including a street lamp, trees, bushes, a path and the entrances. After you have decided together where everything is situated, go "onstage" and explore your set. Concentrate on visualizing everything and imagining all the sounds, smells, etc. that you remembered in the first exercise.

3. Act out the basic situation of the scene *silently*: two girls in the park on a spring afternoon, impatiently awaiting the arrival of two boys. One of the two girls has met her "date"; the other girl wonders who her "blind date" will be. You will be surprised at how much you can communicate to each other simply with looks, movements and gestures. For example, how might one of you, the shyer one, communicate to the other that you are afraid and want to leave? How might the bolder of you reassure the other that there is nothing to be afraid of? How might you tell her that she must remain where she is? How might one of you communicate to the other that you still don't see the boys and you don't believe they are really coming? That you see them at last? At that point what would each of you do? Why?

Don't lose the sense of where you are, which you concentrated on in the first two exercises. From the very beginning of this improvisation, imagine all the sights, sounds, smells, etc. of the park.

4. Act this scene again, only now communicate with words as well as looks and gestures. This improvised scene should take place in the present, so that you can easily invent dialogue natural to you and your friends. What would *you* say if you were in that situation?

5. Amy and Virginia are both naïve young girls, eagerly awaiting the arrival of the two boys, but the girls are not alike. What differences between them can you discover from their words and physical actions in the written scene? For instance, how do they differ in their attitudes toward love? Toward this "double date"? Toward Biff Grimes? How do they each behave after they see the boys? If possible, read the entire play to discover personality characteristics not shown in this scene. You will learn, for example, that Amy has spunk. She is not so timid as she may appear in this one scene. Virginia flirts daringly, but Amy speaks up forthrightly

and says what she feels. When Biff arrives, she says, "I always liked you, Biff." Virginia is shocked at her frankness. When later in the play Biff asks Amy to "go steady," Amy encourages Biff to kiss her. She is even brave enough to elope with Biff despite her mother's fierce objections to him. What other traits can you discover? Amy and Virginia will eventually become utterly different from one another (see the "Introduction" to this selection). The seeds of these differences are present even now.

6. If you perform this scene as a "period piece" (occurring in a bygone era), decide on the specific year. It would be interesting and helpful to learn something about the historical events, customs, manners and dress of the period you select. A librarian may be able to help you find relevant information, pictures and cartoons. The play was first copyrighted in 1930. If you choose to think of the Prologue and Epilogue as taking place about that time, then this scene would be set somewhere around the beginning of the twentieth century.

From *The Drinking Gourd* by Lorraine Hansberry.
Act 1

INTRODUCTION

At the time of this writing, the late Lorraine Hansberry's original television play *The Drinking Gourd* has not yet been produced on television. A play on the subject of slavery by this major American, black playwright was ordered and paid for by a leading TV network in 1961. The play's indictment of slavery, however, may have been more searing than the network had expected or wanted. Perhaps the unprecedented commercial success of Alex Haley's *Roots* will make a difference in the fate of this play. Perhaps by the time you read these words, this outstanding television drama will have received the treatment it deserves at long last.

The title of the play is taken from the familiar Negro spiritual of that name, and refers to the constellation of stars commonly known as the Big Dipper. This formation points to the North Star, which showed the way to freedom to runaway slaves. This spiritual, filled with secret meanings, was used by the Underground Railroad as a guide to slaves making their escape.

The scene preceding this one begins at "Quittin' Time." Exhausted from their long hours of hard labor, the slaves slowly form a line in front of the community outdoor fireplace. Rissa, the cook, is doling out meager portions of bacon and corn pone. When Sarah (pronounced "Say-rah"), "a young girl of about nineteen," takes her place in line, she bends down to play with Joshua, a little boy of seven or eight who has been hanging around Rissa. Sarah quietly asks Joshua where his uncle Hannibal is. Rissa, who is Hannibal's mother, overhears. She pretends not to care but when Sarah informs her that he was missing from the fields that afternoon, she asks whether Coffin, the slave "driver," knows. When she learns that Coffin does know and plans to tell "Marster Sweet," she asks Sarah to find Hannibal. She hands Sarah his supper, already wrapped, "which has been lying in readiness" all along.

"HANNIBAL is a young slave of about nineteen or twenty."

Exterior. Moonlit Woods. SARAH *emerges from the woods into a tiny clearing, bundle in hand.*

SARAH: [*Calling softly*] Hannibal—[*The camera pans to a little hillock in deep grass where a lean, vital young man lies, arms folded under his head, staring up at the stars with bright commanding eyes. At the sound of* SARAH's *voice off camera we come down in his eyes. He comes alert. She calls again*] Hannibal—[*He smiles and hides as she approaches*] Hannibal—[*She whirls about fearfully at the snap of a twig, then reassured crosses in front of his hiding place, searching*] Hannibal—[*He touches her ankle—she screams. Laughing, he reaches for her. With a sigh of exasperation she throws him his food*]

HANNIBAL: [*Romantically, wistfully—playing the poet-fool*] And when she come to me, it were the moonrise . . . [*He holds out his hand*] And when she touch my hand, it were the true stars fallin'. [*He takes her hand and pulls her down in the grass and kisses her. She pulls away with the urgency of her news*]

SARAH: Coffin noticed you was gone first thing!

HANNIBAL: Well, that old driver finally gettin' to be almost smart as a jackass.

SARAH: Say he gona tell Marster Sweet in the mornin'! You gona catch you another whippin', boy . . . ! [*In a mood to ignore peril,* HANNIBAL *goes on eating his food*] Hannibal, why you have to run off like that all the time?

HANNIBAL: [*Teasing*] Don't run off *all* the time.

SARAH: Oh, Hannibal!

HANNIBAL: [*Finishing the meager supper and reaching out for her playfully*] "Oh, Hannibal. Oh, Hannibal!" Come here. [*He takes hold of her and kisses her once sweetly and lightly*] H'you this evenin', Miss Sarah Mae?

SARAH: You don't know how mad old Coffin was today, boy, or you wouldn't be so smart. He's gona get you in trouble with Marster again.

HANNIBAL: Me and you was *born* in trouble with Marster. [*Suddenly looking up at the sky and pointing to distract her*] Hey, lookathere!—

SARAH: [*Noting him and also looking up*] What—

HANNIBAL: [*Drawing her close*] Lookit that big, old, fat star shinin' away up yonder there!

SARAH: [*Automatically dropping her voice and looking about a bit*] Shhh. Hannibal!

HANNIBAL: [*With his hand, as though he is personally touching the stars*] One, two three, four—they makes up the dipper. That's the Big Dipper, Sarah. The old Drinkin' Gourd pointin' straight to the North Star!

SARAH: [*Knowingly*] Everybody knows that's the Big Dipper and you better hush your mouth for sure now, boy. Trees on this plantation got more ears than leaves!

HANNIBAL: [*Ignoring the caution*] That's the old Drinkin' Gourd herself! [*Releasing the girl's arms and settling down, a little wistfully now*]

HANNIBAL: Sure is bright tonight. Sure would make good travelin' light tonight . . .

SARAH: [*With terror, clapping her hand over his mouth*] Stop it!

HANNIBAL: [*Moving her hand*] Up there jes pointin' away . . . *due North!*

SARAH: [*Regarding him sadly*] You're sure like your brother, boy. Just like him.

> [HANNIBAL *ignores her and leans back in the grass in the position of the opening shot of the scene, with his arms tucked under his head. He sings softly to himself*]

HANNIBAL: "For the old man is a-waitin'
            For to carry you to freedom
            If you follow the Drinking Gourd.
            Follow—follow—follow . . .
            If you follow the Drinking Gourd . . ."

SARAH: [*Over the song*] Look like him . . . talk like him . . . and God knows, you sure think like him. [*Pause*] In time, I reckon—[*Very sadly*] you be gone like him.

HANNIBAL: [*Sitting bolt upright suddenly and peering into the woods about them*] You think Isaiah got all the way to Canada, Sarah? Mama says it's powerful far. Farther than Ohio! [*This last with true wonder*] Sure he did! I bet you old Isaiah is up there and got hisself a job and is livin' fine. I bet you that! Bet he works in a lumberyard or something and got hisself a wife and maybe even a house and—

SARAH: [*Quietly*] You mean if he's alive, Hannibal.

HANNIBAL: Oh, he's alive, all right! Catchers ain't never caught my brother. [*He whistles through his teeth*] That boy lit out of here in a way somebody go who don't mean to never be caught by nothin'! [*He waits. Then, having assured himself within*] Wherever he is, he's alive. And he's free.

SARAH: I can't see how his runnin' off like that did you much good. Or your mama. Almost broke her heart, that's what. And worst of all, leavin' his poor little baby. Leavin' poor little Joshua who don't have no mother of his own as it is. Seem like your brother just went out his head when Marster sold Joshua's mother. I guess everybody on this plantation knew he wasn't gona be here long then. Even Marster must of known.

HANNIBAL: But Marster couldn't keep him here then! Not all Marster's dogs and drivers and guns. Nothin'. [*He looks to the woods, remembering*] I met him here that night to bring him the food and a extry pair of shoes. He was standin' right over there, right over there, with the moonlight streamin' down on him and he was breathin' hard—Lord, that boy was breathin' so's you could almost hear him on the other side of the woods. [*A sudden pause and then a rush in the telling*] He didn't say nothin' to me, nothin' at all. But his eyes look like somebody lit a fire in 'em, they was shinin' so in the dark. I jes hand him the parcel and he put it in his shirt and give me a kind of push on the shoulder . . . [*He touches the place, remembering keenly*] . . . Here. And then he turned and lit out through them woods like lightnin'. He was *bound* out this place!

[*He is entirely quiet behind the completion of the narrative.* SARAH *is deeply affected by the implications of what she has heard and suddenly puts her arms around his neck and clings very tightly to him. Then she holds him back from her and looks at him for the truth*]

SARAH: You aim to go, don't you, Hannibal? [*He does not answer and it is clear because of it that he intends to run off*] H'you know it's so much better to run off? [*A little desperately, near tears, thinking of the terrors involved*] Even if you make it —h'you know what's up there, what it be like to go wanderin' 'round by yourself in this world?

HANNIBAL: I don't know. Jes know what it is to be a slave!

SARAH: Where would you go—?

HANNIBAL: Jes North, that's all I know. [*Kind of shrugging*] Try to find Isaiah maybe. How I know what I do? [*Throwing up his hands at the difficult question*] There's people up there what helps runaways.

SARAH: You mean them aba—aba-litchinists? I heard Marster Sweet say once that they catches runaways and makes soap out of them.

HANNIBAL: [*Suddenly older and wiser*] That's slave-owner talk, Sarah. Whatever you hear Marster say 'bout slavery—you always believe the opposite. There ain't nothin' hurt slave marster so much—[*Savoring the notion*]—as when his property walk away from him. Guess that's the worst blow of all. Way I look at it, ever' slave ought to run off 'fore he die.

SARAH: [*Looking up suddenly, absorbing the sense of what he has just said*] Oh, Hannibal—*I* couldn't go! [*She starts to shake all over*] I'm too delicate. My breath wouldn't hold out from here to the river . . .

HANNIBAL: [*Starting to laugh at her*] No, not you—skeerified as you is! [*He looks at her and pulls her to him*] But don't you worry, little Sarah. I'll come back. [*He smoothes her hair and comforts her*] I'll come back and buy you. Mama too, if she's still livin'. [*The girl quivers in his arms and he holds her a little more tightly, looking up once again to his stars*] I surely do that thing!

SUGGESTIONS FOR THE ACTOR

1. According to the dictionary, the seven principal stars of the constellation Ursa Major, known as the Big Dipper, form a shape like "a vessel with a handle, used to dip water." "The two stars forming the edge farthest from the handle are approximately in line with the North Star." The Little Dipper is composed of the "seven principal stars . . . in Ursa Minor, the North Star forming the outer end of the handle."

Find these two constellations in the sky some starry night. If necessary examine pictures of the two constellations beforehand. First look for the Big Dipper. Then find the North Star in the same way that escaping slaves found it. Examine the two constellations carefully. Observe the rest of the sky and the line of the horizon as well as these particular stars. Notice also what happens to your eyes when they focus on objects so far away. Later try to recall all those sights. Concentrate on "seeing" in your mind's eye the starry sky, the line of the horizon, the Big Dipper and the North Star surrounded by the rest of the Little Dipper. When you "see" an imaginary distant object, do your eyes focus differently from the way they focus on an imaginary close object?

For the actor playing Hannibal: You not only "see" the North Star; you also have powerful feelings toward this object. It symbolizes liberty for you and for so many others, and is literally a beacon, lighting the way to freedom. As an exercise, concentrate both on "seeing" the North Star and on thinking the inner thoughts of your character while you (Hannibal) lie on your back in the tall grass. As you gaze up at the North Star, what do you want to do? What actions do you contemplate in order to reach your objective?

For the actress playing Sarah: The North Star has a special significance for you too—a negative one, at this point in the play. You are sure that it will soon lead the man you love away from you, perhaps to his death. What are your inner thoughts as you gaze at this distant object?

2. For the actor playing Hannibal: When you improvise a scene not shown in the play itself but from the life of the character you portray, you are performing an étude. As a preparatory exercise, act some études as Hannibal with your brother Isaiah. You will need the best actor you can find who is willing to play Isaiah. For instance, you may choose to work on a scene in which you try to console Isaiah after his wife is sold. Isaiah cannot be comforted. He may now decide to escape, telling you when and where to bring him food and extra shoes. Then enact your last meeting with your brother, the encounter so vividly described in the written scene. Perform this situation silently. Your eyes communicate worlds to one another, but no word is spoken. You dare not utter a sound for fear of being overheard. His hand on your shoulder says more than verbal goodbyes ever could. Even though you do not speak aloud, you (Hannibal) and Isaiah are each thinking a whole chain of silent thoughts throughout the scene.

3. The scene between Hannibal and Sarah is at its heart a love scene. If there is tremendous love and physical attraction between the two, the anticipated separation becomes almost unbearable.

Much as you, Hannibal, love Sarah, you cannot stay with her; you cannot endure the life of a slave. At the end of the scene in an attempt to comfort her and to resolve your own inner conflict about leaving, you vow to return someday and buy her. Much as you, Sarah, love Hannibal, you cannot run away with him—not yet. The thought of risking death fills you with terror. By the end of the play, however, you have changed. You not only prepare to escape but *you* lead Hannibal, who has been blinded, and you guide little Joshua as well. You even carry a gun. You are still terrified, but nevertheless you do what must be done. (Which requires more courage: braving danger without any thought of what is to be feared, or braving danger despite one's intense fear?)

Act some études together, of earlier encounters, before escape was discussed. You might wish to include the moment when you first realized that you love each other. This moment is not shown in the play. Before you begin each étude, decide specifically when and where the scene takes place and what you were each doing just before the scene. Where are you each coming from? Where are you going? What do you each want to do as the scene opens?

From *Take a Giant Step* by Louis Peterson.
Act I, Scene 1

INTRODUCTION

Take a Giant Step concerns the painful, lonely growing up of a seventeen-year-old black boy named Spencer Scott. His family lives in a middle-class, mostly white neighborhood in a New England town. "If you walked down a rather shady, middle-class street in a New England town, you would probably find a house very similar to the one in which the Scotts live. It was a rather ordinary house when it was built and it is a rather ordinary house now, but it has been well cared for * * * and it gives off an aura of good health and happiness if houses can ever know such things. The house has been cut away to expose to view to the audience the back entrance hall, a kitchen up left [actor's left] a dining room left, a living room and a hall right [actor's right] in which there is a front door and a staircase leading to the upstairs. * * *

The time is the present—Fall—late October. It is a fine day—a golden warm day which is typical of New England at this time of year.

Spence's parents love him, but they both work and have no time for him. His older brother is away at college. His friends from childhood, all white, have recently given him up since they started going out with girls. Of his old pals only Iggie, a Jewish boy, has not rejected him. Spence is closest to his grandma, a semi-invalid who dies later in the play. She is the only member of the family who listens to him. Although her manner to Spence is crusty on the surface, she is his defender.

When the play opens, Spence comes home late from school on the last day before a week-long vacation. Spence, however, has been suspended for the week following the vacation. He "talked back" to a history teacher who had made false and insulting remarks about Negroes during the Civil War. Spence became so angry that he went to the men's room and smoked a cigar. He tells his grandma the whole story. She does not let him know that she approves of his standing up for what is right. Instead she scolds him for using bad language in relating the story to her. Tony, a former pal, comes over supposedly to visit but really to borrow Spence's baseball equipment. (Spence has always been showered with material possessions in place of the attention he craves.) Spence would like to feign indifference to his former friends, but he cannot help revealing his hurt. Angrily he gives Tony all his baseball equipment "for keeps." Spence confides his loneliness to Grandma afterward. He asks her whether the closest bus "will take you right out to the colored section"; he then asks her to lend him five dollars. He pretends that he wants the money to buy flowers for his mother and cigars for his father in order to soften the blow of his suspension. The playwright is clearly indicating to the audience, however, that Spence plans to leave home immediately. He helps Grandma upstairs and she agrees to get the money for him.

It is essential for the actor playing Spence in the scene following to know that Spence does not really have a girl friend as yet, although at this point he is anxious to find himself a girl. He even wants to get married and find a job. Tired of being a lonely "kid," he hopes that being a grown up *now,* right away, "will bring a couple of things with it. Happiness—a nice girl—maybe—"

SPENCE *has just helped* GRANDMA *off. Pause. Then he runs to kitchen, gets suitcase and clothes. Doorbell rings.*

SPENCE: Dear, dear God—if that's my mother, just kill me as I open the door. [*Crosses to door. He hides suitcase left of piano. Opens door*] Hi! Iggie—did you give me a scare!

IGGIE: Hiya, Spence.

SPENCE: I'm in a terrible hurry, Iggie. What do you want?

IGGIE: I just came over to see if you have any stamps to trade.

SPENCE: [*Crosses left, gets shoes*] I haven't got much time. Come on in—but you can't stay long. I've got to go somewhere.

IGGIE: [*Comes in*] Where are you going?

SPENCE: No place. [*Pause*] You sure you came over to trade stamps?

IGGIE: [*At sofa*] Sure—that's what I came over for. I finished my home work early—and so I thought I might—

SPENCE: [*Sits in chair left of table*] You know, Iggie—you're going to be out of school for a week. You didn't have to get your homework done so soon. That's the most disgusting thing I ever heard.

IGGIE: [*Crosses to table*] Now look, if I want to get my homework done—that's my business. I don't tell you it's disgusting when you don't get yours done at all, do I?

SPENCE: [*Crosses back to sofa*] O.K.—O.K., Iggie. I only thought you came over because you heard I got kicked out of school.

IGGIE: No, Spence—I hadn't heard.

SPENCE: You're sure?

IGGIE: I told you I hadn't heard, didn't I? [*Sits right of table*]

SPENCE: [*Crosses right to close door*] That kind of news has a way of getting around. [*Looking at him*] Well, what are you thinking about? [*Crosses back to sofa*]

IGGIE: Nothing. I was just thinking that if I got kicked out of school, I guess I'd just as soon I dropped dead right there on the floor in the principal's office.

SPENCE: O.K., Iggie. You don't need to rub it in. I get the picture. [*Look upstairs*]

IGGIE: I'm sorry, Spence. Is there anything I can do?

SPENCE: Now, Iggie—pardon me for being so damn polite—but what in the hell could you do about it?

IGGIE: I only want to help, Spence.

SPENCE: [*Crosses left to below table*] Well, you can't—so let's drop it, shall we?

IGGIE: I didn't mean that business about dropping dead. I probably wouldn't drop dead anyway. There's nothing wrong with my heart.

SPENCE: [*Sits sofa*] Iggie—will you please cut it out.

IGGIE: Anything you say. I didn't mean to offend you.

SPENCE: You didn't offend me, Iggie. You just talk too much—that's all.

IGGIE: I'll try to do better in the future.

SPENCE: Look, Iggie—I've gone and hurt your feelings—haven't I? Hell—I'm sorry. I've always liked you, Iggie. You're a good kid. I'm apologizing, Iggie.

IGGIE: It's O.K., Spence. I know you're upset.

SPENCE: [*Crosses down left*] I know how sensitive you are and all that and I just mow into you like crazy. I wish someone would tell me to shut my mouth. [*He walks to the stairs*] Gram —hurry up with that dough, will you. Iggie—look—I'll tell you what I'm going to do for you. [*He goes over to the piano and comes back with his stamp album*] Here—Iggie—it's yours. I want you to have it—because you're my friend.

IGGIE: Your album! But don't you want it, Spence?

SPENCE: No, Iggie. I don't want it.

IGGIE: But why? I think you must be crazy. [*Stands*]

SPENCE: Hell, Iggie—because I'm growing up. I'm becoming a man, Iggie. And since I'm going out in just a few minutes with my girl friend—you know it's time for me to quit fooling around with stuff like that.

IGGIE: Have you got a girl friend?

SPENCE: Yeh! Yes—I have—as a matter of fact I might get married soon. Forget all about school and all.

IGGIE: Really. Who is the girl, Spence?

SPENCE: Just a girl—that's all. And if everything works out O.K., I won't be coming back. You know, I'll have to get a job and stuff like that. Now you've got to go, Iggie, cause I've got to finish packing and get dressed. [*Leads* IGGIE *center*]

IGGIE: Where are you going, Spence?

SPENCE: I can't tell you, Iggie.

IGGIE: Are you sure you're feeling all right?

SPENCE: Yes, Iggie, I'm feeling all right.

IGGIE: [*Crossing to door*] Thank you for the gift. I appreciate it.

SPENCE: Forget it.

IGGIE: It's a beautiful album.

SPENCE: It certainly is.

IGGIE: [*Crosses to center*] Hey, I was just thinking—maybe I could go up and talk to old Hasbrook. It might do some good.

SPENCE: [*Crosses to door*] I don't care about that any more, Iggie. I'm pretty sure I won't be coming back to school.

IGGIE: Are you sure you want me to have this, Spence?

SPENCE: Yes, Iggie, I want you to have it.

IGGIE: [*Crossing to door*] Well—I hope I'll see you soon. [*He is opening the door*]

SPENCE: [*At door*] Hey, Iggie! You won't mind if just once in a while—I come over and see how you're doing with it?

IGGIE: I hope you will. Goodbye. [*Exits*]

SPENCE: Geez—I don't know what's wrong with me. I think maybe my brains are molding or something. [*Gets suitcase, shoves clothes inside and runs upstairs*] Hey, Gram—will you

hurry up with that five bucks so I can get the hell out of here
before I really do something desperate!

1. What is your main objective in this scene? What do you
each want to do? Iggie, why have you come here now? What do
you each *claim* that you want to do? Is your real objective
different from your supposed objective?

What are your smaller objectives during the course of the
scene? For example, at one point you, Spence, want to make up
for having hurt Iggie's feelings. When does your objective change?
In other words, when do you want something else?

2. Improvise some scenes (invent them spontaneously as you
perform) as yourselves, the actors, in which you each pretend to
have one objective while you hide your real objective from your
partner.

One possible situation: You really want to find out whether
your friend is secretly dating your girl. You pretend, however, that
you want to get the homework assignment or to borrow something
from him. Your friend really wants to prevent you from learning
the truth, but pretends that he needs help with the math homework, or that he is late for a dentist's appointment.

Invent your own situations. Do not reveal your hidden objective
to your scene partner. Together you plan where you are
(place), when this is happening (time), and a little bit about your
past relationship (a few words only). For instance, you may decide that you are no longer the good friends you once were, or
that one of you just moved next door to the other. Don't invent an
elaborate story beforehand. The scene ends when each of you either succeeds in getting what he really wants or else gives up after
trying his hardest, using a variety of approaches.

The entire group may participate in these improvisations.

3. Spence, your feelings toward Iggie are far from simple. You
like him. In fact in a subsequent scene you tell a girl that you
meet: "Iggie's a friend of mine. He's kind of hard to talk to be-

cause he's real shy. * * * But he knows I like him and I think he's getting a lot better. * * * My theory is that everyone needs somebody else." In the course of this scene, however, you have negative as well as positive feelings toward Iggie. What are your different attitudes toward him during the scene? What causes each change of attitude? Is Iggie ever in your way, interfering with your reaching your objective? If so, when is he an obstacle in your path?

Iggie, what are your feelings toward Spence? How is your attitude toward him affected by his behavior during the scene?

How would you both describe your past relationship? How often have you visited each other's homes?

4. Spence, what are your various attitudes toward your stamp collection during the course of this scene? What does this object represent to you at this moment in your life? Why do you give it to Iggie?

Iggie, what is your attitude toward Spence's stamp collection?

For both actors: In character, improvise a scene not shown in the play itself, in which you work on the stamp collection together. If possible, work with a real stamp album. If you do not own a stamp album and are unable to borrow one, then at least familiarize yourself with an actual collection before you attempt to imagine one.

5. Spence, you do not always tell the truth in this scene. At what points are you lying? Why? Iggie, at what points, if any, do you doubt Spence's word? Why? Are you ever convinced that he is lying? If so, when? Are *you* always telling the truth in this scene? If your real reason for coming here is not the reason you give to Spence, why do you lie?

Generally speaking, these sorts of questions are open to interpretation. Frequently there is no one "right" answer. For instance, your (Iggie's) real reason for visiting Spence might or might not be the same as your stated reason. One interpretation might be more interesting than another, but neither would be wrong. As an actor, however, you should always be able to *justify* your decision. In fact, you should justify (have a reason for, motivate) everything you do onstage. Your motivation, or reason, must fit your general characterization, your character's present circumstances and the basic theme of the play, the point the playwright is making through this play.

You (the actor) have to decide whether you (the character) are telling the truth. If you are telling a lie, are you deceiving another person only or trying to fool yourself as well? Why do you lie in this instance? Do you lie habitually? Occasionally? Rarely? Your partner must decide whether or not to be fooled. You may observe your partner in subtle ways to see whether you are believed. On the other hand, if you are unaccustomed to lying you may be too afraid or too embarrassed to look your partner in the eye. Your partner may show doubt or, for some reason, may pretend to be deceived.

6. For the actor playing Spence: You (Spence) become quite sick by evening. Are you feeling perfectly well now? If not, what are your present symptoms? Have you a headache or other pain? You, the actor, should imagine specifically where and how much you (Spence) hurt. Have you other symptoms of oncoming illness —fatigue, slight nausea or dizziness? You, the actor, should try to recall those sensations and pinpoint any discomfort.

From *Bernardine* by Mary Chase.
Act I, Scene 1

INTRODUCTION

This sometimes hilarious, always tender look at adolescence was written in the early 1950s and depicts that era. The title represents the woman of every boy's dreams, at least every boy in the gang at the Shamrock, beer joint and adolescent haven. The glamorous, sensuous woman of the world "Bernardine Crud" is a figment of their group imagination. The invention of her home town "Sneaky Falls" on "Itching River" is also a collaborative effort. Later in the play a real woman appears who, to the gang's amazement, could be Bernardine in the flesh, but that incredible event has not yet transpired when this scene takes place.

The entire play is a flashback, nostalgically introduced in a Prologue by one of the boys several years later. "The backdrop, dimly visible, is a chalk on blackboard treatment of 'The Land of BERNARDINE,' with the Sneaky Falls area magnified. The Play begins as two of the boys (Tub and McElroy) walk on to set up the first scene in the Shamrock. * * * Tub and McElroy place one table down left with a chair on either side of it, the other table is placed left center, slightly upstage of the first table. The jukebox is moved into position in the upstage area between the two tables." The phone booth is placed in the up center area. For definitions of these technical theatre terms, see page xiii.

The implication is that "a group of high school boys, passing the theatre, has walked in to 'show' an audience these episodes of the recent past." The boys act in character as they set up the scene.

After their exit, Arthur Beaumont (Beau) enters in U. S. Air Force uniform to deliver the Prologue. Beau tells the audience that he is now a lieutenant in the Air Force (evidently during the Korean War), but in high school days he was a "big wheel" at the Shamrock, a "musty, dusty old place," but it was the gang's beloved hangout, their club, where they could freely discuss their favorite subject, girls. He informs the audience that the first scene takes place on a Saturday afternoon in late spring.

Tub and Fudge enter and position themselves for the scene. By the end of the Prologue Tub is leaning on the jukebox, from which he listens intently to a trumpet solo. Fudge sits on a chair on the downstage side of the table down left.

When Beau has finished talking, he removes his Air Force jacket, cap and tie and throws them offstage. "Under the jacket he is wearing either a sports shirt jersey slipover or sweater." He seats himself at the left center table in a chair to the (actor's) right of the table, lights a cigarette and listens to the music. There is "a more or less constant background of music from the jukebox. This can be blues, jazz or swing."

Act I, Scene 1, most of which is reprinted below, has a cast of eight: seven boys and Helen, the waitress.

DESCRIPTION OF CHARACTERS

ARTHUR BEAUMONT. Beau assumes a cloak and dagger manner and comic ferocity to mask a sensitive nature and the heart of a poet. Although he is the leader of "the gang" he is the most insecure of all of them.

Whenever he is about to go into his routines, such as the gruff businessman * * * he draws back from the others a moment, like an actor about to go onstage, and shows his face and body in the process of "becoming" these various poses. For instance, before he speaks in Scene 1 as the gruff businessman, "he's a traveling man—hard candies," etc., he throws out an an imaginary paunch, puts his thumbs into imaginary suspenders. He pantomimes each change of voice and "gag" with quick changes of facial expression and gestures; making a "production" of each one.

He is tall and slender, dreamy-eyed but quick of movement, and always sensitive to the feelings of others—especially suffering.

There is nothing of the extrovert about him. He only wishes there were.

MARVIN (TUB) GRINER. Griner is the prime "wolf" of the gang. He is well built physically with handsome head and shrewd, penetrating eyes. He is completely realistic. He is a good athlete.

GEORGE (FUDGE) FRIEDELHAUSER. Fudge is the gang bouncer. He is slow-witted, whole-hearted and the largest boy physically. He has no success with girls but this doesn't bother him. He is immature emotionally and is happiest when he is roving with the boys, playing pranks. At no time in the play is he dressed up. Fudge is at his best on the football field.

LEONARD (LEN) CARNEY. Carney has a keener intellect than the rest. He is indolent, humorous and brave. He is perhaps the only boy in the crowd who realizes Beau's true nature.

MORGAN (DINK) OLSON. Olson is funny, pessimistic and has no imagination. He is a "kibitzer" by nature, dour but not unhappy. His clothes are casual to sloppiness. His hair is always rumpled.

GIBBS. Gibbs is a pompous boy inclined to be fat. He has no humor or sensitivity. * * * He is still wearing small boy T-shirts, and he has on his head a flat felt hat, stuck with feathers in the ribbon around the crown. This hat is rolled tightly, crown flattened down to the brim and he wears it on the back of his head. He wears a T-shirt and corduroys.

MCELROY. Although he, too, wears a flat hat on the back of his head—a sharp item in the small-fry crowd from which he hopes to escape—he is nothing like Gibbs. Mac is sensitive, sharp eyed and well balanced. In a few years he will be one of the leaders of a gang of his own. He, too, wears a T-shirt and corduroys.

HELEN (THE WAITRESS). She is about thirty years old, wispy-haired and dreary, inclined to be carping. She has no sense of humor.

TUB: [*Indicating the jukebox with a jerk of his thumb*] This guy—he doesn't blow it like he means it.

FUDGE: You're not listening. He means it.

TUB: [*Shakes his head as he listens to another note of the trumpet. Decides and makes sudden gesture of decision*] If he means it—he doesn't make it.

BEAU: [*He hasn't heard them—his expression is rapt. He leans forward. He speaks fiercely*] Dig it—dig that sound! That cool, cool sound. [*The other boys are impressed with* BEAU's *approval of the trumpet player*]

TUB: [*Hesitantly—first glancing at* BEAU] Beau—you SURE that's Martiniz?

FUDGE: [*Grinning happily*] That's Martiniz!

TUB: Oh, he stinks any more. He used to be good but he stinks now. Bevans is hot now.

FUDGE: Bevans is plenty hot.

BEAU: [*Rising, walking forward thoughtfully, hands in pockets*] Martiniz! [*His face is rapt. Then he sighs*] He can no longer run the distance—but he can still hurt you. [*Enter* CARNEY *and* OLSON *from right.* BEAU *is unaware of their entrance until they call him by name. He is still listening to the music*]

CARNEY: Beaumont! Tub, Fudge.

OLSON: Hi, Beau—hi, men.

TUB: 'Lo, Olson.

FUDGE: Hi, Carney.

BEAU: [*His eyes gleam with a mocking light but fond as he looks at them. He makes his expression comically fierce. He gives a wave of the hand, moving each finger as though he were playing the piano in mid-air. There is a weary elegance in this gesture. Behind his back the other boys practice it at home trying to imitate him*] Greetings . . . men!

CARNEY: Hi ya, Beau!

OLSON: Hi, Beau! [CARNEY *and* OLSON *move to the table at which* BEAU *now sits,* OLSON *sitting on chair left of table,* CARNEY *putting one foot on chair upstage of table.* TUB *moves to table down left, pushes* FUDGE's *feet off it, sits down upstage side of table. Music fades*]

TUB: Where you been? We got problems.

OLSON: Oh, messin' around. Say, we brought a couple of fellows with us.

CARNEY: They're a couple of plenty sharp boys.

BEAU: [*Languidly*] Who?

OLSON: Will McElroy and Dave Gibbs. [*Groans from* TUB *and* BEAU]

FUDGE: They're a couple of twinks.

TUB: [*Sneers*] Sharp boys! That Gibbs is still ridin' a bicycle.

OLSON: Listen . . . he claims his old man is gettin' him a '42 Plymouth next month.

TUB: [*To* BEAU] Why should we mess around with that young stuff?

FUDGE: We're takin' a chance lettin' them come in here.

OLSON: [*Turning to* FUDGE] McElroy *looks* old. He's sixteen but he coud pass for eighteen. [*Turns back to* BEAU] You'll like him, Beau. You'll be callin' him Fofo.

CARNEY: And Gibbs . . . he admits he used to be a square. But he's not a square any more. He just said so.

BEAU: We can always throw them out . . . so let them in.

CARNEY: [*Crosses right and bawls out loudly*] Hey, you creeps

. . . haul it on in here! [MCELROY *and* GIBBS *enter from right. They try to appear nonchalant and hide their great eagerness and excitement. But they are like bear cubs trying to walk on two legs.* MCELROY *looks around warily. He will feel his way. But* GIBBS *has already decided on the swaggering, bold "You guys have nothing on me" approach.* CARNEY *stands beside them to do the honors. He points out the members of the gang, who make some desultory individual movement as each name is called*] Guess maybe you guys might know these guys. Art Beaumont, Tub Griner, and Fudge Friedelhauser, Will McElroy . . .

MAC: Hello!

CARNEY: . . . and Dave Gibbs.

GIBBS: Hi! [TUB *and* FUDGE *both mumble a weak "Hi"*]

BEAU: [*He makes the same finger-waving movement*] Greetings! I will try to like you.

GIBBS: [*To their amazement, has the temerity to walk directly over to* BEAU] My dad plays golf with your dad, Beaumont.

BEAU: [*Coolly, with a raised eyebrow*] Oh?

GIBBS: [*Blissfully unaware of his mistake, in this familiarity*] My dad says your dad is the best engineer in the whole state.

BEAU: [*With sarcasm*] Well . . . well . . . well!

GIBBS: He says not another man could have built that Mount Secrist Tunnel with nature against him.

BEAU: [*Very bored, as he turns and flicks ashes off his cigarette*] I barely know the man.

GIBBS: [*He is puzzled but not discouraged. He steps over* BEAU's *outstretched feet and crosses to right of* TUB] I've seen you around, Griner. You've got a '46 Nash.

TUB: [*Rises, glaring at* GIBBS] '48! And that used to be a Nash, but it's not a Nash any more. [*He moves upstage to jukebox, leans against it, puts nickel in*]

GIBBS: [*Although wilting, is not squelched.* MCELROY *watches him and suffers.* GIBBS *moves upstage of table down left and leans across it, looking intently at* FUDGE] Hi, Friedelhauser! I've seen you play football. You're not bad, boy.

FUDGE: [*Rises slowly, glaring at* GIBBS] And I'm not Friedelhauser either. [*He crosses right center, standing right of* BEAU]

BEAU: [*Takes on the deep, gruff tone of a big-time business official*] This man's name is Bidnut . . . Fofo Bidnut. He's a traveling man . . . hard candies. How's business, Mr. Bidnut . . . little slow, eh, little slow?

FUDGE: [*Laughing*] Yeah . . .

GIBBS: [*Puzzled*] But I've seen him play . . .

MAC: [*He is sure that* GIBBS *has ruined both of their chances*] Skip it! Shut up! [*He motions to* GIBBS *to cross right. He turns to* BEAU] Okay if we sit down, Beaumont? *He starts to lower himself to the floor.* GIBBS *has already sat down*]

BEAU: [*In sudden alarm*] Look out for that floor . . . she tips!

GIBBS: [*Jumping up*] She . . . what? [*All boys laugh loudly, except* MAC]

MAC: [*Pulling* GIBBS *down*] Shut up. Sit down. [MCELROY, *who is watching like a cat, offers* GIBBS *a cigarette with a casual air. They both light up as the older boys study them*]

TUB: Watch this. [GIBBS *and* MCELROY *take puffs on cigarettes. Derisively*] Sharp boys! [*Tub moves downstage, sits on edge of down left table, facing right*]

OLSON: How'd I know, huh?

GIBBS: [*He will not be quiet*] This is a pretty nice spot here. But the Rancho . . . that's the real spot. Ever been to the Rancho, Beaumont?

TUB: Been to it? He just sold it!

CARNEY: [*Anxious to get the limelight off* GIBBS] Aw, knock it off, will you. [*Turning to* BEAU] What happened to you last night, Beau?

OLSON: We came by and you weren't here. Did you have a date?

BEAU: Last night? [*Such a long time ago. He finally remembers*] Oh, yes, yes . . . I had a date. This *friend* from out of town, she drove in from Idaho in her '54 Caddy convertible.

GIBBS: [*He inches forward. His eyes are bugged out*] Saaay!

BEAU: [*In confidential tone*] You know something, Griner? She may take that offer from Hollywood after all. They've been driving the little thing nuts.

TUB: [*He plays up*] Well . . . now . . .

BEAU: [*Dreamily*] But it's just like I told her. You don't need them, Sugar. You've got me. And she smiled as I pried her arms from around my neck. I had to pry and pry and pry. She would not let go . . . the little tiger!

GIBBS: Wow!

BEAU: [*Throwing his head forward, putting one hand to the back of his neck*] Take a look there, fellows. She leave any marks? [*While GIBBS and MCELROY stare, the gang leaps forward and gazes with mock solemnity at BEAU's neck. They give forth with a chorus of "Oooh . . . ahhhh . . . look at that . . . jeepers!"*]

OLSON: [*In shocked tone*] You better get a doctor to take a look at that, Beaumont!

GIBBS: [*This is indeed the world he belongs in . . . he thinks*] Saaay . . . who is this babe?

BEAU: Tell him, class.

BOYS: Bernardine.

TUB: Bernardine Crud! [*He moves down left, the others return to their original positions*]

MAC: Bernardine Crud . . . where does she go to school?

BEAU: [*Turns to the two younger boys*] School! She's through school. She's lived. She's a little older . . . little beat up looking but not too much. Just misty and dreamy.

GIBBS: Oh, boy!

MAC: What do you know!

BEAU: You couldn't miss her. When she walks down the street her eyes flash a message . . . live on, boy, dream on. I'm waitin' for you. But as for actual conversation she knows only one word.

MAC: Only one word . . . what's that?

BEAU: The word is . . . yes.

TUB: [*With feeling*] That's a good word.

GIBBS: Jeepers . . . where does this babe live?

BEAU: Now, that's an interesting question. She lives in a little town in the mountains of Idaho, on the banks of Itching River . . . a place called Sneaky Falls.

GIBBS: [*He takes out notebook and pencil*] Sneaky Falls?

MAC: Sneaky Falls?

BEAU: It's away up in the mountains. Terrible roads . . . buses not running. Of course, you could make it in a super jet. [*Rises, walks over to face* GIBBS] You've heard of it, of course.

GIBBS: [*Brightly*] Oh, sure, sure. [*The other boys exchange an amused glance with* BEAU]

MAC: I never did. [BEAU's *eyes linger a moment on* MCELROY *with interest, but he gazes sternly at* GIBBS, *although his voice is dangerously gentle*]

BEAU: You have, Gibbs?

GIBBS: Yeah, seems to me we passed through there last summer on our way home from Winnemucca.

BEAU: Well, well, well . . . very, very interesting. [*Turns now as* HELEN, *a waitress about thirty with dyed red hair and spotted apron, comes in with pad and pencil. She enters from stage left, crosses slowly to tables and puts empty beer bottles on the tray she is carrying*] Greetings, Helen . . . what about a round of beer here?

HELEN: Okay. . . . [*Sees the younger boys. Her lips clamp and she moves slightly toward them*] What's *your* order?

GIBBS: Two beers, light on the head.

HELEN: I said . . . what's your order?

GIBBS: Just gave you the order.

HELEN: Yeah? [*Walks over and stands between them*] Let's see your draft cards.

MAC: [*Slaps at pockets. But he determines to bluff*] Well, what did I do with that thing? Must have left it in my other suit.

HELEN: Your snow suit?

GIBBS: Say, listen, you!

MAC: Aw, what's the difference, we'll get one after a while.

HELEN: [*Crossing back to stage left*] I'll get my old-age pension after a while too. [*Angrily, to older boys*] Don't try to pull this on me! [*Stops at exit left*] Do you want the old man to lose his license? Just because he lets you kids with draft cards have a glass of three-two in here, don't drag in a kindergarten. [*Looks at* MAC *and* GIBBS] Pepsi-cola . . . coca-cola. [*She exits left*]

MAC: [*With disgust*] Two cokes! The deal stinks.

BEAU: [*Who has moved to the jukebox during the scene with* HELEN. *He has put a nickel in the jukebox which plays until end of record*] McElroy, come over here.

MAC: [*He starts to rise with alacrity and then stops. His eyes meet* BEAU's *in a test of character. He slowly drops back down. He speaks and his eyes, gaze are steady*] Why should I?

BEAU: [*Gazes at him silently . . . approvingly. Then he smiles suddenly, a gentle, tender smile. The other boys are looking at* MAC *with the same silent approval.* MAC *doesn't realize it yet but he has passed a milestone in his life. The boys are beginning to suspect that he may be a "hep" character . . . eager to make the gang but not willing to give everything to do it. When* BEAU *speaks his voice is soft*] No reason at all, Mac . . . none at all.

MAC: Okay.

BEAU: You're all right, Mac. Yep . . . you may be perfectly all right.

GIBBS: [*Feeling this is the time to wade in with both feet and establish himself and* MAC *as big men*] Me and Mac sure had a time last night . . . didn't we, Mac?

MAC: Sssh . . . shut up!

GIBBS: Mac swiped his old man's car and we picked up a couple of babes. Boy . . . we made pretty good time with those babes . . . eh, Mac?

BEAU: [*During end of* GIBBS' *speech,* BEAU *has been crossing slowly right, stops upstage of chair, wheels it around sharply, and sits*] Eh, Mac?

MAC: [*With a look of disgust at* GIBBS] Last night? I forgot last night already. [BEAU *looks at the other boys over* MAC's *head and makes an approving circle in the air with his thumb and forefinger. They nod in agreement*]

TUB: [*With a stern voice gives his attention to* GIBBS] You knew these girls, of course?

GIBBS: [*Happily*] Knew 'em? Of course not. We picked 'em up.

TUB: [*With an air of regret makes a disapproving clucking sound with his tongue. He sighs*] Hear that, Beaumont?

BEAU: [*Covering his face with hands*] I wish I hadn't.

TUB: You were taking an awful chance, Gibbs, taking strange tomatoes into your car.

GIBBS: Chance? It was them that was taking the chance.

BEAU: Gibbs, never slap it down like that. If you see a chance to slide it in, slide it in. But that "didn't we make time with those babes last night." Don't do it. It sounds boastful . . . it sounds . . . [*Snaps his fingers toward* OLSON *for the right word*]

OLSON: Immature.

BEAU: [*Turning to* OLSON] Yeah.

GIBBS: But you just did it. You said last night you and Bernardine . . . [*They all laugh*]

BEAU: Gibbs, I am afraid you are the type of character who gives our school a bad name.

FUDGE: Weldy's old lady thinks it's us . . . but it's you.

GIBBS: Hey, with the reputations you guys have got for smooth operators and big wheels, what is this?

BEAU: [*Rises, walks over and faces* MAC] McElroy, tell us the story of your life in two words.

MAC: [*Puzzled, worried*] Two words . . . gosh . . .

BEAU: Gibbs could do it in two words. [*Wheeling sharply toward* GIBBS] I stink. . . . Beat it, Gibbs!

GIBBS: What?

FUDGE: Wanta get hurt (*moves menacingly toward* GIBBS. *The others rise, threateningly*] . . . blow!

GIBBS: [*Getting to his feet, angrily*] Comin', Mac?

MAC: I don't know yet. . . .

GIBBS: All right for you, Mac, next time you . . .

TUB: [*As they all move toward him, more threateningly*] Beat it! [*With a reproachful glance at* MAC, GIBBS *exits right quickly.* MAC *rises, facing* BEAU]

BEAU: Two words, Mac . . . like this. . . . Fudge . . .

FUDGE: I slug . . .

BEAU: Carney . . .

CARNEY: I scheme . . .

BEAU: Olson . . .

OLSON: I bull . . .

BEAU: Tub . . .

TUB: I . . .

BEAU: [*Breaking in quickly*] Better use the nice word . . . to-morrow's Sunday. . . .

TUB: I conquer!

BEAU: And I laugh! [*He gives a mocking, horrible, and yet comic laugh*] Now you, Mac . . .

MAC: [*Bewildered*] I . . . I wonder! [*The boys all laugh*]

BEAU: [*Grabs his hand eagerly*] You're all right, Mac. Fellows, I want you to meet Mr. Bidnut of Sneaky Falls, Idaho. . . . Mr. Bidnut . . . Mr. Bidnut . . . Mr. Bidnut . . . Mr. Bidnut. [*All cross to stage right, shaking* MAC'S *hand eagerly He is in. His face is jubilant*]

SUGGESTIONS FOR THE ACTOR

1. For the actor playing Beau: When Olson asks, "Did you have a date?" you, Beau, reply, "Last night? * * * Oh, yes, yes . . . I had a date. This *friend* from out of town, she drove in from Idaho in her '54 Caddy." After you say, "Last night?" you have a mood change (known as a transition) from reality to the dream of Bernardine.

In a full-scale production a change in lighting at that moment might help you by emphasizing your change in mood. But in a scene-study class or workshop you probably will have to depend solely on your own inner change of thoughts, and the outward projection of that change with your own body and voice, to stress the transition. How will your manner change when you are about to re-create the Bernardine myth? Will a change in the tempo of your words and physical actions help to reflect your inner change? Note what the playwright tells us in the "Description of Characters" about Beau's behavior "whenever he is about to go into his routines."

2. Discuss: Why does the gang accept McElroy but reject Gibbs? What do we learn about the differences between these two boys? What do we learn about the standards of the gang from their reactions to the behavior of Gibbs and McElroy?

3. After you have tentatively answered the questions on the "Actor's Check List," beginning on page 336, get together as a group and discuss your answers. Change some of them, if necessary, to create more variety of characterization. For instance, it would be fine for one member of the gang to slouch all the time, but it would certainly seem odd if four or five of the boys had the same distinctive physical characteristic. Begin with the clues provided in the "Description of Characters" and the play itself. Then add more traits of your own invention.

4. Discuss: Do you want to act the scene exactly as written, a nostalgic, comic view of male adolescence in the 1950s, or would you prefer to bring it up to date? Can this scene be brought up to date by changing such minor details as the years of the cars, the references to draft cards (Helen could demand to see the younger boys' birth certificates instead) and the vintage of the jukebox music? Are the values and dreams of adolescent boys today similar to what they were then, or are they radically different?

5. This scene does not really begin at the beginning. No scene ever does. Every character is already engaged in some activity as the scene opens. Decide what the character you portray was doing beforehand. Those of you playing the characters already at the Shamrock can improvise (make up spontaneously, as you perform) a scene showing the action that might have occurred before Tub speaks his opening line. Those of you who arrive afterward (Carney, Olson, Gibbs and McElroy) can improvise a different episode: what you might have been doing and discussing before your arrival. Do not attempt these études (improvisations in character) until you are thoroughly familiar with the scene itself and the characters you portray.

From *Bernardine* by Mary Chase.
Act II, Scene 3

INTRODUCTION

See pages 203–4 for background.

One of the members of the gang is Buford Weldy, "called Wormy by his friends. He is a muscular blond boy with a cleft in his strong chin."

Wormy is never consciously funny. He is always warmhearted, sincere and dogged. He is always dressed more neatly than the other boys because of his mother's vigilance. * * * He is always astonished, bewildered and then delighted at the humor of the other boys but he has none himself.

Not so long ago Wormy was a "wild kid," his escapades constantly getting him into trouble at school. (He was expelled three times!) Now he is "girl crazy," but he has scared away one girl after another, including Jean Cantrick, with his crude "passes." "Jean is a typical, pretty, arrogant appearing young American girl, trying to be like the other girls in her group. * * * Basically she is sweet and kind but tries to conceal it." Wormy and Jean had really cared about each other once; in fact, they still care although neither will admit it. Since their breakup, Wormy's friends have tried hard to "fix him up" with dates, but without success. His reputation has spread even beyond the confines of his home town.

Wormy's parents are divorced. His father is remarried and lives in another town. Wormy's mother still treats him like a child. She gives the orders and Wormy at least pretends to obey. He complains: "She's always half a mile behind me. When I wanted a car, she bought me a tool chest. When I want a girl, she buys me a dog."

She also thrusts Vernon Kinswood on him. She invites Vernon, an obnoxious boy Wormy's age, to come over that afternoon to do homework with Wormy, have dinner and spend the night.

Kinswood is always well dressed. An opportunist by nature, he discovered cannily and very early, how to get along with adults. In his heart he is not shocked at the gang, he only believes they are stupid. He has taken a long look at the world and decided it doesn't pay to have their kind of fun. Kinswood was never young. He is the only one of the boys who can wear glasses. He is pompous but not effeminate.

Vernon's mother suffers from all sorts of physical complaints, either real or imagined. Vernon positively relishes describing her symptoms in minute detail to any willing (or even unwilling) listeners.

Pretending that he and Vernon are going out only to walk the dog that Saturday afternoon, Wormy gets permission to leave the house, although his mother wants him back in an hour to meet an old friend of hers. Wormy manages to "ditch" Vernon, and he arrives at the Shamrock. Vernon follows him there, but the gang tosses him out. Wormy's friends try hard to find him a date, but no girl is willing. He then announces that he is not going to chase after young girls any more; he plans to find himself a real woman "with the come-on look and the warm, warm glance." Outside the Shamrock the woman of his dreams passes by—Bernardine in the flesh! (Her real name is Enid Lacey.) "She is glamorously dressed. There is a faint siren smile on her face." With "panting appreciation," the gang follows her to the Barclay Hotel.

Miracle of miracles, Enid, a sophisticated divorcée in her thirties, is attracted to Wormy, deeply touched by his youth, his loneliness and confusion. Although she is not fooled by the line he hands her—he claims to be an orphan named Ralph, a sailor about to be shipped off to South America for seven years—she invites him to her hotel suite. She is so nice to him, so warm and encouraging, that Wormy feels compelled to tell her the truth before making any serious "passes." When he tells her his real name, Enid realizes with horror that Wormy is the son of one of her oldest friends. (Enid was Ruth Weldy's guest for tea earlier that afternoon.) Regretfully, she sends him away.

Meanwhile Wormy's mother has been frantically searching for him. She returns home briefly, instructs Vernon to stay there and take any phone calls, and leaves again. She does not plan to return until she has found her son.

The Weldy living room "is suggested by the use of a love seat, two armchairs, an oblong table upstage of [behind] the love seat, and a coffee table below [in front of] the love seat. Love seat is placed stage center, slightly downstage [toward the audience], with armchair on either side, turned out three quarters. The room is dainty, feminine, and tasteful."

Before this scene, Vernon had sat down at the love seat, placing his root beer on the coffee table. He had carelessly thrown his left leg over the arm of the love seat. As the scene opens, he is comfortably reading a book.

Both boys in the scene wear suits, white shirts and ties.

The telephone rings, and he [VERNON] *rises, crosses around left of love seat and upstage to answer it.*

VERNON: Hello. No, Buford isn't here. His mother has just gone out to look for him. Is this Mrs. Beaumont? Mrs. Griner? Would you care to leave a message? No? Well, listen! If this should turn out to be Len Carney, you haven't fooled me one bit! [*Slams down receiver angrily.* WORMY *enters right. His head is lowered, his hands are in his pockets. He walks slowly, thoughtfully, crossing from down right to the armchair down left*] Weldy! About time you showed up. Your mother is crazy. She's out looking for you. Where have you been?

WORMY: Over at your house.

VERNON: [*He is right of the love seat*] At my house!

WORMY: [*His knee on the armchair down left, he gradually sinks into it*] Vern, I think I'm beginning to see the light.

VERNON: I'm glad to hear you say it. Frankly, I was about ready to give you up, Weldy.

WORMY: I can see what you mean, Kinswood.

VERNON: [*Reaching down at coffee table to pick up root beer float*] Carney just called you.

WORMY: [*Suddenly*] Carney! Jeepers! The guys! I was supposed to file a report with them. [*He jumps up from the chair*]

VERNON: [*Suspicious*] A report? What kind of a report?

WORMY: On a deal I was working on.

VERNON: [*More suspicious*] What kind of a deal?

WORMY: Listen, Vern! If Carney or any of them call, I'm *not here!* Vern, old paint, [*Crossing right, he pats* VERN *on shoulder*] you've got the right idea! [*Turns, goes back left to armchair, sitting*] You get along with your folks. You never give a thought to dames. You've got it figured out right.

VERNON: I've waited a long time to hear you say that, Weldy. You've been skating on some pretty thin ice. [*He crosses up to love seat, sits center*] Hanging around with those guys at the Shamrock and over at Beaumont's basement. [*Looking off right cautiously, then continuing*] I hear they pull some pretty raw stuff over there. I hear Beaumont sneaks liquor from his old man's cellar. You'd think he'd have a little more feeling for his old man. [*Now talking man to man,* WORMY *and* VERNON *near a new rapprochement, each making reluctant concessions to the other*]

WORMY: [*Turning to him*] Listen, Vern, I know how you feel about those guys. But I know Beaumont pretty well. The one person in the world he's got plenty of feeling for is his old man. It's the only thing he never cracks wise about, never even talks about. All the guys know that about Beaumont.

VERNON: [*Grudgingly*] Well, he's got some fine way of showing it.

WORMY: [*A half wistful sad smile plays over his face. His tone is reminiscent and nostalgic as though he were talking about a world now lost to him*] Beau's got a record collection . . . what a collection, sweet and hot, bebop and long hair. I never knew a guy so crazy about music.

VERNON: But Griner is a crude specimen. Thinks he's a wolf, but he's just a lazy bum.

WORMY: Griner *is* a wolf and he's not a lazy bum, Vern. He worked nights all last year in a garage to buy his clothes. His old man had to give up his law practice on account of a brain operation.

VERNON: Well, I didn't know that about Griner. I sympathize with anybody's got illness in the family.

WORMY: [*Wistful again*] Those bull sessions in Beau's basement and the Shamrock! There wasn't anything they didn't talk about . . . politics, jet planes, dames, and God.

VERNON: God! Those guys talk about God? [WORMY *nods*] They've got a nerve.

WORMY: [*With great feeling*] Gee, I've had a lot of fun with those guys. I've had more fun with those guys than I ever had in my life.

VERNON: But face it. There isn't one of them will ever amount to a damn.

WORMY: I don't think they even plan on it.

VERNON: You've got to keep on the beam in this world.

WORMY: You're right, Vern. You stay on the beam, you get along with your folks. You never give a thought to dames.

VERNON: [*Jumping up sharply, facing* WORMY] Quit saying that! I give 'em plenty of thought.

WORMY: [*Amazed*] You, Kinswood! [WORMY's *mouth drops open*]

VERNON: [*Nodding assent, he crosses right, below coffee table*] I got it all figured out. [*Turning left to* WORMY] Do you know a fellow in town named R. L. Pomfrey?

WORMY: [*Nodding*] An old guy?

VERNON: [*He nods*] About thirty-five. He drives a yellow Jaguar. And those girls that ride with him . . . are they dreams . . . are they gorgeous! He's got the prettiest girls in town. When he walks in a restaurant with 'em [*Sits armchair down right*] everybody turns around to stare. Sometimes he has two or three . . .

WORMY: Yeah? No kiddin'!

VERNON: When Pomfrey was in school I hear he didn't date at all. He didn't have a car, didn't have any dough. But he kept sluggin' till he got out of school and got established in his profession. Then he got this Jaguar. He's got a place in the mountains for weekends and an apartment in town. He can have anybody he wants . . . now. [VERNON *leans back against armchair, puts his hands behind his head, his legs sprawled*] I think I'll paint my Jaguar maroon color. These snoot-faced girls like Hobbs and Johnson and Cantrick who wouldn't look at me now . . . they'll be glad to look at me then. But I won't look at them. Because by that time they'll be old and washed up and I'll drive by with a car load of beauties. [*There is a vindictive smile on his face and his eyes glow*]

WORMY: [*His tone is full of astonishment*] Old! Cantrick old! I can't imagine Cantrick . . . ever growing old. [*He looks at* VERNON *with a sudden wave of revulsion and jumps up from the chair*] Kinswood . . . you slob! [*Running quickly, he crosses right and exits, below* VERNON]

VERNON: [*Jumping to his feet and following* WORMY *off right*] Weldy, where are you going?

SUGGESTIONS FOR THE ACTOR

1. When you, Vernon, answer the telephone, you, the actor, must imagine the voice on the other end, probably speaking in falsetto

to imitate a woman's voice. "Hear" the words spoken. When do you (Vernon) begin to suspect a trick? When do you surmise that the voice belongs to Carney? You are not telling the exact truth when you say, "You haven't fooled me one bit." You certainly were deceived at first; that's what makes you so angry.

2. You, Wormy, are depressed, not only because Enid made you leave, but because you blame yourself for losing this incredible opportunity. You are disgusted with yourself. Later you make this shameful confession to the gang: "I told her my name. I didn't have to do that but I did. Why? Because I haven't got the wolf teeth, that's why. * * * And if you haven't got them you never get them. * * * I'm a chicken, that's all. A natural-born chicken." Your plan to give up your old friends because you don't consider yourself good enough for them—you are sure that you will never become a "smooth operator."

In your state of mind at the beginning of this scene, what is your new attitude toward Kinswood? Why? Notice that as you grow friendlier, you start calling him "Vernon." At your friendliest, you even address him as "Vern." At the end of the scene, however, you demote him; he is "Kinswood" once again.

3. This conversation between you is not only unusual; it is unique—the two of you become almost close on this one occasion until you, Vernon, show your true colors. Despite Wormy's notorious reputation for being a "wolf," it is really you, Vernon, not Wormy, who look upon girls and women merely as "sex objects" (to use an expression more recent than the play). You, Wormy, cannot be the "smooth operator" you think you want to be, because your nature is really tender and loving, not hard-boiled or cynical. Vernon's ugly, vindictive remark about the girl you still care for nips this "new rapprochement" in the bud. (Definition of "rapprochement": "A coming together; establishment or state of cordial relations.") Disgusted with Vernon now as well as with yourself, you head for the Shamrock. You want to see your friends for the last time and bid them all farewell, but in a "masked" and "casual" fashion, "according to the rules."

As an acting exercise, improvise a scene *typical* of the relationship between you (Wormy and Vernon), a scene not shown in the play. Invent the dialogue and your character's physical actions as you perform. What are you (Wormy and Vernon) each doing as the scene opens? Why? What were you each doing beforehand? Where are you now? Where were you previously? Where will you be afterward? When is this (the time of day, the day of the week, the date, the season, the year)? What do you want of each other? Why is it important for each of you to reach your objective right now?

For instance, you might wish to enact this situation: You, Wormy, are walking your dog with Vernon in the park or on the street earlier this Saturday afternoon, before your encounter with "Bernardine" (Enid).

Wormy, your objective is to get rid of Vernon (whom you call "Kinswood") and join your friends at the Shamrock. You are hoping that they will be able to "fix you up" with a date.

Vernon, your objective is to follow Mrs. Weldy's instructions: You want to keep Wormy (whom you call "Weldy") away from the gang and see that he returns home within the hour to meet an old friend of his mother's.

4. Each of you should visualize the people you mention who do not appear in the scene. See the descriptions of the boys in the gang on pages 204–6. What is the attitude of the character you play toward each of the individuals you mention? You, the actor, should think of people you know in real life who can elicit in you the appropriate feeling. For example, you, Wormy, and everyone else in the gang hero-worship Beaumont (Beau). You, the actor, should recall a young man whom you admire tremendously.

Have you, Vernon, ever set eyes on Mrs. Griner and Mrs. Beaumont? (You, the actor, must make that decision.) If so, then you should visualize these mothers when you wonder whether you are addressing one of them on the telephone. Has either of you (Wormy or Vernon) ever seen Beaumont's father? If so, then you (the actor) should picture him when you refer to him.

5. You, Wormy, unintentionally reveal to Vernon that you were "supposed to file a report" with the "guys." Your "report" is of course your account of how you "made out" with Bernardine. Naturally you wouldn't share that confidence with Vernon, not even at this moment, when your relations are cordial. You therefore reply vaguely to his questioning and then change the subject.

From *Fiddler on the Roof,* book by Joseph Stein, based on Sholom Aleichem's stories. Act II, Scene 1

INTRODUCTION

This world-renowned musical based on Sholom Aleichem's delightful stories takes place in Anatevka, a small village in Czarist Russia in 1905, "on the eve of the revolutionary period." The insulated Jewish community, however, is not aware of any imminent changes. They live as best they can, according to time-honored traditions, without which their "lives would be as shaky as—as a fiddler on the roof!" The play concerns the milkman Tevye and his family—his wife, Golde, and their three daughters of marriageable age, Tzeitel, Hodel and Chava.

At the beginning of the play Yente the Matchmaker has arranged a match between Tevye's eldest daughter, Tzeitel, and a middle-aged butcher. When Tevye arrives home for the Sabbath, one of the villagers reports news of the outside world. In another village all the Jews were evicted and forced to leave their homes. As the men curse the powers that be, a strange, hungry young university student from Kiev arrives and lambasts them for merely cursing their lot instead of trying to change society. He tells them that someday the wealth of the rich will be theirs. The "radical" young student, Perchik, arranges with Tevye to give lessons in the Bible to Tevye's five daughters (the youngest two are small roles) in exchange for food and lodging. Tzeitel begs her father not to force her to marry the butcher, as she has pledged her love to Motel, a poor tailor. Tevye is shaken by their pledge, a break with the tradition of arranged marriages, but being a loving father, he agrees.

The wedding between Tzeitel and Motel takes place onstage. At the festivities Perchik shocks everyone by dancing with Hodel. (They had danced together before, but in private.) They are attracted to each other, although their verbal exchanges have been sharp. Perchik has admired Hodel's quick wit and intelligence, but he has critized her for being tradition-bound. She in turn has attacked his strange ideas and lack of "respect" for girls. Custom has prevented men and women from dancing together until now. Nevertheless, others follow Perchik's lead until the celebrations are interrupted by what the Constable has referred to as "a little unofficial demonstration." The Russian Constable and his men enter with clubs, destroying dishes and wedding gifts, knocking over everything in sight. This anti-Semitic demonstration is not really "unofficial" at all. The Constable is acting under orders. Perchik grapples with one of the Constable's men, is hit with a club and falls. Hodel rushes over to him and helps him into the house. At the end of Act I, Tevye orders the wedding party to "clean up."

The first scene of the second act follows a short Prologue, a soliloquy in which Tevye adresses heaven, as is his habit.

The exterior of TEVYE'S *house. Afternoon.* HODEL *enters, petulantly, followed by* PERCHIK.

PERCHIK: Please don't be upset, Hodel.

HODEL: Why should I be upset? If you must leave, you must.

PERCHIK: I do have to. They expect me in Kiev tomorrow morning.

HODEL: So you told me. Then goodbye.

PERCHIK: Great changes are about to take place in this country. Tremendous changes. But they can't happen by themselves.

HODEL: So naturally you feel that you personally have to—

PERCHIK: Not only me. Many people. Jews, Gentiles, many people hate what is going on. Don't you understand?

HODEL: I understand, of course. You want to leave. Then goodbye.

PERCHIK: Hodel, your father, the others here, think what happened at Tzeitel's wedding was a little cloudburst and it's over and everything will now be peaceful again. It won't. Horrible things are happening all over the land—pogroms, violence— whole villages are being emptied of their people. And it's reaching everywhere, and it will reach here. You understand?

HODEL: Yes, I—I suppose I do.

PERCHIK: I have work to do. The greatest work a man can do.

HODEL: Then goodbye, Perchik.

PERCHIK: Before I go [*He hesitates, then summons up courage*], there is a certain question I wish to discuss with you.

HODEL: Yes?

PERCHIK: A political question.

HODEL: What is it?

PERCHIK: The question of marriage.

HODEL: This is a political question?

PERCHIK: [*Awkwardly*] In a theoretical sense, yes. The relationship between a man and woman known as marriage is based on mutual beliefs, a common attitude and philosophy towards society—

HODEL: And affection.

PERCHIK: And affection. This relationship has positive social values. It reflects a unity and solidarity—

HODEL: And affection.

PERCHIK: Yes. And I personally am in favor of it. Do you understand?

HODEL: I think you are asking me to marry you.

PERCHIK: In a theoretical sense, yes, I am.

HODEL: I was hoping you were.

PERCHIK: Then I take it you approve? And we can consider ourselves engaged, even though I am going away? [*She nods*] I am
very happy, Hodel. Very happy.

HODEL: So am I, Perchik. * * * And when will we be married,
Perchik?

PERCHIK: I will send for you as soon as I can. It will be a hard
life, Hodel.

HODEL: But it will be less hard if we live it together.

PERCHIK: Yes.

SUGGESTIONS FOR THE ACTOR

1. This brief scene is, of course, a love scene despite all your
(Perchik's) speechmaking. The charm as well as humor of the situation springs from the fact that your sometimes pompous-sound-
ing words mask your deepest feelings, even though they honestly
express your intellectual views. For all your glib talk when it
comes to political affairs, you are the shy, awkward lover when it
comes to affairs of the heart. Hodel, you are undoubtedly "on to"
him, at least by the time he proposes marriage; you sense the emotions he dares not express. Otherwise, it would be out of character
for a girl of your intelligence and sensitivity to fall in love with a
young man so unfeeling that he would marry strictly for political
and sociological reasons.

What is communicated, then, are not the words alone, but the
meaning, intentions, emotions beneath the words. The thoughts
beneath the words are called the subtext. A good exercise when
working on this scene, after you have studied the play and carefully investigated the characters you are portraying, would be for
you, Perchik, to speak your inner thoughts and feelings as well as

the words in your text aloud. You, the actor, use a different tone of voice, perhaps a lower, deeper tone, to express your character's inner thoughts. The actress playing Hodel pretends that she does not hear the words of your subtext and *inner monologue* (the character's private thoughts while others are speaking or during pauses). Then rehearse the étude (an improvisation in character) again, this time only whispering your secret thoughts. Lastly, think your subtext silently, expressing these thoughts and feelings with your eyes only, without grimacing in any way. Hodel will of course respond to the feelings you silently communicate to her.

Another étude can be performed in which you, Hodel, speak your inner thoughts as well as your written lines aloud while Perchik speaks only his written text. You, the actress, now work on the three stages of the étude (subtext and inner monologue expressed aloud, in a whisper and with eyes only).

The great Russian teacher-director Stanislavsky invented this exercise, applicable to any scene, in connection with his teaching of the inner monologue. His inspiring success with this technique is described in the first chapter of *Stanislavsky Directs* by Nicolai M. Gorchakov, translated by Miriam Goldina (New York, Funk & Wagnalls Company, 1954).

2. Where are you (Perchik and Hodel) coming from at the beginning of the scene? What were you doing? This written scene is a continuation of a discussion begun previously offstage. Improvise the "scene before the scene," the discussion not shown in the play itself. Let your words and physical actions come spontaneously, in response to your partner's behavior. Perchik, you initiate the conversation. You must break the news of your departure to Hodel. You long to marry her, although you dread proposing marriage. How do you plan to tell her you are leaving? When you begin the conversation, do you get right to the point or do you "beat around the bush"? When is this discussion taking place (time of day, day of week, date, season, year)? What is the weather? Is either one of you engaged in a physical task? What are you each doing? Hodel, what do you want of Perchik? Let this improvised scene lead you naturally into the written scene, which you act first in your own words, then in the playwright's words.

3. In the play script, your (Hodel's) line "So am I, Perchik" is followed by a song, a romantic duet entitled "Now I Have Every-

thing." If you wish to sing the song, you can purchase sheet music and lyrics at a music store. (For any public performance you would, of course, need to obtain written permission for the use of all copyrighted material.) When the song ends, Hodel adds, "And when will we be married, Perchik?"

4. You, the actor playing Perchik, should imagine your (Perchik's) life before you came to Anatevka. Answer the questions on the "Actor's Check List," beginning on page 336. Is your (Perchik's) family living? If so, where are they now? It would be helpful for both of you to learn a little about social conditions in Czarist Russia shortly before the Russian Revolution. Learn all you can about life in the Jewish communities. What were pogroms?

From *A Raisin in the Sun* by Lorraine Hansberry.
Act I, Scene 2

INTRODUCTION

The action of this deservedly famous play by the late black play-wright Lorraine Hansberry takes place sometime between World War II and "the present" (the play was first produced in 1959). The setting is a cramped apartment on Chicago's South Side, a black ghetto. The furnishings of the Younger living room were once "selected with care and love and even hope," but by now "Everything has been polished, washed, sat on, used, scrubbed too often." A section of the room provides "a small kitchen area, where the family prepares the meals that are eaten in the living room proper, which must also serve as dining room. The single window that has been provided for these 'two' rooms is located in this kitchen area. The sole natural light the family may enjoy in the course of a day is only that which fights its way through this little window."

The crowded apartment is shared by Mama, a woman of strength and inner beauty, her twenty-year-old daughter, Beneatha, her son, Walter, a man in his thirties, his attractive wife, Ruth, and their ten-year-old son, Travis.

It is a Saturday morning in the fall, house-cleaning time. "Furniture has been shoved hither and yon." Mama has been washing down walls in the kitchen area; Beneatha has been spraying insecticide into the cracks in the walls. She wears dungarees, "a handkerchief tied around her face."

This is no ordinary day. "In spite of all the other conversations and distractions of the morning," including Asagai's visit in the following scene, the entire family is anxiously awaiting the arrival of the mail—they are expecting Mama's insurance money, a check for ten thousand dollars! This money has been the source of friction within the family for a long time. Walter wants Mama to invest in a liquor business; he is desperate, utterly frustrated by his job as a chauffeur. He dreams of becoming a wealthy businessman someday. Beneatha hopes Mama will offer to pay for medical school; her ambition in life is to become a doctor. The other women in the family work as domestics. Mama has not made up her mind yet, but she is thinking of using some of the money for a down payment on a house, and putting some aside for Beneatha's education.

Mama tells Beneatha that she thinks Ruth went to the doctor this morning; she is sure Ruth is pregnant.

The telephone rings and Beneatha answers it. She is delighted to hear Asagai's voice. Beneatha is a college student, eager to learn and to grow. Joseph Asagai (Ah-sah-guy) is a handsome, intellectual, idealistic young African she met on campus. He comes from Nigeria; his tribal origin is Yoruba. His great dream is African independence. He spent the summer in Canada studying, and has just returned. He tells Beneatha that he has a present for her which he would like to deliver right away. She agrees despite the disarray of the apartment.

Ruth returns, distraught over her unwanted pregnancy. Beneatha blurts out a remark which she instantly regrets. Referring to the expected baby, she asks, "Where is he going to live, on the roof?" Ruth makes a slip of the tongue which leads Mama to suspect that she went to see an abortionist instead of a doctor. Mama massages Ruth to help her relax, but Ruth "collapses into a fit of heavy sobbing." Just then the doorbell rings as Ruth and Mama leave the room.

Although not as pretty as Ruth, Beneatha's "lean, almost intellectual face has a handsomeness of its own." She is "slim and intense," with thick hair. "Her speech is a mixture of many things; it is different from the rest of the family's in so far as education has permeated her sense of English—and perhaps the Midwest rather than the South has finally—at last—won out in her inflection; but not altogether, because over all of it is a soft slurring and transformed use of vowels which is the decided influence of the South Side."

Her mother and sister-in-law think she flits from one interest to another; she is always seeking new ways of "expressing" herself. She has at various times taken up (and dropped) horseback riding, play acting, etc. She has recently begun guitar lessons. Africa fascinates her; she wants to learn all about her heritage.

"Alaiyo" is Asagai's nickname for Beneatha. It is a Yoruba word, meaning, appropriately, "One for Whom Bread—Food—Is Not Enough." Beneatha hungers for mental, emotional, spiritual fulfillment, not just satisfaction of bodily needs.

The doorbell rings.

BENEATHA: Oh, my God—that must be Asagai. [*Profoundly disturbed, she opens the door to admit a rather dramatic-looking young man with a large package*]

ASAGAI: Hello, Alaiyo—

BENEATHA: [*Holding the door open and regarding him with pleasure*] Hello— [*Long pause. She crosses left to above the table, folds towel*] Well—come in. And please excuse everything. My mother was very upset about my letting any one come here with the place like this.

ASAGAI: [*Coming into the room, up center*] You look disturbed — Is something wrong?

BENEATHA: [*Continues to fold and "neats" up the towel* MAMA *had left on chair left of table*] Yes—we've all got acute ghetto-itus. [*She smiles and comes toward him, finding a cigarette and sitting on sofa*] So—sit down! No! Wait! [*Business straightening sofa cushions*] So, how was Canada? [*She crosses down center*]

ASAGAI: [*A sophisticate*] Canadian.

BENEATHA: [*Looking at him as they sit: she on the chair right of sofa, he on the left of the sofa*] Asagai, I'm very glad you are back.

ASAGAI: [*Places the gift box on the coffee table. Looking at her*] Are you really?

BENEATHA: Yes—very.

ASAGAI: Why—you were quite glad when I went away. What happened?

BENEATHA: You went away.

ASAGAI: Ahhhhhhhh.

BENEATHA: Before—you wanted to be so serious before there was time.

ASAGAI: How much time must there be before one knows what one feels?

BENEATHA: [*Stalling this particular conversation. Her hands pressed together deliberately childish*] What did you bring me—?

ASAGAI: [*Indicating the package*] Open it and see.

BENEATHA: [*Rises from the chair down right, gets package, crouches on sofa with* ASAGAI, *and eagerly opens the package. Drawing out some records and the colorful robes of a Nigerian woman*] Oh, Asagai! You got them for me! How beautiful— And the records, too! [*She lifts out the cloth and runs down right to mirror with it and holds the drapery up in front of herself*]

ASAGAI: [*Rising from the sofa and coming down right to her at the mirror*] Wait! I shall have to teach you how to drape it properly. [*He drapes the material about her for the moment and stands back to look at her*] Ah— Oh-pay-gay-day! Oh-bah-mu-shay! [*"Opegede! Ogbamushe!"*] You wear it well—very well— mutilated hair and all.

BENEATHA: [*Turning suddenly*] My hair—what's wrong with my hair?

ASAGAI: [*In front of sofa. Shrugging*] Were you born with it like that?

BENEATHA: [*Reaching up to touch it*] No—of course not. [*She looks back to the mirror, disturbed*]

ASAGAI: [*Smiling*] How then?

BENEATHA: [*Embarrassed and a little demure to discuss the Great Hair question*] You know perfectly well how—as crinkly as yours—that's how.

ASAGAI: And it is ugly to you that way?

BENEATHA: [*Quickly*] Oh, no—not *ugly*— [*More slowly, apologetically*] But it's so hard to manage when it's well—*raw*.

ASAGAI: And so to accommodate that—you mutilate it every week?

BENEATHA: It's not mutilation!

ASAGAI: [*Laughing aloud at her seriousness*] Oh—please! I am only teasing you because you are so very serious about these things. [*He stands back from her and folds his arms across his chest as he watches her pulling her hair and frowning in the mirror*] Do you remember the first time you met me at school —? [*He laughs. Takes stage slightly right center*] You came up to me and you said, and I thought you were the most serious little thing I had ever seen— You said, [*He imitates her*] "Mr. Asagai—I want very much to talk with you. About Africa. You see, Mr. Asagai, I am looking for my *identity!*" [*Crossing to her, he folds over and roars*]

BENEATHA: [*Turning to him, not laughing*] Yes— [*Her face is quizzical, profoundly disturbed*]

ASAGAI: [*Still teasing, he crosses right to her and, reaching out, takes her face in his hands and turns her profile to him*] Well—it is true that this is not so much a profile of a Hollywood queen as perhaps a Queen of the Nile— [*A mock dismissal of the importance of the question. He crosses left to center*] But what does it matter? Assimilationism is so popular in your country.

BENEATHA: [*Wheeling, passionately, sharply*] I am not an assimilationist!

ASAGAI: [*The protest hangs in the room for a moment and* ASAGAI *studies her, his laughter fading*] Such a serious one. [*There is a pause between them, then*] So—you like the robes? You must take excellent care of them—they are from my sister's personal wardrobe.

BENEATHA: [*With incredulity*] You—you sent all the way home —for me?

ASAGAI: [*With charm*] For you—I would do much more— Well, that is what I came for. I must go. [*He crosses to center door*]

BENEATHA: [*Crosses up right and above sofa to center*] Will you call me Monday?

ASAGAI: Yes— We have a great deal to talk about, you and I. I mean about identity and time and all that.

BENEATHA: Time?

ASAGAI: Yes—about how much time one needs to know what one feels.

BENEATHA: [*Crosses down left of sofa to front of sofa*] You see! You never understood that there is more than one kind of feeling which can exist between a man and a woman—or at least— there should be.

ASAGAI: [*Shaking his head negatively but gently, crosses down center to meet her in front of the sofa*] No—between a man and a woman there need be only one kind of feeling. I have that for you— Now even—right this moment—

BENEATHA: I know—and by itself—it won't do. I can find that anywhere.

ASAGAI: For a woman it should be enough.

BENEATHA: I know— That's because that's what it says in all
the novels that men write. But it isn't. Go ahead and laugh—
but I'm not interested in being someone's little episode in
America or— [*With feminine vengeance*]—one of them! [*She
removes the robe and folds it.* ASAGAI *has burst into laughter
again*] That's funny as hell, huh!

ASAGAI: It's just that every American girl I have known has said
that to me. White—black—in this you are all the same. And
that same speech, too!

BENEATHA: [*Angrily*] Yuk, yuk, yuk! [*Places folded robe in box*]

ASAGAI: It's how you can be sure that the world's most liberated
women are not liberated at all. You all talk about it too much!

SUGGESTIONS FOR THE ACTOR

1. Why are you, Beneatha, "profoundly disturbed" as the scene
begins? What are you thinking when the doorbell rings? Gradually
your pleasure at seeing Asagai again pushes your unhappy
thoughts into the background. You, the actress, should read the
entire play carefully, more than once. (*A Raisin in the Sun* should
be easy to obtain; it is included in many anthologies.) Read the
scene just before Asagai's entrance a number of times. Are you
(Beneatha) feeling sorry for Ruth? Regretting your hurtful remark, wishing you could "strike it off the record"? Are you also
somewhat embarrassed by your appearance? Are you afraid your
mother may embarrass you by revealing her complete ignorance
of Africa?

Have you completely forgotten the ten-thousand-dollar check
arriving in today's mail? If not, when might you think of it? You
expect the mailman to ring the doorbell this morning, as he always
does.

2. When you, Beneatha, look in the mirror, you, the actress,

must imagine both the mirror itself and your own reflection, unless you use a real mirror. Visualize one small part of your reflection at a time. Which feature or part of yourself can you recall most easily—your eyes—your mouth—your hair? Whatever it is, concentrate on "seeing" that small part first, then other bits of your reflection until, little by little, you visualize your entire self. "See" the reflection of the multicolored Nigerian robe which Asagai drapes about you. Remember that the mirror image *reverses* the way the robe is actually draped. (If it really hangs over your left shoulder, it will appear to hang over your right shoulder in the mirror.) "See" the imaginary mirror itself. Is it framed or decorated? Does the mirror need cleaning? Is it cracked anywhere? What is its shape? What are its dimensions?

3. For the actor playing Asagai: To develop a full characterization, it is essential to know something about your (Asagai's) life in Africa. Find out as much as possible about daily life in Nigeria in the 1940s after World War II or in the 1950s. Since you (Asagai) are a highly political individual, it is also important for you (the actor) to learn something about the struggle for African independence during those years.

You, Asagai, are far from a typical Nigerian young man. You are cosmopolitan, sophisticated, intellectual. Are you wealthy enough to pay for your own education in America? If not, who is subsidizing you? What are you studying? For what career are you preparing yourself?

4. For both of you: Study the play to learn more about your relationship, your attitudes and feelings toward one another. Beneatha does not yet realize that you, Asagai, want her to be your wife. Her fear of being merely another "romantic little episode" in your life here is unfounded. In a later scene you propose marriage to her; you want her to accompany you to Africa and practice medicine there eventually, if that is her desire. At the end of the play you, Beneatha, are seriously considering his proposal. Your romantic feelings toward him are evidently stronger than you have been willing to admit, even to yourself.

5. Act some études together: improvise scenes *in character* which depict incidents not shown in the play. (Make up the words and physical actions as you perform.) For instance you might wish to enact your first meeting at school, when you, Beneatha,

said so earnestly, "Mr. Asagai—I want very much to talk with you. About Africa." How had you known Asagai's identity before you met him?

You might wish to improvise another incident—your last meeting before the summer, when you, Beneatha, were glad Asagai was leaving for Canada.

Get together beforehand and plan some of your specific circumstances—where you (Asagai and Beneatha) are, when this is happening and what you were each doing before the scene opens.

From *Splendor in the Grass,* the screenplay by William Inge, adapted to the stage by F. Andrew Leslie. Act II, Scene 3

INTRODUCTION

Originally a movie, *Splendor in the Grass* was later adapted to the stage from William Inge's screenplay.

The locale of most of the play is eastern Kansas; the time is the late 1920s. The main characters are Wilma Dean Loomis, called "Deanie," and Bud Stamper. At the beginning of the play Deanie and Bud are high school sweethearts, passionately in love. They are the envy of their classmates. Deanie is beautiful, sweet and innocent. She worships Bud, to whom she is practically engaged. Bud is the captain of the football team; his family is extremely rich—his father has made a fortune in oil, and oil stocks keep going up. Bud adores Deanie, but he is deeply disturbed by his strong physical desire for her. His father warns him that there are two kinds of girls: "nice girls," with whom one must not "fool around," and the "other" kind. Bud wants only Deanie, however, and he is filled with frustration. He wants to marry Deanie now, but his father extracts a promise from him that he will wait until he is graduated from college, Yale. Bud reluctantly agrees, although he really wants to attend an agricultural college and then take over his father's ranch.

Deanie's mother is relieved to learn that Bud and Deanie have not "gone too far," but she nevertheless fills Deanie with feelings of guilt and shame when she tells her that "nice girls" never experience physical desire.

Bud's older sister Ginny is the "other" kind of girl; "her youthful good looks are already coarsened by fast living and too much makeup." At a local dance Bud discovers, to his horror, that Ginny is parked in a car outside, apparently granting sexual favors to a number of boys. He is overwhelmed with a sense of guilt and fear that Deanie's innocence may also be "spoiled," as Ginny's was. He knows that Deanie would never refuse him anything he demanded of her, and he does not trust his own self-control. He decides that he must stop seeing her. Instead he takes up with Juanita, a classmate with a reputation for being promiscuous.

Deanie becomes severely distraught. When her high school English teacher asks her to explain the poet Wordsworth's lines,

> Though nothing can bring back the hour
> Of splendour in the grass, of glory in
> the flower,

she becomes hysterical, reminded of her own unbearable loss. Later she attends a high school dance with a new escort, Toots, who plies her with liquor. She meets Bud outside the dance and "throws herself" at him, but he resists. She then attempts suicide. Her parents place her in a mental hospital in Wichita. Bud wants to marry her now, despite his father, but he is told by her doctor that she is mentally unstable and that it may be a long time before she will be released from the hospital.

Bud attends Yale, but he has no interest in his studies, and he fails his courses. Depressed and homesick in New Haven, he is comforted by Angelina, a "lovely Italian girl, about Bud's age," who works as a waitress in a pizza parlor. A serious relationship develops. Bud's father learns of this relationship and theatens to break it up, but this time Bud stands up to his father. In the big stock market crash of '29, Bud's father loses his entire fortune. Shortly afterward, Bud learns of his father's suicide.

Deanie eventually gets well and becomes engaged to John, formerly a patient at the mental hospital, now a doctor practicing in Cincinnati. Her hospital psychiatrist convinces her that she should see Bud again before she marries John, in order to face her fears and to find out how she really feels.

When Deanie first arrives home, her old girl friends Kay and June visit her. Her mother warns them to keep Deanie away from Bud. She fears that her daughter will have another breakdown. When Deanie insists on seeing Bud again, her father informs them all that Bud is now staying at his father's old ranch, a distance from town.

In an earlier scene, set several months before this one, we learned that Kay's family had become wealthy before the Depression and had sent her to a finishing school, Miss Finch's school. We also learned that June, who had been Deanie's closest girl friend in high school, had become engaged to Rusty, another classmate.

The following scene ends the play.

* * * KAY, JUNE *and* DEANIE *step onstage from down left, and pause.*

KAY: [*Looking around*] Gee, the old place sure doesn't look like it used to, does it?

JUNE: Remember all the swell parties Bud used to throw out here for the gang?

KAY: Isn't it a shame? [*Both girls look at* DEANIE. *Now that she's here,* DEANIE *is quite frightened.* KAY, *gently*] Want me to go looking for Bud?

DEANIE: Please, Kay.

KAY: Okay. [*She crosses right as the others wait down left, and calls out*] Bud . . . Bud . . .

DEANIE: [*A painful sigh*] Oh, June. [JUNE *hugs her*]

KAY: [*Calling again*] Bud . . . [*She crosses farther right.* BUD *appears at upper right and crosses down to her, alongside the right platform. He doesn't see* DEANIE *and* JUNE, *who still stand at far down left. He is very soiled from head to foot with grease. He wears dirty denim work clothes and cowboy boots*]

BUD: Well, hi, Kay!

KAY: [*Turning to him*] Hi, Bud! Jeepers, you're a mess.

BUD: [*Laughs*] I been working over some rigging out in the backyard. We got a little gas coming in now, and we're eating a little more regularly. [*He pauses at the down right end of the right platform*]

KAY: [*Stepping to him*] Bud . . . Deanie's here.

BUD: Deanie! [*He wipes his hands nervously on an old rag . . . hesitates*] Golly, Kay, I hate to see Deanie when I'm so . . . so soiled.

KAY: She won't mind, Bud.

BUD: How is she, Kay? [*Then he looks left.* DEANIE *is crossing toward him*]

KAY: She seems just wonderful, Bud, really.

BUD: [*Looking at* DEANIE] I'm glad. [DEANIE *walks up to them. She and* BUD *look at each other*]

DEANIE: Hello, Bud.

BUD: Hello, Deanie, long time no see.

DEANIE: Yes—a long time. [*Automatically, they reach for each other's hands, but it is no longer an awkward clutching or an erotic fumbling.* BUD *merely holds her hand in his. Both seem relaxed*]

BUD: It's *good* to see you, Deanie.

DEANIE: Thanks, Bud, it's awfully good to see you.

KAY: Look—you two have lots to talk about. I'll wait in the car with June. [*She crosses left quickly, and she and* JUNE *exit.* BUD *and* DEANIE *scarcely notice*]

BUD: [*Trying to be lighthearted*] Hey, wanta meet my wife?

DEANIE: [*She wasn't expecting this. Her composure slips*] Of course . . .

BUD: [*Stepping center and onto the center platform. Calling to-*

ward up right. Lights come up at center] Angie. Angie . . . [*He looks at* DEANIE, *noticing that she is upset. His face clouds*] Say . . . didn't they tell you? [DEANIE *shakes her head*] Oh gosh, Deanie . . .

DEANIE: It's all right, Bud.

BUD: [*Turning up right again*] Angie! Come out here, honey. I want you to meet someone. [ANGELINA *appears up right*]

ANGELINA: You call, Bud? [*She crosses to the step at up center*]

BUD: Angelina, this is Deanie. An old friend of mine.

ANGELINA: [*Crossing down to* DEANIE] How do you do? [DEANIE *steps onto the center platform to meet her*]

DEANIE: [*Shaking hands*] Hello, Angelina.

ANGELINA: [*Gesturing toward up right*] Won't you come in? The house, it doesn't look like much, but I offer you some wine.

DEANIE: Thanks, but I can't stay. My friends are waiting.

ANGELINA: Oh, then maybe you can come back again? Come back some time for dinner.

DEANIE: Thank you, Angelina. I'd like that. [*Pause.* ANGELINA *senses that there is something* BUD *and* DEANIE *have to say to each other*]

ANGELINA: Well, I'd better get back to the kitchen. I've got things on the stove. It was nice to meet you, Deanie.

DEANIE: It was good to meet you, Angelina. [ANGELINA *turns and exits as she came, crossing up center and then off up right.* BUD *and* DEANIE *watch her go*]

BUD: I married Angelina when I left New Haven. I didn't even finish my first year there in school. Angie was wonderful to me . . . when things began to go wrong.

DEANIE: Are you happy, Bud?

BUD: I guess so, Deanie. I never ask myself that question very often though. How about you?

DEANIE: I . . . I'm getting married next month.

BUD: Are you, Deanie?

DEANIE: Yes. A boy in Cincinnati. [*Then she dares to look at him*] I think you might like him.

BUD: Things work out awfully funny sometimes, don't they, Deanie?

DEANIE: Yes, they do.

BUD: I hope you'll be awfully happy, Deanie.

DEANIE: Like you, Bud, I don't think much about happiness either.

BUD: What's the point? You gotta take what comes.

DEANIE: Yes. [*Pause. They have said what they have to say to each other*]

BUD: Let me walk you back to the car.

DEANIE: That's all right, Bud. Don't bother.

BUD: [*Holding her hand*] Goodbye, Deanie. [*She doesn't answer. She turns down, steps off the center platform, and starts left. Bud calls after her*] Deanie! [*She turns back to him*] I'm . . . I'm awfully glad to see you again, Deanie.

DEANIE: Thanks, Bud. [*He stands watching her, as the lights fade out at center and right. He turns and goes out up right as* DEANIE *moves down left.* KAY *and* JUNE *step onstage to meet her*]

KAY: [*Gently*] Deanie, honey, do you think you still love him?

DEANIE: [*A sense of wonder*] I don't know. He's a totally different person to me now.

JUNE: How do you mean?

DEANIE: I'd always worshiped Bud like he was a god. But all this time he's been a man, hasn't he? Like other men all over the world, trying to get along.

KAY: [*Thoughtfully*] I guess so, Deanie. I guess that's really all there is to it.

JUNE: [*Pause. Then a smile, as she links arms with* DEANIE *and* KAY] Come on, gang, let's go home. Unless I'm very much mistaken, we've got a wedding to get ready for! [*They go off down left together quickly*]

SUGGESTIONS FOR THE ACTOR

1. Before you begin to act the scene, it is important to understand its relation to the rest of the play and to the point the playwright is making. If at all possible, read the entire play. If you cannot obtain the script, carefully read the introduction to this scene.

What is the over-all mood of the scene? It is sad surely, or at least there are many sad moments, and yet the scene is not tragic. If actors perform this play honestly, the audience may well be moved to tears by this final scene. Yet the actors themselves should not weep. Bud and Deanie are not heartbroken. They know what they have lost, but at last they have come to terms with life. They accept what life still offers them. "You gotta take what comes," says Bud. Then too, Deanie now realizes for the first time that she had loved an illusion, not the real Bud. She had worshiped a "god" who had never really existed. Bud and Deanie "don't think much about happiness" any more. Never again will they experience the splendor, the wild joy (or the pain) of their first love, but in a different way Deanie loves her fiancé and Bud loves his wife.

To quote the entire key passage from Wordsworth's poem "Intimations of Immortality" which Deanie's English teacher had read earlier in the play:

> Though nothing can bring back the hour
> Of splendour in the grass, of glory in the flower,
> We will grieve not, rather find
> Strength in what remains behind.

2. For Bud and Deanie: How did your feelings of guilt and shame about your bodies affect your lives? How did you acquire these attitudes? If you, Deanie, had possessed a greater sense of self-worth (before your hospitalization) might your life have turned out differently? How? Why?

3. No scenery is necessary, but all of you must plan the imaginary setting specifically. Before a word is spoken, you, the actresses playing Kay, June and Deanie, must visualize not only what the ranch looks like now, but also what it looked like in the old days when Bud would throw "swell parties" out here. It would be useful to walk all over your "stage," visualizing the physical setting before beginning the scene itself. The entire cast should perform this exercise. Imagine the sounds and smells of the ranch too. "Feel" the ground beneath your shoes. "Feel" the fresh air on your body. The season is late fall or early winter. What is the time of day? What is the weather? How are you dressed?

4. When you act a "sad" moment, do not concentrate on being sad. If you try for sadness you will produce only some outward indications of sadness such as a woeful expression, hunched shoulders, a catch in the voice. You will not be acting honestly. Instead, concentrate as usual on what your character is thinking at every moment, on what your character wants, what he or she says and does to reach that objective, on communicating with others and on imagining the physical surroundings.

This is an uncommonly quiet scene. Not very much happens to the characters outwardly. Outwardly, Bud and Deanie meet after a long separation; Deanie discovers that Bud is married and she meets his wife. After a brief conversation, the former sweethearts part. Not much to it. But what happens to the characters *inwardly* during the course of the scene? What is your character thinking at every moment?

Inventing an excuse, Angelina leaves you, Bud and Deanie, alone. She senses that you two have something to say to each other. You, Bud, and you, Deanie, must concentrate so strongly on your inner thoughts that they actually show on your faces. Your expressions must "motivate" (cause, impel) Angelina's action—leaving.

For Bud and Deanie: As an exercise (invented by Stanislavsky), act the private conservation between you in the following manner. You, Bud, speak your inner thoughts, as well as the playwright's words, aloud. Speak your secret thoughts in a softer voice than you normally use. You, the actress playing Deanie, pretend that you do not hear these inner thoughts. Then act this portion of the scene again, reversing the procedure. This time you, Deanie, speak your inner thoughts aloud, as Bud did previously. Now you, the actor playing Bud, pretend that you hear only the playwright's words.

5. For the actresses playing Kay, June and Angelina: The play does not provide a great deal of information about the characters you play, but you must each imagine the whole past and present life of your character anyway. It would be helpful to answer all the questions on the "Actor's Check List." (See pages 336–39.)

From *West Side Story* by Arthur Laurents and Stephen Sondheim.
Act I, Scene 4

INTRODUCTION

This celebrated musical drama (book, or words other than song lyrics, by Arthur Laurents) parallels the tragedy of Shakespeare's teen-age lovers Romeo and Juliet. In *Romeo and Juliet* the lovers' two noble families have long been feuding. In *West Side Story* the lovers belong to rival teen-age street gangs on Manhattan's West Side, the Jets and the Sharks. In this version it is hatred between warring ethnic groups that destroys the lovers. The Sharks are Puerto Rican, struggling to make a place for themselves in a new, often hostile environment, New York City. The Jets, of various ethnic backgrounds, were here first and consider themselves "American." Their struggle is to keep the territory they have already won.

The action of the play begins on a West Side street at 5 P.M. at the end of summer. The Jets are onstage, "in possession of the area: owning, enjoying, loving their 'home.' Their leader is RIFF: glowing, driving, intelligent, slightly whacky. His lieutenant is DIESEL: big, slow, steady, nice. The youngest member of the gang is BABY JOHN: awed at everything, including that he is a Jet, trying to act the big man. His buddy is A-RAB: an explosive little ferret who enjoys everything and understands the seriousness of nothing. The most aggressive is ACTION: a catlike ball of fury." Snowboy is "a bespectacled self-styled expert."

Each gang "has its own prideful uniform. The boys—
sideburned, long-haired—are vital, restless, sardonic."

Bernardo, leader of the Sharks, enters. He is "handsome,
proud, fluid, a chip on his sardonic shoulder." The Jets "flick him
off." He returns with more Sharks. The beginnings of warfare
occur, mild at first. Then A-rab is cornered by the Sharks and
Bernardo pierces his ear. A free-for-all follows until "the arrival
of a big goonlike cop," Officer Krupke, and a plainclothesman,
Schrank, who orders the Jets to quit fighting with the Sharks.
"You hoodlums don't own the streets," warns Schrank. The boys
fiercely resent this attitude. Determined to prevent the Sharks
from capturing their turf, they plan a "rumble." The leaders of the
two gangs must have a "war council" to choose weapons. Riff decides to challenge Bernardo at the gym dance that night at 10 P.M.
He wants to take his friend and "lieutenant," Tony, with him, but
Tony seems to have lost interest in the Jets lately.

In the ensuing scene Riff convinces Tony to go to the dance for
the sake of their old friendship, although Tony admits he no
longer gets a "kick * * * from being a Jet." He is "a good-looking sandy-haired boy" who works for "Doc," the druggist. Tony is
waiting, reaching out for something great that is coming. He
doesn't know what it is, but he is certain it will come soon,
"Maybe tonight . . ."

The next scene takes place at 6 P.M. in a bridal shop. "ANITA, a
Puerto Rican girl with loose hair and slightly flashy clothes, is
finishing remaking what was a white communion dress into a
party dress for an extremely lovely, extremely young girl: MARIA.
ANITA is knowing, sexual, sharp. MARIA is an excited, enthusiastic,
obedient child, with the temper, stubborn strength and awareness
of a woman." She was brought to New York City from Puerto
Rico one month before by Bernardo, her brother. Anita is Bernardo's girl friend. Bernardo brought Maria here to marry Chino,
"a shy, gentle sweet-faced boy." But she does not love Chino.
"When I look at Chino, nothing happens." Like Tony, Maria is
restless. Her days here have been spent sewing; her evenings, just
sitting. At first she does not wish to be the only girl wearing a
demure white dress at the dance, but then suddenly she sees the
advantage of being "the only one" and she is happy. When Chino

and Bernardo join them, Maria excitedly tells her brother, "tonight is the real beginning of my life as a young lady of America!"

The following scene in the gym, reprinted here, may be acted by an entire class or group at once. The cast includes all the Jets and all the Sharks, girls as well as boys, and two adults. Gladhand, a social-director type, tries to run the dance and keep the peace, vastly assisted in the latter endeavor by the presence of a police officer, Krupke. This scene requires a large playing space. If a large stage is not available, it can be acted in a large room cleared of desks and tables. A real gym would be even better.

10:00 P.M. *The gym.*

Actually, a converted gymnasium of a settlement house, at the moment being used as a dancehall, disguised for the occasion with streamers and bunting.

Both gangs are jitterbugging wildly with their bodies, but their faces, although they are enjoying themselves, remain cool, almost detached. The line between the two gangs is sharply defined by the colors they wear: the Jets, girls as well as boys, reflecting the colors of the Jet jackets; the same is true of the Sharks. The dancing is a physical and emotional release for these kids.

MARIA *enters with* CHINO, BERNARDO *and* ANITA. *As she looks around, delighted, thrilled by this, her first dance, the Jets catch sight of* BERNARDO, *who is being greeted by* PEPE, *his lieutenant, and other Sharks. As the music peters away, the Jets withdraw to one side of the hall, around* RIFF. *The Sharks, seeing this, draw to their side, around* BERNARDO. *A brief consultation, and* RIFF *starts across—with lieutenants—to make his challenge to* BERNARDO, *who starts—with his lieutenants—to meet him. The moment is brief but it would be disastrous if a smiling, overly cheerful young man of about thirty did not hurry forward. He is called* GLADHAND, *and he is a "square."*

GLADHAND: [*Beaming*] All right, boys and girls! Attention, please! [*Hum of talk*] Attention! [KRUPKE *appears behind* GLAD-HAND; *the talk stops*] Thank you. It sure is a fine turnout tonight. [*Ad libs from the kids*] We want you to make friends here, so we're going to have a few get-together dances. [*Ad libs: "Oh, ginger peachy," etc.*] You form two circles: boys on the outside, girls on the inside.

SNOWBOY: Where are you?

GLADHAND: [*Tries to laugh at this*] All right. Now when the music stops, each boy dances with whichever girl is opposite. O.K.? O.K. Two circles, kids. [*The kids clap their hands back at him and ad lib: "Two circles, kids," etc., but do not move*] Well, it won't hurt you to try.

SNOWBOY: [*Limping forward*] Oh, it hurts; it hurts; it—

[KRUPKE *steps forward.* SNOWBOY *straightens up and meekly returns to his place.* RIFF *steps forward and beckons to his girl,* VELMA. *She is terribly young, sexy, lost in a world of jive. She slithers forward to take her place with* RIFF. *The challenge is met by* BERNARDO, *who steps forward, leading* ANITA *as though he were presenting the most magnificent lady in all the world. The other kids follow, forming the two circles* GLADHAND *requested*]

GLADHAND: That's it, kids. Keep the ball rolling. Round she goes and where she stops, nobody knows. All right: here we go!

[*Promenade music starts and the circles start revolving.* GLADHAND, *whistle to his mouth, is in the center with* KRUPKE. *He blows the whistle and the music stops, leaving Jet boys opposite Shark girls, and vice versa. There is a moment of tenseness, then* BERNARDO *reaches across the Jet girl opposite for* ANITA'S *hand, and she comes to him.* RIFF *reaches for* VELMA; *and the kids of both gangs follow suit. The "get-together" has failed, and each gang is on its own side of the hall as a mambo starts. This turns into a challenge dance between* BERNARDO *and* ANITA—*cheered on by the Sharks*—*and* RIFF *and* VELMA—*cheered on by the Jets. During it,* TONY *enters and is momentarily embraced by* RIFF, *who is delighted that his best friend did turn up. The dance builds wilder and wilder, until, at the peak, everybody is dancing and shouting, "Go, Mambo!" It*

> *is at this moment that* TONY *and* MARIA—*at opposite sides of the hall—see each other. They have been cheering on their respective friends, clapping in rhythm. Now, as they see each other, their voices die, their smiles fade, their hands slowly go to their sides. The lights fade on the others, who disappear into the haze of the background as a delicate cha-cha begins and* TONY *and* MARIA *slowly walk forward to meet each other. Slowly, as though in a dream, they drift into the steps of the dance, always looking at each other, completely lost in each other; unaware of anyone, any place, any time, anything but one another*]

TONY: You're not thinking I'm someone else?

MARIA: I know you are not.

TONY: Or that we have met before?

MARIA: I know we have not.

TONY: I felt, I *knew* something-never-before was going to happen, had to happen. But this is—

MARIA: [*Interrupting*] My hands are cold. [*He takes them in his*] Yours, too. [*He moves her hands to his face*] So warm. [*She moves his hands to her face*]

TONY: Yours, too.

MARIA: But of course. They are the same.

TONY: It's so much to believe—you're not joking me?

MARIA: I have not yet learned how to joke that way. I think now I never will.

> [*Impulsively, he stops to kiss her hands; then tenderly, innocently, her lips. The music bursts out, the lights flare up, and* BERNARDO *is upon them in an icy rage*]

BERNARDO: Go home, *"American."*

TONY: Slow down, Bernardo.

BERNARDO: Stay away from my sister!

TONY: . . . Sister?

[RIFF *steps up*]

BERNARDO: [*to* MARIA] Couldn't you see he's one of them?

MARIA: No; I saw only him.

BERNARDO: [*As* CHINO *comes up*] I told you: there's only one thing they want from a Puerto Rican girl!

TONY: That's a lie!

RIFF: Cool, boy.

CHINO: [*To* TONY] Get away.

TONY: You keep out, Chino. [*To* MARIA] Don't listen to them!

BERNARDO: She will listen to her brother before—

RIFF: [*Overlapping*] If you characters want to settle—

GLADHAND: Please! Everything was going so well! Do you fellows get pleasure out of making trouble? Now come on—it won't hurt you to have a good time.

[*Music starts again.* BERNARDO *is on one side with* MARIA *and* CHINO; ANITA *joins them.* TONY *is on the other with* RIFF *and* DIESEL. *Light emphasizes the first group*]

BERNARDO: I warned you—

CHINO: Do not yell at her, 'Nardo.

BERNARDO: You yell at babies.

ANITA: And put ideas in the baby's head.

BERNARDO: Take her home, Chino.

MARIA: 'Nardo, it is my first dance.

BERNARDO: Please. We are family, Maria. Go.

[MARIA *hesitates, then starts out with* CHINO *as the light follows her to the other group, which she passes*]

RIFF: [*To* DIESEL, *indicating* TONY *happily*] I guess the kid's with us for sure now.

[TONY *doesn't even hear; he is staring at* MARIA, *who stops for a moment*]

CHINO: Come, Maria.

[*They continue out*]

TONY: Maria . . .

[*He is unaware that* BERNARDO *is crossing toward him, but* RIFF *intercepts*]

BERNARDO: I don't want you.

RIFF: I want you, though. For a war council—Jets and Sharks.

BERNARDO: The pleasure is mine.

RIFF: Let's go outside.

BERNARDO: I would not leave the ladies here alone. We will meet you in half an hour.

RIFF: Doc's drugstore? [BERNARDO *nods*] And no jazz before then.

BERNARDO: I understand the rules—Native Boy.

[*The light is fading on them, on everyone but* TONY]

RIFF: Spread the word, Diesel.

DIESEL: Right, Daddy-o.

RIFF: Let's get the chicks and kick it. Tony?

TONY: Maria . . .

[*Music starts*]

RIFF: [*In darkness*] Tony!

DIESEL: [*In darkness*] Ah, we'll see him at Doc's.

TONY: [*Speaking dreamily over the music—he is now standing alone in the light*] Maria . . .

SUGGESTIONS FOR THE ACTOR

1. This scene will work only if every single one of you creates a three-dimensional, flesh-and-blood human being, acting and reacting in character at every moment, whether or not you have lines in the script. Remember that we do not all express the same emotion in the same way. It is not only important to react to what is happening at all times, but to react as your character would. How true the motto for the old Moscow Art Theatre, "There are no small parts, only small actors!"

Answer the questions on the "Actor's Check List," beginning on page 336, even though the play itself may make no mention of your role. Use your imagination!

2. Each of you must have a definite attitude toward every other character in the scene. It would probably be a good idea to break this very large group into smaller groups. There are already two subgroups: the Jets and the Sharks. Each subgroup can be further divided into a number of smaller groups, such as three or four male friends, girl friend and boy friend, two sisters. The members of these small groups converse at times, in character, of course. For example, early in the scene there is undoubtedly some murmuring about the challenge everyone is expecting. One or two "loners" may not have heard about it until now. Improvise the conversation you might hold when there is a "Hum of Talk" and Gladhand has to call "Attention!" Be sure you know your character's relationship with each member of your small group. Keep in mind, however, that such activity serves only as background; it should never take the audience's attention away from the main line of action.

3. In rehearsing a large-group scene, even for performance in a class or workshop, it is useful to have a director, either the teacher or a student. The director can judge whether background reactions are not enough, just right or overdone. The director should position the players so that no vital action or reaction is obscured from the view of any member of the audience (if there is to be an audience—with the entire group participating, there may not be). For scene work not leading to any formal production it is unnecessary for the director to block every small movement and gesture. (Blocking a scene means *positioning the actors and providing pat-*

terns of movement.) In fact, the more that can be left to the individual actor's imagination, the more creative the experience for each participant. But a director is probably needed to block large group movements, or chaos may result.

It is often worthwhile at some early rehearsals for you, the actors, to invent your own words instead of speaking the lines in the script, while you follow the line of action of the written scene. At least one of these improvisations should take place before the scene is blocked. During this rehearsal move and group yourselves wherever you like. Some exciting self-blocking may occur, which the director may choose to retain. At later rehearsals if the scene sounds stilted and lacks spontaneity, try reanimating it by improvising your own words again.

4. In the play script, this scene ends with Tony's lovely ballad "Maria" (immediately following the last word of the excerpt printed above). If you, the actor playing Tony, wish to sing the song, you can obtain sheet music and lyrics at a music store. If you do not wish to sing, perhaps you (Tony) can exit dreamily at the end of the scene; entranced, you speak Maria's name over to yourself with all the joy and wonder of first love.

5. The dance music may be brought up to date. Use any dance music you wish (records or tapes), whatever dances the whole group knows, as long as the music fits the mood. But be sure that the music played during the lovers' meeting is slower, softer, more romantic than what comes before or after.

6. For the director: One directorial problem this scene presents is the shift of focus from one group to another, or from the whole group to Tony and Maria alone. In a performance onstage, these shifts of focus are easily accomplished by lighting one area and darkening the rest. If stage lighting is not available, you must find another way to focus on only one grouping. Here are some devices, not all of which would suit this particular scene.

(a) Everyone out of the focus "freezes" (assumes statuelike positions) as in the children's game of Statues. During the dialogue between the lovers, all but Tony and Maria freeze in the positions they were in last. Even if an actor assumes a dance position, it must be comfortable enough to hold throughout the dialogue. During a freeze the actor does not act or react at all. Later in the scene when Gladhand says, "Now come on—it won't hurt you to have a good time," instead of *light* emphasizing the first group, the *second* group withdraws from the focus by freezing. The audience's attention is thus directed toward the first group. When according to the script the light is supposed to follow Maria to the second group, instead the *first* group freezes.

(b) Or, instead of freezing, the actors out of focus continue to act soundlessly, making sure that their movements are very small, and not so sudden as to distract the audience. If possible they take the least conspicuous stage positions, which usually are as far away from the audience as possible, and far to the (actor's) left or right (upstage left or right). They may even keep their backs to the audience.

(c) The actors out of focus do not move, but they do not freeze either. They continue to act, to concentrate on the thoughts and desires of the characters they portray, but without any physical activity. These actors must invent logical reasons for their characters to remain still. How many possible reasons can *you* think of for remaining motionless, in one position? For intensive work on taking the focus, and withdrawing from the focus without either moving or freezing, study the exercise "Two Scenes" in *Improvisation for the Theatre* by Viola Spolin (Evanston, Northwestern University Press, 1963), in the chapter entitled "Non-Directional Blocking." Incidentally, a group of actors highly trained in this technique of "nondirectional blocking" may be able to block a large-group scene without a director.

(d) In certain situations actors out of the focus may find a way to motivate an exit.

Your group of actors may wish to discuss this question with you: Which of the techniques for shifting focus listed above would best suit *this* scene? Why?

7. Although your understanding of this play does not depend upon familiarity with *Romeo and Juliet,* a knowledge of Shakespeare's play would certainly add to your appreciation of *West Side Story.* A comparison of the two plays could make for interesting discussion. For example, you could compare Tony and Maria's first encounter at the gym dance with Romeo and Juliet's first meeting at the Capulet ball. (A paperback edition containing both plays is published by Dell Publishing Co., Inc., 1 Dag Hammarskjold Plaza, New York, New York 10017.)

Monologues for Young Women

From *Green Grow the Lilacs* by Lynn Riggs.
Scene 2

INTRODUCTION

This lovely folk play may be familiar to some of you in another
form, the world-famous Rodgers and Hammerstein musical version entitled *Oklahoma!*. The tale is a simple one, "which might
have been the substance of an ancient song." The characters,
however, are more complex.

Green Grow the Lilacs is laid in Indian Territory in 1900 before Oklahoma became a state.

Laurey Williams has been reared for the last five years, ever
since her parents died, by her good-natured aunt Eller. They are
farmers. Laurey "is a fair, spoiled, lovely young girl about eighteen." She is still only half-aware of her own feelings. She tries to
deny the stirrings of love and desire within her for Curly, a handsome young cowboy. Nor does she really understand her instinctive terror of Jeeter, a strange, "growly" hired hand. Both men are
in love with her. Curly invites her to a party but she refuses. She
has already consented to go with Jeeter. She was afraid to refuse,
she confesses to Aunt Eller. This discussion is interrupted by the
arrival of a peddler and a farm girl, Ado Annie. This peddler had
cheated them before. Nevertheless, they want to see his wares.

The simple objects he displays—combs, perfumes, etc.—give
Laurey great sensuous delight. Most of us, with our convenient
all-purpose drugstores and "five-and-dimes," take such things for
granted, hardly notice them. But Laurey lives a pioneer's existence. To her, the peddler's visits are a rare treat.

This monologue takes place in Laurey's primitive but feminine bedroom. The peddler, Aunt Eller and Ado Annie are also present.

LAUREY: What do I want, Mr. Pedlar Man?* [*In a kind of abstracted ecstasy*] Want some hairpins, a fine-tooth comb, a pink 'un. Want a buckle made out of shiny silver to fasten onto my shoes! Want a dress with lace! Want pe'fume, face whitenin'! Wanta be purty, wanta smell like a honeysuckle vine!

* * *

[*Her mood rising*] Want things I c'n see and put my hands on. Want things I've heared of and never had before—pearls in a plush box, diamonds, a rubber-t'ard buggy, a cut glass sugar bowl. Want things I caint tell you about. Caint see 'em clear. Things nobody ever heared of. [*Passionately, in a low voice*] Not only things to look at and hold in yer hands. Things to *happen* to you! Things so nice if they ever did happen yer heart ud quit beatin', you'd fall down dead. They ain't no end to the things I want. Everything you got wouldn't be a starter fer me, Mister Pedlar Man! [*Breaking off*] So jist give me a bottle of shoe blackin', and make it quick!

SUGGESTIONS FOR THE ACTOR

1. One could not hope for a better monologue to study in connection with work on sensory awareness. It is ideal, not only because of its succession of recalled and imagined sensory impressions, but also because of your character's intense emotional response to these impressions.

If you, the actress, hope to make vivid for your audience all these "things to look at and hold in yer hands," you must first visualize them yourself. As an actress, whenever you speak lines that refer to people, places or things that do not appear onstage, you

*This line has been added by this editor to make the context clear.

should have concrete images in mind. You should always select an image meaningful to you. It should be something, someone or some place that can evoke in you the desired response or feeling. If the character you play refers to a loved one not actually present, you, the actress, should "see" a real person, preferably one that you love in real life. In life, images come to you automatically, all the time. You do not have to plan them. But on the stage it is often necessary to make a conscious effort to visualize what you are saying. Make these selections in advance, but if a fresh image flashes through your mind spontaneously onstage, that's fine.

You should also select nonvisual sense memories that can lead you to the desired emotion. Suppose, for example, that you want to capture Laurey's delight over the smell of honeysuckle, but in real life you dislike that smell. You can recall the smell of lilacs instead if that aroma delights you, even though you *say,* as the character Laurey, "wanta smell like a honeysuckle vine!"

Visualize an appropriate image for every object mentioned in your monologue, one that will evoke in you Laurey's feeling. Recall appropriate scents, sounds and textures as well.

2. Here is an exercise you can do at home by yourself, to heighten your sensory awareness. Try to recall a varied succession of sights, smells, sounds, tastes and textures. For instance, "Imagine that you smell: wood smoke; tobacco smoke; gasoline; turpentine; banana oil; roses; lilies; violets; a chest lined with cedar; a chest containing damp and rotting papers; a delicate cheese." (These sensory impressions were suggested by H. D. Albright in *Working Up a Part* [Boston, Houghton Mifflin Company, 1947], page 37.)

3. This short monologue contains several distinct changes of mood and purpose. These changes are called "transitions." Find where each one occurs. Each change begins a new little section (called a "beat"). Give each section a label, a title, by composing a sentence beginning with the words, "I want ———" or "I need ———." Each sentence should express as concisely as possible what you (Laurey) desire or need at that moment. For example, one section might be labeled, "I need to return to reality." Which section would that label suit? When you act the role, concentrate on what you, as Laurey, want or need at each moment.

From *A Raisin in the Sun* by Lorraine Hansberry.
Act III

INTRODUCTION

See pages 231–33 for a description of the beginning of the play.
When Mama refuses to invest in a liquor business, making a down payment on a house in an all-white neighborhood instead, Walter loses all hope for the future. Seeing what she has done to her son, Mama confesses to him that she was wrong. Nothing is worth destroying her "boy." She tells him that the down payment on the house was thirty-five hundred dollars. That leaves sixty-five hundred. She wants Walter to take all the remaining money, put three thousand dollars in a savings bank for Beneatha's medical schooling and keep the rest in a checking account in his own name, to use as he sees fit.

Walter is overjoyed. Not even an attempt on the part of a community "improvement" association to buy their new house in order to keep them from moving into the neighborhood can deflate his spirits. He is filled with love for the whole family.

Suddenly the bubble bursts. It is Saturday, moving day. A little man named Bobo brings the terrible news. Walter had given all the money, every cent, including Beneatha's three thousand dollars, to a shady character named Willy. Bobo and Willy were supposed to go to Springfield and pay out some graft to speed up the approval of their liquor license. Walter was planning to go into business with them. Bobo had given Willy his own life savings too. But Willy never showed up at the train station. He disappeared with all the money!

It is an hour later. As the curtain rises

* * * There is a sullen light of gloom in the living room * * * BENEATHA sits at the kitchen table, still surrounded by the now almost ominous packing crates. We feel that it is a mood struck perhaps an hour before, and it lingers now, full of the empty sound of profound disappointment. * * * Presently the doorbell rings and BENEATHA rises without ambition or interest to answer. It is ASAGAI, smiling broadly, striding into the room with energy and happy expectation and conversation.

He has come to help with the moving. Beneatha informs Asagai that her brother gave the money away, that he invested it "with a man even Travis wouldn't have trusted." Asagai expresses his sympathy. "And you, now?" he asks.

BENEATHA: Me?— Me? Me, I'm nothing— Me. When I was very small—we used to take our sleds out in the winter time and the only hills we had were the ice covered stone steps of some houses down the street. And we used to fill them in with snow and make them smooth and slide down them all day—and it was very dangerous, you know—far too steep—and sure enough one day a kid named Rufus came down too fast and hit the sidewalk—and we saw his face just split open right there in front of us— And I remember standing there looking at his bloody open face thinking that was the end of Rufus. But the ambulance came and they took him to the hospital and they fixed the broken bones and they sewed it all up—and the next time I saw Rufus he just had a little line down the middle of his face— I never got over that—

* * *

That that was what one human being could do for another, fix him up—sew up the problem, make him all right again. That was the most marvelous thing in the world— I wanted to do that. I always thought it was the one concrete thing in the world that a human being could do. Fix up the sick, you know—and make them whole again. This was truly being God—

* * *

I wanted to cure. It used to be so important to me. I wanted to cure. It used to matter. I used to care.

SUGGESTIONS FOR THE ACTOR

1. Your (Beneatha's) disappointment is so profound that you are not even angry. You are beyond anger; you feel dead inside.

Until today your desire to "express yourself" had led you to take up one hobby after another, but your desire to be a doctor had evidently withstood the test of time. Your mother would never have told Walter to set aside three thousand dollars for your medical education if your ambition had been merely a passing fancy. Not only have you been deprived of the opportunity to study medicine, but you have been betrayed by your own family— by your brother, who invested your money without your knowledge, and even by your mother, who entrusted your money to your brother.

Have you, the actress, ever been cruelly disappointed? If so, how was the crushing message transmitted to you? Through something someone said to you? Through someone's tone of voice? Through something you saw? Something you read? Was the message communicated through touch? Through various sense impressions? How did you react at that moment? Why? What did you do afterward? Try to recall vividly everything you saw, heard, smelled, touched and tasted when the blow first struck and for the next few hours.

2. Why do you, Beneatha, say, "Me?— Me? Me, I'm nothing — Me"? Your present negative attitude toward yourself is not at all like you; you don't ordinarily consider yourself "nothing." You say the word "Me" four times, but each "Me" has a somewhat different shade of meaning. Exactly what are you thinking each time you say the word? What thoughts or images flash through your mind during the breaks indicated in your monologue by dashes?

3. Take the time to "remember" the incident from your (Beneatha's) childhood. "See" the ice-covered stone steps. Imagine

packing the steps with snow, making them smooth. "Feel" the snow in your hands. Was your face cold? What part(s) of your face? Where else did you feel the chill? Were you dressed warmly? "See" the sleds whizzing down the steep decline. Can you, the actress, recall how it felt to ride a sled down a steep hill when you were small? "Hear" the shrieks, the shouting, the nervous laughter.

When you (Beneatha) speak of Rufus, you (the actress) should visualize a little boy whom you knew when you were a child. Can you picture the accident? If not, as you work on your part, try to picture any gory accident that you once witnessed in real life. How were you affected by what you saw? What did you want to do? What did you do? What did Beneatha want when she saw the accident? What did she do?

4. To you (Beneatha), the saving of Rufus seemed like a miracle. The accomplishments of modern medicine filled you with awe.

Can you, the actress, share that feeling? Have you ever marveled over a doctor's capacity to save lives? Has a doctor ever saved the life of someone you loved, or even someone you knew casually? What was your reaction? If you were never thrilled by the skills of modern medicine, then substitute something else, any accomplishment that you consider, or once considered, miraculous.

As a child, you (Beneatha) were so impressed and excited by a doctor's ability to make a person "all right again" that you wished to possess that power yourself. From that moment until now you longed to practice medicine. In your present (temporary) state of depression, however, you no longer believe that doctors can cure the hurts of mankind. You are now convinced that the real ailments are not physical.

Have you, the actress, ever believed in something (or someone) with all your heart, only to become disillusioned? If so, in what (or in whom) did you believe? Why did you change? As you prepare to act your role, recall both your own original ideal and your own subsequent disillusionment. What did you do when your dream was shattered? What physical actions did you perform? As you rehearse the monologue, appropriate actions for your character may occur to you spontaneously because of this personal memory.

From *Dance to the Piper* by Agnes de Mille.
"Adolescence"

See pages 97–99 for background.

Agnes de Mille's mother had reached "definite conclusions" about everything, from economic reform (she was the daughter of economist Henry George) to the budgeting of one's time. Because she did not believe in wasting anything, not even five minutes, she regularly failed to allow for sufficient traveling time in her schedule. Hence she invariably brought Agnes late to her dance classes, after the "warm-ups" were over. Her ideas of dress and hair-do were definite too, and distinctly different from the current vogue. Agnes de Mille writes, "When I started going to parties she piled a crown of curls on the top of my head surmounted with laurel leaves. This arrangement did much to militate against any social success I might have had." Nevertheless, she was a selfless, devoted mother, who in later years sacrificed all luxury for the sake of Agnes' career.

In the following selection Agnes describes her adolescence—after she had turned sixteen.

AGNES: I had been a pretty child. My nose was small and pert, my skin white. I was skinny, spider-legged and quick. I found myself suddenly imprisoned in someone else's body, heavy, deep-bosomed, large-hipped. My skin went muddy and on my face there developed seemingly overnight a large hooked nose, my father's nose. "Roman," my mother called it. "Aristocratic," the family said. "Full of character," people have told me since. But it would fool no girl. It was ugly. And it was mine for life. From that unmarked day when as a narcissistic youngster I looked in a mirror and realized I was not going to be a beautiful woman, I gave up caring how I looked—or thought I did. Except in costume * * *

Mother continued her losing battle to bring me up as a normal girl, and boys seemed indicated. * * *

She signed me up for the Junior Cotillion and forced me to go. I used to enter the cotillion room clad in a pink or flowered crepe de Chine dress made by her, a little sash tying my precocious torso in two like a sack, a frill at my neck and frills at my elbow, pink silk socks and sandals (all the other girls wore taffeta frocks and silver cloth slippers with pointed toes). My hair was arranged by Mother in a nest of curls and crowned by a laurel wreath. How I hated my hair! All the excitement of putting it up was canceled out by the visual result. Mother elected to arrange it before every party and reserved time in her day to do this while I sat before the glass sinking into deeper and deeper melancholy. Great tears stuck in my eyes. My mouth grew sour with rage and disappointment. I knew I would never look like the others. Then jabbing the final pin into place with last-ditch conviction and remarking that I was unco-operative and ungrateful, she would kiss me and dispatch me to an evening of enchantment.

I always bobbed a curtsy when I met my partners until requested to stop. They used to break into sweats of embarrassment. I was, by general consensus, a perfectly rotten dancer, pointing my toes and performing little variations on the basic shuffling that completely unnerved my doggedly pushing escort. I also snapped my head smartly on every turn as one does in pirouettes. Indeed I responded to every musical suggestion so enthusiastically and variously as to take the boy off guard and leave him with no plan. He generally suggested lemonade and talk. I began to talk.

"The music is excellent tonight. Don't you think?"

"Gee—yes!"

"The floor's good."

"Sure."

Pause.

"Do you play tennis?"

"A little."

"Oh—" Pause.

"Do you like music?"

"You mean what they're playing now—'I'm Always Chasing Rainbows'?"

"No, real music."

"Gee, I don't know much about that stuff."

Pause.

Very slowly—"I see."

I tried again.

"What grade are you in?"

"First year high."

"Oh, I'm finishing. I thought you were older."

"I guess I'm not bright like you."

I sat out alone as many as thirteen or fourteen dances in a row. I sat with that alert indifferent air of one who has too much on her mind of interest and charm to notice that she is bleeding to death at the heart. I held my head very high and turned it vigorously with an exaggerated interest in every single thing that was in no way connected with the stag line. I told myself with somber pride that when I was a great dancer with all the capitals of Europe at my feet, they would be very surprised indeed to remember they had passed me up. Very surprised. I used to go outside and look at the night sky and the line of hills against the stars and tell myself that these boys and girls never in their lives could know the deep emotions I felt. The next day I always practiced like a maniac.

Still, I was not unhappy. On the contrary I got through adolescence without a pang. I postponed it.

SUGGESTIONS FOR THE ACTOR

1. This selection reveals one of Agnes de Mille's greatest gifts, evident in her dances as well as her writing: her superb sense of

humor. In this piece she exhibits that rare quality we all could use —the ability to laugh at oneself. The laughter here is never pure joy, however; it is wry, liberally sprinkled with memories that still hurt. Chances are that when you, Agnes, manage to retain an aesthetic distance from these past events, you are able to see and emphasize their ironic humor. But at moments these events become so real to you that you mentally relive them. At these times you would probably feel anguish or, at the least, embarrassment rather than amusement. As an actress you must decide just when you, as the character Agnes, view the incidents from the distance of time (which soothes, even if it fails to heal all wounds) and when you view them from up close, as if they were happening in the uncomfortable here and now.

2. The dialogue between Agnes and her unnamed partner can be very funny (although not to the adolescent Agnes). Try to imagine this boy—visualize a gawky, graceless, not-overly-intelligent teen-ager of your acquaintance. Recall his manner of speech as well as his appearance and try to imitate him when you repeat his words. Agnes would probably do just that when repeating the conversation. Both you (Agnes) and the boy are dreadfully awkward, but in entirely different ways. He is practically tongue-tied, not much of a conversationalist even under ordinary circumstances, but at this moment he is utterly overwhelmed by you. You attempt to make up for your feeling of awkwardness by trying too hard. You are much too enthusiastic, much too determined, much too everything. And of course much too bright for this dull fellow. You are intellectually precocious, but socially backward. The art of small talk, light banter, is totally beyond you.

3. Take your time before speaking the last paragraph. Before you speak these words, you must pull yourself out of the past and back into the present. You are not really contradicting yourself when you say, "Still, I was not unhappy." You are reflecting now on your life *in general* during your adolescent years. You conclude that your life was not an unhappy one. The last line of your monologue, "I postponed it," could be called a surprise ending. You mean that you did not go through the period of turbulence, "storm and stress" that is usually associated with adolescence, until later on.

From *Dance to the Piper* by Agnes de Mille. "Decision"

INTRODUCTION

See pages 97–99 and 268–70 for background.
Agnes' younger sister Margaret possessed the social graces from childhood on. Agnes would follow her mother's unfashionable dictates in dress even as an adult. Margaret, on the other hand, decided all such matters for herself, even as a teen-ager. Naturally pretty, she customarily looked "ravishing." Unlike Agnes, she was "mistress of the wisecrack" and surrounded by boy friends from the age of eleven on. Agnes was cast in the role of chaperone by the ripe old age of fifteen.

Douglass Montgomery, a young actor in this excerpt, was to remain Agnes de Mille's lifelong friend. They would share their driving passion for the stage. Agnes would soon wish to share another kind of passion with her friend "Dug," but no such luck. As for romance, Agnes would be a "late bloomer." Years later she was to fall madly in love with Walter Foy Prude and marry him.

Before her first meeting with Douglass, Agnes had become so terribly discouraged by her lack of proficiency in ballet technique that, at least consciously, she had renounced all thought of going on the stage professionally. Instead she attended the University of California and devoted herself to her academic studies with the same zeal previously reserved for dancing. Yet she still practiced ballet and gave an occasional amateur performance.

Agnes de Mille captures and examines one of the most significant moments in her life in the following selection from her autobiography. As a writer, she has an almost uncanny knack of immortalizing such moments.

AGNES: At the Pasadena Playhouse, Margaret had spotted a young actor she thought she'd like to get better acquainted with. She engineered a meeting, that is, she gave out the order that he was to be brought to the house on a Sunday night, and he was brought. His name was Douglass Montgomery and he turned out to have good manners and a pleasant husky charm. Mag liked him fine. She arranged to take him through the Fairbanks studio, which was the second step in her softening-up routine. He came the following Sunday. Mag was dressed to kill in white silk, a dazzling white coat, a white cloche on her sleek dark hair. She sported gardenias and fake pearls. I thought she looked, as always, just ravishing. I was dressed in a dirty red practice tunic and I had all the living room rugs rolled back to the wall. Mag met him at the garden gate and whisked him around to the tennis court where the lively twanging of rackets and the yelping of our seven dogs gave evidence of Father's Sunday fun. "But what is that going on in the house?" said Douglass, turning his head. "Oh that," said Mag, "never mind about that. That is just my sister Agnes, who practices dancing on Sunday afternoon."

"I would like to see," said Douglass, and although she resisted, he maneuvered her back. There was no use in apologizing for the way I looked. Nobody looked the way I did who expected to be seen by anyone else. "Do you do this where people can watch you?" he asked.

"Well," I said with great misgiving. "This Friday . . . it's just amateur . . ."

"I'll come," said Dug.

Dug came. He stood backstage at the Friday Morning Club and looked me hard in the face. He trembled a little. There were tears of excitement in his eyes. (Dug was only seventeen.) He spoke in a very low voice. He put a cigarette in his mouth, but his lips shook. "Look here. You're no amateur. You're a very great performer. You belong to the world. Get out of the university. Stop this nonsense. Get into the theater. You've got a calling. You've got a duty. It's hard to say. Are you listening to me? You're a great dancer."

No trumpets sound when the important decisions of our life are made. Destiny is made known silently. The wheels turn within our hearts for years and suddenly everything meshes and we are lifted into the next level of progress. In a crowd of fussing clubwomen, overdressed, chattering, impatient to get to their chicken patties and ice cream, the laborious battlements my father had erected with all the sincerity of his heart and life care fell before one sentence. This boy simply said what I had waited all my life to hear.

SUGGESTIONS FOR THE ACTOR

1. When you, as the character Agnes de Mille, describe your sister, Margaret, you the actress should visualize a stunning girl, elegantly dressed, someone you know. Choose for this purpose someone who arouses in you the sorts of feelings Margaret probably evokes in Agnes. What do you think Agnes feels toward her sister? Does she admire her? Envy her? Any other possibilities?

When you speak of Douglass Montgomery, picture a sensitive-looking, charming boy about seventeen years old, someone who attracts you in real life. When he first sees you (Agnes) looking your worst, all dirty, disheveled, perspiring (in contrast to Margaret, who is not only immaculate but dazzling in white silk), what do you want to do? Run and hide? Become gorgeous by waving a magic wand? Apologize for your appearance? Pretend indifference? What *do* you do?

2. Imagine the Friday Morning Club. Visualize it concretely. Exactly where is the stage? Can you describe it? Describe the backstage area. "See" the rows of tables, set for luncheon, facing the stage. What color and material are the tablecloths? Describe the table settings. Picture the overdressed clubwomen, "hear" their noisy chatter and the clatter of dishes as the waiters serve the

food. "Smell" the chicken patties, coffee, etc. "Feel" the floor beneath your ballet slippers, your own dripping perspiration, your rapid heartbeat right after your performance.

3. Now, years after the event, you (as the older Agnes) remember the exact words Dug spoke to you at the club. You treasure the memory. You vividly recall not only his precise words, but his tone of voice and all the visual signs of his excitement. He spoke quietly but with tremendous intensity. He wanted desperately to convince you that you must become a dancer. As you recall his words, you probably cannot help but *act* as he did, even though in all likelihood you (Agnes) are not consciously trying to imitate him.

4. It might be dramatically effective to react silently, as the young Agnes, to Dug's words before returning to the present, that is, before you say, "No trumpets sound when the important decisions of our life are made."

As the young Agnes, how do you react to Douglass' words? First allow his words to "sink in." Once you grasp what he has just told you, what do you want to do? What crucial decision do you make right now, in these unlikely surroundings? Work on your "inner monologue": the actual words that go through your mind as you silently formulate your decision. If you have a strong urge to react physically in some way, go ahead. Do it. You (the actress) can always tone down your reaction later.

When you say, "the laborious battlements my father had erected with all the sincerity of his heart and life care fell before one sentence," you are referring to his repeated attempts to dissuade you from dancing. Throughout your youth, your father, whom you worshiped, made it all too clear that he did not consider dancing a worthy occupation for a person of your intelligence. He had been greatly relieved when you had announced to him that you were giving up your struggle to become a dancer and were registering for college instead. But these words from a seventeen-year-old boy were enough to overturn that decision, permanently.

From *Portrait of Myself* by Margaret Bourke-White. "The Enchanted Steel Mills"

INTRODUCTION

World-famous photographer Margaret Bourke-White began her career almost accidentally. A senior at picturesque Cornell University in the 1920s, where she was preparing for a career as a naturalist, Margaret needed extra cash. All the waitress and student-librarian jobs were filled. Inspired by Cornell's magnificent waterfalls, she turned to her old camera with its cracked lens, took a number of scenic shots and sold them to fellow students. She also sold cover photographs to Cornell's alumni news bulletin and received complimentary letters from alumni. Several suggested that she consider a career as an architectural photographer. Intrigued by this idea, Margaret wanted an unbiased opinion of her work. During her spring vacation she approached a well-known architect in New York City. He and other members of his firm assured her that with her portfolio of photographs she could get work in any architect's office in the country.

After graduation she went to Cleveland and pounded the pavements for work. She began to have moderate success selling photographs of gardens and estates to landscape architects. She hoped to earn enough money from architectural photographs to pay for experimenting with photographs of industry, especially Cleveland's steel mills, which had always fascinated her. Margaret Bourke-White may have derived her sense of excitement about industry from her father, an inventor who had helped to develop new types of printing presses. During her childhood, he had once taken her to see a foundry for presses. The sight of the flowing metal and flying sparks against the blackness had filled her with wild joy. In her autobiography she writes, "This memory shaped the whole course of my career."

Margaret sold her first industrial photograph to a bank, the Union Trust Company, which needed covers for its monthly magazine *Trade Winds*. After that the Union Trust bought one of her pictures every month. The bank allowed her to take whatever industrial shots she fancied and to develop her own style.

She was still not free, however, to conduct the photographic experiments that interested her most, for women were unwelcome inside the steel mills. In *Portrait of Myself* she writes, "They had been prohibited ever since a visiting schoolteacher twenty years earlier had inconsiderately fainted from the heat and fumes."

Margaret had photographed Mrs. John Sherwin's garden. Coincidentally John Sherwin was president of the Union Trust Company and was on the board of directors of "half the firms in town." Margaret decided to ask him for a favor.

MARGARET: John Sherwin, president of Union Trust, was puzzled that a "pretty young girl should want to take pictures in a dirty steel mill." But he was quite willing to send a letter of introduction to his friend Elroy Kulas at Otis Steel.

Mr. Kulas was forceful, short of stature, able. In the twelve years since he had become president, his company's output of steel ingots had quadrupled.

This of course I did not know, but I knew very well why I wanted to photograph the making of those steel ingots; and Mr. Kulas eyed me kindly while I tried to explain.

I do not remember the words I used, but I remember standing there by his massive carved desk, trying to tell him of my belief that there is a power and vitality in industry that makes it a magnificent subject for photography, that it reflects the age in which we live, that the steel mills are at the very heart of industry with the most drama, the most beauty—and that was why I wanted to capture the spirit of steelmaking in photographs.

He must have been a little surprised at the intensity of this twenty-one-year-old girl, possessed of this strange desire to photograph a steel furnace. And I, too, was a little surprised to find myself talking so fearlessly to the first industrial magnate I had ever faced.

But during my camera explorations down in the Flats among the ore boats and bridges I had done a good deal of thinking about these things. To me these industrial forms were all the more beautiful because they were never designed to be beautiful. They had a simplicity of line that came from their direct application to a purpose. Industry, I felt, had evolved an unconscious beauty—often a hidden beauty that was waiting to be discovered. And recorded! That was where I came in.

As I struggled to express these ideas to Mr. Kulas, I remembered to tell him certain things I had decided in advance I must say—to assure him I was not trying to sell him something, that at this stage I wanted only permission to experiment. And he in turn expressed a polite interest in seeing and perhaps purchasing for the company some of the pictures if they turned out well. I said, "Wait till we see what I get, first." And then of course I heard again about the fainting schoolteacher and about the "dangers": the acid fumes, the overpowering heat, the splashing hot metal. I wasn't the fainting kind, I insisted.

Mr. Kulas turned to the portfolio I had brought, looked at the pictures one by one, and stopped to study a photograph of the Sherwin rock garden. It showed little rills from a spring falling through moss-covered stones, with a little lead figure of a Cupid or nymph guarding each rill.

"I think your pictures of flower gardens are very artistic," said Mr. Kulas, looking up, "but how can you find anything artistic in my mill?"

"Please let me try."

And he did.

SUGGESTIONS FOR THE ACTOR

1. Visualize the bank president, John Sherwin, and the president of the steel mill, Elroy Kulas. Picture two important men you have

met in real life, men who bear great responsibility—a school principal, for example. You (Margaret) describe Mr. Kulas as "forceful, short of stature, able." As you describe him, "see" him in your mind's eye. These magnates are busy men, yet both have granted you interviews. What is your (Margaret's) attitude toward each of them? What are their attitudes toward you?

Also visualize your photograph of the Sherwin rock garden, with its little streams guarded by nymphs and cupids.

2. You, Margaret Bourke-White, are relating the story of a significant conversation that took place sometime in the past. Why are you telling this story now? Are you speaking aloud to yourself as you write your autobiography? Are you talking to a friend or an interviewer? Are you lecturing to an audience? Where are you? When is this happening? How old are you? You, the actress, must make all these decisions. As you speak, you (Margaret) gradually begin to relive that experience of long ago. You "see" Mr. Kulas' impressive office as if you were there once more; you even recall the details of the carving on his massive desk.

Here is one possible approach to the end of the monologue: When you say, "Please let me try," you are still deep, deep in the past. This plea is the most intense, urgent line of the entire selection. You want this chance more than anything else in the world. Then you recall how his affirmative decision changed your whole life from that moment on. After many months of struggle, you eventually took pictures the likes of which had never been seen before. Back in the present now, you add, "And he did."

3. The following suggestion is one possible interpretation, by no means the only one. When you expressed your beliefs to Mr. Kulas, you became so caught up in what you were saying that you were almost carried away by your youthful enthusiasm. But you caught yourself in time; you remembered that you must not appear to be selling him "a bill of goods." You wanted only permission to experiment. Your manner changed then, and it changes now as you relive the event. When you say, "As I struggled to express these ideas to Mr. Kulas, I remembered to tell him certain things I had decided in advance," you become more subdued.

4. If you, the actress, are unable to identify with Margaret Bourke-White's passionate desire to photograph steel mills, you will have to substitute a real passion of your own in preparing this

role, something you wish for with all your heart. You should then transfer the intensity of your own desire to the particular circumstances of the character you play. But I suggest that you do not *begin* work on this role with a hunt for a substitute desire; first try to view the world through Margaret's eyes. If possible, read her autobiography, *Portrait of Myself,* and study her photographs, especially the industrial shots. Most important of all, start looking at the world around you, the physical world, in a new way. Even if you have never in your life taken so much as a snapshot with a Brownie camera, find beautiful, interesting, exciting subjects for photographs. Plan the angle from which you would photograph your subject if you had a camera with you. Plan your composition. Try to select at least one good pictorial composition every time you take a walk. Avoid subjects that are commonly considered beautiful, such as pretty faces, fields of daisies, willow trees and the like. Instead, hunt for subjects that are primarily functional, useful, such as bridges or smokestacks or machinery or whatever industrial forms catch your eye and capture your imagination. Sometimes a man-made object against a natural setting can be magnificent, as, for example, Margaret Bourke-White's photograph, captioned, "A coal rig rises like a dinosaur on the shore of Lake Superior," reproduced in her autobiography. Sometimes a natural object juxtaposed against a man-made setting can be striking, such as a lone flower forcing its way through a crack in the concrete.

Nowadays, since the pioneering work of Margaret Bourke-White and others, the concept that industrial forms contain "a hidden beauty * * * waiting to be discovered," is no longer novel. When she was first experimenting, however, Margaret Bourke-White's ideas were unfamiliar and puzzling, even to some of those individuals who helped her most.

From *The Madwoman of Chaillot* by Jean Giraudoux, English text by Maurice Valency.
Act I

INTRODUCTION

This witty, poetic fantasy could be called a modern fairy tale. In the course of a single afternoon all the evil people of the world disappear forever, and the good people live happily ever after. As in fairy tales, each character is either one of the good people or one of the bad ones. The bad people are those who worship money; their greed leads to their downfall.

"SCENE: The café terrace at Chez Francis, on the Place de l'Alma in Paris. * * *

"Chez Francis has several rows of tables set out under its awning. * * *

"TIME: * * * the Spring of next year."

At the beginning of the play it is almost noon. Two of the evil people, "the President" and "the Baron," have formed an international business combine without a name or even a commodity to sell. They join forces with a third customer at the café, "the Prospector," who supplies both. His commodity is oil; he detects it in the drinking water right here. Together they devise a plot to dig up this very section of Paris for petroleum.

The President is more than a little disgruntled by the "raffish individualism" of the inhabitants of this café, for these are the last of the "free people of the earth." One of these good people is Irma, the waitress. "She is twenty. She has the face and figure of an angel."

Irma sees Pierre, a young man, for the first time when a policeman carries him, unconscious, to the café. The policeman had
slugged him in order to prevent his jumping off a bridge. As soon
as Irma sees his face, she falls in love with him.

When he "comes to," the wildly eccentric Countess Aurelia, another of the good people, makes a bet with the police sergeant that
she can convince Pierre life is worth living. She wins her bet easily; Pierre has already seen Irma. Pierre had tried to kill himself
rather than continue in the employ of the wicked Prospector.
Partly for Irma's sake the Countess, affectionately known as "The
Madwoman of Chaillot," refuses to allow the Prospector to take
Pierre away. "I'm holding him because Irma wants me to hold
him," she confesses. "Because if I let him go, it will break her
heart."

When the villains leave, and the Countess learns of the Prospector's horrible scheme, she refuses to take it seriously. She naïvely
supposes the world to be still beautiful and happy. But when she
learns the truth, that the world has changed, she devises a simple
plan to rid the earth of evil: She has Pierre forge a letter supposedly from the Prospector to the President, a letter claiming the
existence of crude oil in the cellar of her home. Since the greedy
ones are all connected like parts of a machine, "If one comes the
rest will follow," and she will then dispose of them all at once.
Pierre escorts the "Madwoman" home. "The others disperse."
Irma is left alone onstage.

IRMA: [*Clearing off the table*] I hate ugliness. I love beauty. I
hate meanness. I adore kindness. It may not seem so grand to
some to be a waitress in Paris. I love it. A waitress meets all
sorts of people. She observes life. I hate to be alone. I love people. But I have never said I love you to a man. Men try to make
me say it. They put their arms around me—I pretend I don't
see it. They pinch me—I pretend I don't feel it. They kiss me—
I pretend I don't know it. They take me out in the evening and
make me drink—but I'm careful, I never say it. If they don't
like it, they can leave me alone. Because when I say I love you
to Him, He will know just by looking in my eyes that many

have held me and pinched me and kissed me, but I have never said I love you to anyone in the world before. Never. No. [*Looking off in the direction in which* PIERRE *has gone, she whispers softly*] I love you.

SUGGESTIONS FOR THE ACTOR

1. Even though you, Irma, do not refer to Pierre at the beginning of your soliloquy, your last line, "I love you," addressed to him, is certainly no afterthought. Earlier in Act I, you fall in love with Pierre, literally at first sight. Ordinary experience is transfigured by your love. The extraordinary simplicity of your soliloquy is close to poetry. The lyricism of your words reflects the wonder, even the rapture, in your heart.

If you, the actress, feel this emotion easily, well and good. If you are having difficulty, however, an "emotion-memory" exercise may be helpful. (If you were to act the entire play, it would probably be easier to build up to this emotional peak.)

Try to recall an important event in your own life that produced in you a feeling similar to your character's. It might be an experience of love or an intense "crush," but it could also conceivably be a different sort of occurrence that produced a sense of joy, wonder, exaltation. Don't pick an event so recent that you are still overwhelmed by emotion. When you have chosen an appropriate incident, *do not* strive to recapture the emotion directly. Sit comfortably, close your eyes and try to recall all the specific sights, sounds, smells and other physical sensations that led up to and accompanied the emotion. Try to remember each sensation in great detail. Speaking these recollections aloud will help set them in your mind, but don't mention what happened, or how you felt about it. Don't say, for example, "After the dance we walked home in the moonlight," or, "I was so happy!" *Describe your sensory impressions only*. The feelings you want to evoke should come back to you automatically, without being forced. Repeat the procedure several times, adding more detail if you can. If the incident you first selected fails to produce the desired emotion, select a different event. This valuable exercise was described by Edward Dwight Easty in his book *On Method Acting* (New York, House of Collectibles, Inc., 1973) in the chapter entitled "Affective Memory."

2. You, the actress, may choose to speak this soliloquy as if to yourself, or you may prefer to address the audience directly.

If you decide to speak this monologue to yourself in a realistic style, your first lines may refer to something in your (Irma's) recent experience. For example, when you, as Irma, say, "I hate ugliness," you may be thinking of the Prospector or the President, his face contorted with greed. When you say, "I love beauty," you may be thinking of Pierre.

On the other hand, since this play is not written in a straight, realistic style, you may decide to speak directly to the audience. If you choose to take the audience into your confidence, you (Irma) may simply be telling them at first what you are really like and how you feel about your work.

3. But no matter which of the above choices you, the actress, make, when you say the abstract words "ugliness" or "beauty," "meanness" or "kindness," think of a vivid, concrete image. It can be anything or anyone that will produce in you (Irma) an intense feeling of hate or love. If, for example, you choose to think of the Prospector when you say, "I hate ugliness," then you must "see" an ugly, hateful person. Since you are not performing the entire play, you must draw upon your own real-life memories for your ugly image. Similarly, when you say "I love you" to the absent Pierre, you must visualize him. Think of someone you, the actress, really love.

From *His Eye Is on the Sparrow,* an autobiography by Ethel Waters (with Charles Samuels)

INTRODUCTION

Ethel Waters was born out of wedlock in Chester, Pennsylvania, to a twelve-year-old rape victim. Her mother, Louise, did not give her the love she craved, probably because Louise could not help associating Ethel with that terrifying experience. In her early years Ethel lived with her grandmother, Sally Anderson, whom she called "Mom." Since her grandmother worked as a sleep-in domestic, Ethel was left on her own most of the time. She was poor and she was tough. Sally Anderson wanted a better life for Ethel, but Sally was seldom around. From earliest childhood Ethel was exposed to the sordid side of life—drunkenness, prostitution and drug addiction, which she always associated with misery and suffering. She was therefore never tempted by any of these vices. She did steal food, however, when she was hungry. Her aunts, with whom she sometimes lived, spent what little money they had on liquor. Her own mother, whom she called "Louise" and then "Momweaze," never drank heavily. For comfort Louise turned to fundamentalist religion. Ethel married at the age of thirteen and soon regretted it; her husband mistreated her badly. After leaving him, she worked in a Philadelphia hotel as a chambermaid, among other menial jobs.

On Ethel's seventeenth birthday she sang publicly for the first time, as an amateur, in a Philadelphia saloon. Two professional vaudevillians heard her; they hired her for a Baltimore engagement. Ethel became a singing sensation when she introduced a

new blues number: "The St. Louis Blues." She became known as
"Sweet Mama Stringbean" because she was so tall and thin. From
honky-tonk vaudeville entertainer, she became a top Harlem
night-club performer (at such night spots as Edmond's Cellar)
and recording star, then a leading actress. She made famous such
all-time song hits as "Dinah," "Takin' a Chance on Love" and
"Stormy Weather." According to her autobiography, when she appeared on Broadway in the musical revue *As Thousands Cheer,*
she became the highest-paid woman performer on Broadway.

At a party some years later Ethel spoke with a stranger, a white
woman, about a novel that had deeply affected her. She did not
realize that she was talking to the wife of Dubose Heyward, author of that novel, *Mamba's Daughters.*

And I went on to tell her how and why *Mamba's Daughters* had
held me spellbound. * * * Mamba's family was just like my own,
with Mamba herself almost the image of Sally Anderson; her daughter Hagar like Momweaze, and Hagar's daughter Lissa being a girl
like myself, illegitimate and going out into the world to become a
successful singer.

To everyone else, I know, Mamba is the main character in the
story * * * but not to me. Hagar dies in the middle of the book, but
for me she lived right on through the last page, and ever afterward.

Hagar had held me spellbound. In Hagar was all my mother's
shock, bewilderment, and insane rage at being hurt and her fierce,
primitive religion. But Hagar, fighting on in a world that had
wounded her so deeply, was more than my mother to me. She was all
Negro women lost and lonely in the white man's antagonistic world.

Dorothy Heyward was impressed. The Heywards subsequently
dramatized the story, making Hagar the dominating role, and
offered the lead to Ethel.

Mamba's Daughters was now a straight and simple melodramatic
story, the story of Hagar, a lumbering, half-crazy colored woman
with a single passion: seeing that her beautiful Lissa has a better life
than she's known. The climax of the play comes when Hagar stran-
gles Gilly Bluton, a sporting man who has raped Lissa and is planning to blackmail her.

Ethel Waters later received wide acclaim for her performance in the play *The Member of the Wedding*. She received Academy Award nominations for her excellent acting in the movie *Pinky* and in the film version of *The Member of the Wedding*. She performed on television and radio as well as in more than a dozen Broadway productions and nine motion pictures. She devoted herself to religion until her death in 1977, at the age of eighty.

ETHEL: *Mamba's Daughters* had its preview opening on New Year's Eve and its regular opening on January 3, 1939, which I still remember as the most thrilling and important experience of my life as a performer. And my whole life, too, except for when I found God.

I was the first colored woman, the first actress of my race, ever to be starred on Broadway in a dramatic play. And we opened at the Empire Theatre, which has the richest theatrical history of any showhouse in America.

And the Empire's star dressing room was mine on that opening night. While the carriage trade was arriving outside, I sat at the dressing table where all the great actresses, past and present, had sat as they made up their faces and wondered what the first-night verdict would be—Maude Adams, Ethel Barrymore, Helen Hayes, Katharine Cornell, Lynn Fontanne, and all the others, now dead, who had brought the glitter of talent and beauty and grace to that old stage.

Yes, there I was, the Ethel who had never been coddled or kissed as a child, the Ethel who was too big to fit, but big enough to be scullion and laundress and bus girl while still a kid. And I could have looked back over my shoulder and blown a kiss to all my yesterdays in show business. I had been pushed on the stage and prodded into becoming Sweet Mama Stringbean and the refined singer of risqué songs in Edmond's Cellar, and on and up to best-selling records, Broadway musicals, and being the best-paid woman in all show business.

That was *the* night of my professional life, sitting there in that old-fashioned dressing room that was a bower of flowers. The

night I'd been born for, and God was in the room with me. I
talked to God until the callboy came to say:

"Five minutes, Miss Waters."

Five minutes more to get ready to be Hagar and tell the story
of my mother in front of the carriage trade. I asked God, "Oh,
stay with me! Lord, keep Your hand on my shoulder! Please,
God!"

Then I got up and started off on that terrifying last mile a
performer has to walk every opening night. Into the wings, a
pause there for a moment waiting for the cue—and then on,
Ethel Waters, to glory or . . .

I was Hagar that night. Hagar and Momweeze and all of us.

Seventeen curtain calls that opening night for me alone.

I couldn't stand it. Half collapsing with joy and humility, I
pushed through the kissing mouths and the slaps on the back to
my dressing room where Elida was waiting.

"How do you feel now, Miss Waters?" she said. "And what
are you thinking?"

"Elida, if I died here and now," I told her, "it would be all
right. For this is the pinnacle, and there will never be anything
better or higher or bigger for me."

SUGGESTIONS FOR THE ACTOR

In this monologue you, Ethel, mentally relive a past experience
as if it were happening in the here and now.

1. Imagine the physical surroundings. Visualize the elegant, his-
toric old theatre, the star dressing room filled with flowers, the
backstage area, the "wings" (offstage area on each side of the
stage) and the brightly lit stage facing the darkness of the audience. "See" your own reflection in the dressing-room mirrors as
you apply finishing touches to your makeup. Can you, the actress,
recall the contours of your own face? What are you wearing as
you (Ethel) apply makeup? As you make your first stage entrance? "Feel" the makeup on your skin; "feel" the warmth of the
stage lights focused on you. "Smell" the flowers in your dressing

room, the grease paint, the face powder. As you wait in the wings for your cue, "hear" the voices from onstage.

2. What is your (Ethel's) attitude toward these physical surroundings? In your mind, what do they represent? In this monologue you list the great actresses who once used this star dressing room. As you (the actress) prepare this portion of your role, think of particular people whose outstanding accomplishments fill you with awe, reverence. They need not necessarily be actresses. Of course, if you do feel awed and inspired by these first ladies of the theatre, so much the better. In that case, visualize each of these stars in turn. You may need to hunt for their photographs and brief biographies in your local library.

When you (Ethel) speak of the "carriage trade," you are referring to the wealthy, who rode in carriages in days gone by.

3. Give yourself time for a drastic mood change after you speak with reverence of "all the others, now dead, who had brought the glitter of talent and beauty and grace to that old stage." For then you remember your own sordid youth. What a contrast! You were always unwanted, too big to fit comfortably on anyone's lap. What is your attitude toward your own past? Are you bitter or nostalgic, or a little of both as you remember your beginnings? What do you mean when you say, "And I could have looked back over my shoulder and blown a kiss to all my yesterdays in show business"? Do you mean that you could have kissed your past goodbye and good riddance? Or do you feel nostalgia, even affection for the old days and the old Ethel?

4. Do you, the actress, believe in God? Have you ever asked God for help? If so, remember that occasion as you work on the section of the monologue in which you (Ethel) turn to God. If you, the actress, have never turned to God for support, what was your source of emotional or spiritual strength at a time of great need?

5. When you say, "and then on, Ethel Waters, to glory or . . ." what are the words you think to yourself but do not express aloud? Why do you stop talking at that moment?

6. Take ample time to remember your (Ethel's) act of artistic creation—your transformation into Hagar onstage—before you go on to think, and then speak, of the curtain calls. Seventeen curtain calls would thrill any actress; you (Ethel), who never knew

love as a child, would be especially overwhelmed by all that approval. Nevertheless, it is not primarily the applause that gives you your feeling of supreme fulfillment. It is your own artistic creation that makes you happy. The performance itself is "the most thrilling and important experience" in your professional life, even more exciting and satisfying than the applause and praise which you receive afterward.

Have you, the actress, ever accomplished anything in your life which makes you proud and happy whenever you think of it? If so, concentrate on recalling in minute detail all your sense impressions at the time of that achievement, when you prepare this part of the monologue. Also remember an occasion in your own life when you were highly praised for a real accomplishment. How did you react to that expression of honest appreciation?

Keep in mind, however, that if the character's emotion comes easily to you, if a particular circumstance in the scene seems completely real to you, then you need not seek a comparable experience in your own life to substitute for your character's experience. The outstanding actress and teacher Uta Hagen makes this point in her excellent book about acting, *Respect for Acting*, written with Haskel Frankel, in the chapter entitled "Substitution" (New York, Macmillan Publishing Co., Inc., 1973): "If you ask me if it is necessary to make a substitution for something that is already real to you, my answer is NO." If that particular circumstance in the play is already real to you, then "you have already made the substitution" without conscious effort, "intuitively."

In her discussion of substitution Miss Hagen stresses the following concept, a difficult but important one to grasp. Onstage, in performance, you should no longer be recollecting the details of the personal event in your own life that you chose as a substitution for something in the play. Dwelling on all those details (sights, sounds, smells, tastes, etc.) was, or should have been, your "homework." You should then have transferred "the *essence* of the experience (not the original event) to the scene." I interpret the word "essence" in this context to mean *the way the experience affected you physically and psychologically, what it made you do*. The ultimate purpose of remembering your own personal experience is to help you find truthful, "spontaneous" *actions* for the character you play, according to Uta Hagen. In performance, concentrate on your character's circumstances.

7. What is your (Ethel's) relationship to Elida, evidently your backstage dresser? There is no other mention of her in this autobiography. You (the actress) are therefore free to imagine her, her behavior toward you and vice-versa in any way you wish, so long as your imaginings are not contradicted by the quoted conversation.

Monologues for Young Men

From *The Amen Corner* by James Baldwin.
Act III

INTRODUCTION

This play by the world-famous American black author James
Baldwin takes place in the tenement home and church of Sister
Margaret Alexander in the black ghetto of Harlem. "The church
is on a level above the apartment and should give the impression
of dominating the family's quarters." On the lower level is a
kitchen and a bedroom with a small door leading to the rest of the
apartment.

Margaret is the pastor of this fundamentalist Negro church. We
learn during the course of the play that ten years before, she had
left her husband, a jazz musician named Luke, to devote her life
to religion instead of to husband and family. She had taken her
small son, David, with her to New York and tried to instill in him
a similar "merciless piety." David is now eighteen years old. Until
recently, he would often play the piano for the congregation,
showing remarkable talent even though he has been attending
music school for only three months.

We learn that Margaret did not really turn to religion because
of any great "calling." Her motive was fear, terror of the pain of
living in the world. At the time that she left Luke, she had given
birth to a dead baby, a little girl. Margaret had suffered unbearable anguish. She loved Luke deeply, passionately then, and she
still does. But she believed that God would protect her and her
son from the pain and evil of life, life in the black community,
only if they both renounced the world completely.

Commenting on white-black relations in this country, James Baldwin wrote in his introduction to this play:

> There has certainly not been enough progress to solve Sister Margaret's dilemma: how to treat her husband and her son as men and at the same time to protect them from the bloody consequences of trying to be a man in this society. * * * She is in the church because her society has left her no other place to go.

A few months before, some jazz musicians entered the church and heard David play. Instead of David's drawing them into the church, they drew him out. They wanted him to join a jazz "combo." At that crucial moment came David's realization that his true calling is music, not religion. He has not been able to pray since then. He has been feeling guilty and confused, unable to go and unable to stay, afraid to tell his mother the truth.

Then one day his father arrives in New York to play his trombone in a jazz club. David goes downtown to hear him and discovers that his father is a gifted musician, one of the best. Luke recognizes his son. The next day he comes to Margaret's house, just "to say hello," but Luke is dying of tuberculosis. The disease has been aggravated by bad living—whiskey, cigarettes, etc. David helps him to the bed onstage, where he remains throughout the play. Earlier, Margaret had wanted David to accompany her to Philadelphia, where she had agreed to preach a sermon, but David now decides to stay home instead. As a child David had been told that his father had deserted his mother; he learns now that Margaret had left Luke.

Margaret leaves for Philadelphia despite her husband's condition. During her absence members of her congregation notice David entering bars, smoking cigarettes and associating with "common-looking" girls.

David has one intimate conversation with his father on the Saturday following Luke's arrival. He tells Luke how much he had needed him as a child. He wants to cry whenever he thinks of his father. Luke then gives David this advice: "Son—don't try to get away from the things that hurt you." Unlike Margaret, Luke wants his son to live in this world—to experience joy and pain, both part of living and loving.

It is early the next morning, Sunday, before church service. "A bright, quiet day." David enters the apartment "suffering from a hangover, still a little drunk." He looks in on Luke, then enters the kitchen. His mother (who had returned from Philadelphia the previous afternoon) walks into the room, dressed in white for the service. David claims that he was visiting friends, and that it grew so late he had to stay overnight, but Margaret smells the whiskey on his breath. She slaps him. Furious, heartbroken, she asks him why he got drunk. He says that he can never play the piano in church again. He is leaving tonight, "going on the road with some other guys." Margaret urges him to pray, to seek safety in the church. She warns him: "There's boys like you all over this city, filling up the gin mills and standing on the corners, running down alleys, tearing themselves to pieces with knives and whiskey and dope and sin!" But she knows he won't listen to her. She tells him that young folks never listen until it's too late.

DAVID: And if I listened—what would happen? What do you think would happen if I listened? You want me to stay here, getting older, getting sicker—hating you? You think I want to hate you, Mama? You think it don't tear me to pieces to have to lie to you all the time. Yes, because I been lying to you, Mama, for a long time now! I don't want to tell no more lies. I don't want to keep on feeling so bad inside that I have to go running down them alleys you was talking about—that alley right outside this door!—to find something to help me hide—to hide—from what I'm feeling. Mama, I want to be a man. It's time you let me be a man. You got to let me go. [*A pause*] If I stayed here—I'd end up worse than Daddy—because I wouldn't be doing what I know I got to do—I *got* to do! I've seen your life—and now I see Daddy—and I love you, I love you both!— but I've got my work to do, something's happening in the world out there, I got to go! I know you think I don't know what's happening, but I'm beginning to see—something. Every time I play, every time I listen, I see Daddy's face and yours, and so many faces—who's going to speak for all that, Mama? Who's going to speak for all of us? I can't stay home. Maybe I can say something—one day—maybe I can say something in music that's never been said before. Mama—*you* knew this day was coming.

SUGGESTIONS FOR THE ACTOR

1. You, David, are described at the beginning of the scene as "suffering from a hangover, still a little drunk." You probably have a splitting headache. Loud noises may make your head feel even worse. The inside of your mouth may feel dry and have a sour taste. You may be suffering from nausea and other effects of an upset stomach. Where were you last night? Did you sleep at all? If not, you may have additional problems caused by the combination of liquor and lack of sleep—grogginess, occasional dizziness (especially when you move suddenly), lack of complete motor control and slightly slurred speech.

Try to recall occasions in your own life when you had these symptoms, either singly or in combination. Recall these physical sensations as precisely as you can. You need not have experienced a hangover to know how a terrible headache feels, or nausea, etc. Have you ever stayed up all or nearly all night? If so, remember exactly how you felt the next day.

Be careful not to exaggerate your (David's) outward condition. You are not roaring drunk. You were only slightly intoxicated when you first entered the apartment. In fact, your mother's hard slap may have sobered you up completely. Your speech may be slightly slurred at times, your movements not quite steady, but these would be subtle, slight deviations from your normal speech and movement.

Here is an old but still valid bit of advice on how to act drunk: Drunken people do not *try* to stagger or to slur their words. They *try*, unsuccessfully, to walk steadily and to pronounce their words correctly.

2. Visualize Margaret. Picture a woman you love in real life, your own mother, perhaps. You (David) want to convince her to let you be a man. How do you go about it? If you fail to convince her one way, you try another tack. You are aware of her reactions to your various arguments. When you pause, you probably expect

her to respond to your demand—"You got to let me go!" She says nothing, however; you must try a new approach.

Your (David's) attitude toward your mother is ambivalent. You love her, yet you fear her. You resent her in many ways. Because she never allowed a phonograph in the house, you never heard any of your father's beautiful recordings until this week. She took you away from your father when you needed him most, and she lied to you about him all these years. He never walked out on you; he never would have done such a thing. She makes you feel guilty all the time, although that is not her intention. Why then do you love her so much? Imagine the good as well as the bad aspects of your relationship. Imagine some tender moments which you two have shared.

Most of us have mixed feelings sometimes about those we love. Do you (the actor) ever resent your own mother? Are you sometimes afraid of her? Why? Remember some of the best and worst moments that you two have shared.

3. Have you, the actor, ever been tortured by feelings of guilt? If so, what did you do to rid yourself of those feelings? Did you find relief? Was the relief permanent? As the character David, you sought "something" to help you hide, bury your bad feelings. You found temporary solace in liquor and sex, but now you want to cast out those guilt feelings once and for all. You face your mother with the truth.

4. Your dream, your vision of your future is not clear to you yet, but you (David) are "beginning to see—something." When you play or listen to music, you see the faces of your family and a great many other faces as well. You, the actor, should visualize the faces of people important to *you* as you act this passage. You (David) want to speak for all your people through your music. What feelings might you express musically?

Do you, the actor, have a burning ambition? If so, it may be helpful to "see" a vision of your own future as you work on your role.

5. You (David) probably notice the change that has come over your mother when you say, "Mama—*you* knew this day was coming." Before you speak this last line, take the time to visualize her change of expression. Then allow this insight to dawn on you: In her heart, she knew all along that you would go. You have at last succeeded in convincing her to let you be a man. You are free!

From *The Rainmaker* by N. Richard Nash.
Act I

This romantic play is set "in a western state on a summer day in a time of drought." The Curry ranch has been hard hit. Vegetation has withered everywhere and great numbers of livestock have died.

The Curry family consists of a father, his two grown sons and his grown daughter, Lizzie. "At first glance, she seems a woman who can cope with all the aspects of her life." Lizzie runs the household with tender care and admirable efficiency. But "Here she is, twenty-seven years old, and no man outside the family has loved her or found her beautiful." Although she tries to hide her loneliness from her sympathetic family, she hungers for love.

Her father and brothers are not deceived. They have been trying their best to find a husband for her, but without any success. They rode into town that afternoon to invite File to supper that evening. He is the Sheriff's deputy, a divorced man, whom Lizzie secretly likes. She has prepared a company meal "fit for a king," dressed for the occasion and placed an extra chair at the table. When the men return, however, they reluctantly admit that File refused the invitation. Her brothers cause her further distress when they tell her that to catch a man, a woman must hide her intelligence and pretend to be a silly, giggling flirt. Aching inwardly, Lizzie rebels to the core against this advice.

Just then the outside door swings open and a stranger steps

onto the threshhold. Bill Starbuck "is a big man, lithe, agile—a loud braggart, a gentle dreamer. He carries a short hickory stick— it is his weapon, his pointer, his magic wand, his pride of manhood."

He calls himself a "rainmaker"; he tries to convince the family that he can produce rain for their parched land. Lizzie calls his claim "bunk." Noah, the oldest son, rigid, ever practical, self-righteous, the only completely unromantic member of the family, agrees with Lizzie. Jim, the youngest, naïve, childlike despite his manly appearance, is easily taken in by Starbuck's tall tale and ingratiating manner. H. C. Curry, their father, is a powerfully built, capable man, but he has his dreams too. He recognizes Starbuck for the fake he is; nevertheless something about this "rainmaker" captures H.C.'s imagination. He wants to hear more. Starbuck offers him a deal: "One hundred dollars in advance—and inside of twenty-four hours you'll have rain!" Lizzie's father asks Starbuck how he would do it. Starbuck replies, "Now don't ask me no questions." Lizzie argues, "Why? It's a fair question! How will you do it?"

(Starbuck has noticed the extra place at the table; he is extremely observant. He later asserts that he knew he had a deal here the minute he saw *four* people and *five* places set. He said to himself, "Starbuck, your name's written right on that chair!")

The Curry house "is strongly masculine in its basic structure— brick and hand hewn beams and such—but it shows LIZZIE's hand" in the furnishings and decorations. "We see a comfortable kitchen on the [actor's] left; the rest of the downstairs living area is a combination of living and dining room."

It is a scorchingly hot day, around suppertime.

STARBUCK: [*left center*] What do you care how I do it, sister, as long as it's done! But I'll tell you how I'll do it! I'll lift this stick and take a long swipe at the sky and let down a shower of hailstones as big as canteloupes! I'll shout out some good old Nebraska cuss words and you turn around and there's a lake where your corral used to be! Or I'll just sing a little tune maybe and it'll sound so pretty and sound so sad you'll weep and your old man will weep and the sky will get all misty-like and shed the prettiest tears you ever did see! How'll I do it?! Girl, I'll just do it! * * *

Sister, the last place I brought rain is now called Starbuck—they named it after me! Dry? I tell you, those people didn't have enough damp to blink their eyes! So I get out my big wheel and my rolling drum and my yella hat with the three little feathers in it! I look up at the sky and I say: "Cumulus!" I say: "Cumulonimbus! Nimbulo-cumulus!" And pretty soon—way up there—there's a teeny little cloud the size of a mare's tail—and then over there—there's another cloud lookin' like a white-washed chicken house! And then I look up and all of a sudden there's a herd of white buffalo stampedin' across the sky! And then, sister-of-all-good-people, down comes the rain! [*Crosses to door right*] Rain in buckets, rain in barrels, fillin' the lowlands, floodin' the gullies! And the land is as green as the valley of Adam! And when I rode out of there I looked behind me and I see the prettiest colors in the sky—green, blue, purple, gold—colors to make you cry! And me?! I'm ridin' right through that rainbow!—Well, how about it? Is it a deal?

SUGGESTIONS FOR THE ACTOR

1. You, Starbuck, are indeed a liar and a "con" man, but your intentions are far from evil. You want to help these people; in fact you do help nearly every character in the play. Not only do you succeed for the first time in bringing rain; you enable Lizzie to see herself through your admiring eyes. Once she stops thinking of herself as plain and undesirable, she can and does find true love.

You are a dreamer and a poet. Fervently, desperately you long for real magical powers.

Later in the play you tell Lizzie that you have two brothers with special gifts. Fred is a doctor with marvelous healing powers. Arny can sing, "and when he's singin', that song is *there!*—and never leaves you!"

You confide in her: "I used to think—why ain't *I* blessed like

Fred or Arny? Why am I just a nothin' man, with nothin' special to my name?"

We, the audience, never know whether there is any truth to this story, but the *feeling* you express is real enough.

Your most serious fault is that you see beauty, romance only in your dreams. Always on the move, you don't take the time to recognize the beauty, the miracle of ordinary life. As Lizzie tells you, "You ain't got no world—except the one you make up inside your head."

You both agree finally that while it is no good to live only in dreams, it is no better to live without any dreams at all.

By the end of the play we learn these few facts about you: You are wanted by the police in several states for deceiving the public. In Kansas you sold four hundred tickets to a Rain Festival, but "No rain, no festival!" In Nebraska you peddled a thousand pairs of smoked eyeglasses to see an eclipse of the sun, but "No eclipse." You sold six hundred "Tornado Rods" to save a town from tornado damage. That town was later blown off the map.

You, the actor, must supply the rest of your (Starbuck's) past life yourself, out of your own fertile imagination. After reading the play several times if possible, answer the questions on the "Actor's Check List," beginning on page 336.

2. Has anyone ever tried to sell you (the actor) a "bill of goods"? Have you ever encountered a high-pressure, smooth-talking salesman? Try to remember his physical appearance, his voice, manner, gestures and movements as clearly as you can. Which, if any, of his outer traits, including his way of talking, can you incorporate into your role? What did his outer traits suggest to you about his inner character? Can you use any of his character traits in developing your role? If so, which ones?

3. The following is a useful theatre game described in *Improvisation for the Theatre* by Viola Spolin (Evanston, Ill., Northwestern University Press, 1963). It involves the use of gibberish, or meaningless combinations of nonsense sounds, "the substitution of shaped sounds for recognizable words. It should not be confused with 'double talk,' where actual words are inverted or mispronounced in order to scramble the meaning." Gibberish should be spoken fluently, so that it sounds to the listener like a foreign language spoken by a native. The sounds do not really

symbolize ideas, however, the way words do. Practice making as many different sounds as possible, exaggerating your mouth movements and varying your tone.

Before beginning this game, try asking other members of the group to perform simple physical actions such as standing up, sitting down or opening a window. Indicate your command with a gesture accompanied by gibberish; use a variety of meaningless sounds such as *"Gallorusheo!"* or *"moolosay!"* or *"rallavo!"*

Here is the game itself, which Viola Spolin entitles "Gibberish ⌗1—Demonstration": Sell or demonstrate something to the audience in gibberish. Then repeat the procedure, but this time "pitch" what you are selling or demonstrating—in other words, *direct* what you are saying to specific members of the audience. Sell directly to them. See them; don't just stare, pretending to see.

What was the difference between the first selling or demonstration and the second? Which playing was more intense? Why?

4. Another game: Now, as Starbuck, sell your "magic" directly to Lizzie. Really see her. In both this exercise and the monologue itself, deliver your sales pitch to a particular member of the audience whom you think of as Lizzie, or to an actress playing the part onstage. In this game speak only in gibberish, or if you prefer, you may utter sounds which have no meaning in this context, such as letters of the alphabet or numbers. Don't try to translate individual words or phrases of your monologue into an invented language. You (Starbuck) want to convince Lizzie that you can make rain, but you (the actor) may not use words to help you. You must depend solely on your tone of voice, your face, your body, movements and gestures, including the gestures you make with your (Starbuck's) hickory stick—your "weapon * * * pointer * * * magic wand * * * pride of manhood." Try to capture the intense enthusiasm, the fast talking and loud bragging of the supersalesman, as well as your (Starbuck's) gentler moods, your dreamlike flights of lyricism.

If an actress plays Lizzie onstage either in this game or during your performance of the monologue, she should keep in mind that Lizzie was deeply hurt and angry just before your (Starbuck's) arrival. She may therefore treat you in a more hostile manner than she would otherwise have done, in happier circumstances.

Observe Lizzie's reactions. The more she resists, the harder you try, changing your approach if necessary.

5. "Feel" the heat. Are you (Starbuck) dripping with perspiration? Where? Are your clothes sticking to your skin? What do you do to cool off?

From *Native Son* (The Biography of a Young American) by Paul Green and Richard Wright. Scene 4

INTRODUCTION

This play, based on the novel *Native Son* by Richard Wright, depicts the rage and frustration of a poverty-stricken young black man living in a Chicago slum around 1940. Bigger Thomas' rage is caused by degrading, brutalizing social conditions and by his sense of utter powerlessness. The inevitable result of his consuming hatred and fear of white society is tragedy—and death.

The play begins in the Thomas apartment, where all four members of the family sleep in the same room. Bigger, "a Negro youth about twenty or twenty-one years old," sleeps on the floor with his twelve-year-old brother. His mother and teen-age sister share the only bed. The family is on relief. Bigger's rage is first depicted when he kills a rat with ferocious intensity, calling it "old Dalton." Mr. Dalton is, on the one hand, the wealthy white landlord who owns this terrible slum, charging exorbitant rent; on the other hand, he contributes to Negro charities. A well-meaning social worker arrives. She plans to help Bigger get a job as chauffeur in Mr. Dalton's own household.

In the next scene Bigger and some of his friends are about to commit a robbery, but when the others learn that Bigger is carrying a gun and knife, they "want no part of him." Bigger terrorizes two people in this scene, revealing the depths of his hate and rage.

In Scene 3, Bigger is hired by the Daltons. Two of his duties will be to act as chauffeur and to tend the furnace. The final deci-

sion in his favor is made by Mrs. Dalton. "Thin, almost ascetic"
and totally blind, she is kind to Bigger. Her daughter, Mary Dalton, "a slender, pale-faced girl of some twenty-two or three," is a
rebel. Bored, disillusioned, often drunk, she is a leftist politically.
She urges Bigger to join a union and asks him a number of personal questions. As with everyone else in the Dalton household,
he barely responds to her, afraid to say much more than "Yes-
sum." She orders him to drive her to a political meeting that night,
to be followed by a celebration. She wants him to meet her leftist
friends.

At the opening of Scene 4, Bigger and Mary Dalton have just
returned from the celebration, late at night. She is quite drunk and
he helps her to her bedroom. Mary pulls Bigger into the room,
against his will. He keeps saying, "ain't my job." She tells him she
wishes she were black too—"down there with you." She touches
his hair and his cheek. Bigger is terrified of being found there.
"They kill me—" he says. She falls and he lifts her into his arms.
She wants him to let her go now but he doesn't. She is so drunk
that she loses consciousness. He stares at her, fascinated, then carries her to the bed. He touches her body, then desperately wants
to get away. Suddenly the blind Mrs. Dalton calls Mary's name
and enters the room. Bigger panics, but he makes no sound. She
checks on her daughter and is about to leave, when Bigger sighs.
Mrs. Dalton turns, startled, and Mary begins to mumble as if waking up. "Quick as a flash and with an instinctive action, BIGGER
picks up a pillow and pushes it down against MARY's face," to prevent her from revealing his presence. He ignores her struggle, concentrating on Mrs. Dalton, who remains unaware of what is happening. He presses the pillow with tremendous strength. At last
Mary stops struggling. Mrs. Dalton leaves.

*For a moment there is no sound or movement; then with a
deep, short gasp of relieved tension, BIGGER falls to the
floor, catching the weight of his body upon his hands and
knees. His chest heaves in and out as though he had just
completed a hard foot-race. Gradually, his breathing sub-
sides, and he stands slowly up, looking at the door. His*

body is relaxed now, the burden of fear gone from him. Then he looks toward the bed, his whole attitude changing, his body becoming taut again. He takes a step forward, then stops uncertainly. He stares at the white form, his face now devoid of that former hard concentration. With a quick movement, he springs to the bed, bends, and stares down at MARY'S *face. Slowly his right hand goes up into the air, the fingers sensitively poised, until again he assumes the same position in which he was standing and looking when the white blur of* MRS. DALTON *first roused him. He stares anxiously at* MARY'S *face, as though a dreadful knowledge were on the threshold of his consciousness. His right hand moves timidly toward* MARY *and touches her, then is jerked quickly away. He touches her head, gently rolls it from side to side, then puts his hands behind him as if they had suffered some strange and sudden hurt.*

BIGGER: [*In a whisper*] Naw—naw —— [*For a moment he stands looking at the still form, as though it had in some manner deeply offended him. Once more he places his hand upon* MARY'S *head. This time it remains there and his body does not move. He mumbles frenziedly*] Naw—naw—naw —— [*He is silent for an instant, then whispers*] I didn't do it —— [*He takes a quick step back*] I didn't, I tell you, I didn't. Wake up, wake up, Miss Dalton. [*His voice takes on a note of pleading*] Miss Dalton, Miss Mary —— [*For a second he stands, then straightens up suddenly. He turns, walks swiftly to the door, opens it, and looks out into the darkness. All is quiet. He walks back to the center of the room and stands looking at the bed. He mumbles piteously*] Naw—naw—naw— I didn't do it —— I didn't go to do it —— [*In a clear, sober, deep voice, as if all his faculties were suddenly alive*] They'll say I done it—I'm black and they'll say I done it —— [*Again he bends over the bed*] I didn't go to do it. You know I didn't. I'm just working here. I didn't want to come here to work. You know I didn't. I was scared—I didn't want to come to your room—you made me come —— [*His voice dies out of him in a sob, and he is silent. Far away a clock booms the hour. Slowly his body straightens with intent and purpose. Looking back over his shoulder, at the door, he slides his hands under* MARY'S *body and lifts her in his arms. He turns un-decidedly about and sees himself in a mirror on the dressing-table*] Don't you look at me—don't say I done it—I didn't, I tell you —— [*For a moment the image in the mirror holds him fascinated. He clasps* MARY *tightly to him as if to protect her and himself. Then suddenly, vehemently, to the image in the mirror, as the hum of the furnace switching itself on is heard below*] Naw—ain't nothin' happened—ain't nothin' happened —— [*He listens to the furnace draft. He jerks his head up as if struck by a smashing thought. He goes through the door with the body of* MARY *in his arms*]

SUGGESTIONS FOR THE ACTOR

1. You need to find a way to build up to this intensely emotional monologue, the devastating climax of Scene 4. One possible approach: As a preparatory exercise, act Scene 4 in its entirety. You will need two actresses to help you out. For the smothering sequence, however, use a doll or some other inanimate object to represent Mary, so that you can really press down on the pillow with all your strength. By the time Mrs. Dalton leaves the room, you should be utterly exhausted, physically as well as emotionally. You may wish to act the scene leading up to your soliloquy in your own words, keeping to the actions provided in the script.

2. To act any portion of Scene 4 you must first make a number of decisions regarding the thoughts and feelings of Bigger Thomas. Why are you, Bigger, in such a frenzied, unreasoning state of terror when Mrs. Dalton enters the room? What do you believe will be the consequences if you are caught in Mary's room? Why do you think so? When you smother Mary, is terror your only emotion? Do you also feel hatred toward Mary Dalton? If so, why? When Mary, drunk, first loses consciousness in your arms, why do you gaze at her face "fascinatedly," your "lips open and breathless"? Are you physically attracted to her? Or is it the fascination of "forbidden fruit"? Or is there a different reason? What is your attitude toward Mrs. Dalton? Read the play care-

fully, several times, for clues. The play script, however, will not provide clear-cut answers to all these questions. You will have to use your own imagination—one of the exciting challenges of this role.

3. You begin to act this monologue long before you speak a word. You perform physical actions from the moment the bedroom door closes. Each of these physical movements is impelled by inner thought, inner feeling, desire. As an exercise, speak aloud your (Bigger's) "inner monologue": all your silent, inner thoughts from the moment the door closes behind Mrs. Dalton to your first words "Naw—naw—." Work on this "inner monologue" privately before trying it in front of others. Do not actually memorize your silent thoughts, though; feel free to change your "inner monologue" every time you perform.

Also work on your inner thoughts *after* you begin to speak "Naw—naw—." There are numerous pauses between the spoken words, filled with physical actions as outlined in the stage directions. What thoughts and feelings motivate each of your physical movements? You, Bigger, must have a reason for your every movement and gesture. What do you want at each moment? What do you say or do to get what you want? At the end of your monologue you want to find a way to get rid of her body. The sound of the furnace draft makes you think of burning it in the furnace.

From *The Glass Menagerie* by Tennessee Williams.
Act II, Scene 8

INTRODUCTION

"The play is memory. Being a memory play, it is dimly lighted, it is sentimental, it is not realistic." The action takes place in the mind of the narrator, Tom, who is also one of the characters in this delicate, poetic drama by one of our greatest playwrights, Tennessee Williams.

As narrator, Tom is in a sense the voice of the playwright. He speaks directly to the audience. He is now a merchant sailor, remembering the past with nostalgia—his family and himself in those days. At times the actor removes his seaman's cap and jacket and steps into the play itself as the character Tom, "a poet with a job in a warehouse. His nature is not remorseless, but to escape from a trap he has to act without pity."

Tom Wingfield, his mother, Amanda, and sister, Laura, live in a small apartment in an overcrowded, lower-middle-class section of St. Louis in the 1930s. Tom's father had deserted the family long before. "He was a telephone man who fell in love with long distance," the narrator tells the audience with typical Williams humor.

The character Tom is deeply unhappy, frustrated by his dull job which fails to satisfy his longing for adventure, and frustrated by his mother's incessant nagging at home. She never allows him to live or to write in peace.

Amanda does not mean to be cruel, but she is; she lacks the perceptiveness to realize that her children cannot possibly fit the mold into which she foolishly, doggedly, valiantly struggles to place them. She lives "in her illusions." Tom is a poet; a job in an office or factory, even an executive's position, could never satisfy him. Laura is two years older than Tom, but she is childlike, withdrawn. She spends all her time in a world of her own imagination, playing with her collection of tiny glass animals, her "glass menagerie," and listening to her father's old records. "A childhood illness has left her crippled, one leg slightly shorter than the other, and held in a brace. * * * Stemming from this, Laura's separation increases till she is like a piece of her own glass collection, too exquisitely fragile to move from the shelf."

Refusing to recognize the seriousness of Laura's problem, Amanda tries to prepare Laura for a business career. When that attempt fails miserably, Amanda determines to get her married. She keeps urging Tom to bring home a nice young man from work, a "gentleman caller" "for sister." She informs him that she knows about his desire to join the Merchant Marine. He will be free to leave home once Laura has a husband to take care of her, Amanda tells him. Tom realizes that Laura seems "peculiar" to outsiders, but he does bring home a friend for dinner, the long-awaited "gentleman caller." The evening ends in failure, inevitably, despite Amanda's elaborate preparations. Unknown to Tom, Jim is already engaged to another girl.

Amanda loses her struggle; Tom leaves home and Laura remains. Yet Tom cannot really escape; no matter how far he travels or how long he stays away, his memories of Laura pursue him. He can escape his mother's harsh nagging, but he cannot break free of stronger bonds—Laura's gentle sweetness, her dependence, her fragility.

After the "gentleman caller" leaves, Amanda blames Tom for not knowing that his friend Jim was engaged. She accuses him of selfishness. Tom had intended to go to the movies, but now he says, "The more you shout at me about my selfish pleasures, the quicker I'll go, and I won't go to the movies either." He leaves, slamming the door behind him.

Amanda yells after his departing figure, "Go, then! Then go to the moon—you selfish dreamer!"

Tom, as narrator, wearing seaman's jacket and cap, walks

across the stage for the last time to the fire-escape landing, where he stands and speaks. He may lean against the grillwork at times. He is coming from one of the alleys which flank the Wingfield's apartment building. The alley is in darkness. We do not see the tangled clotheslines, garbage cans or neighboring fire escapes.

In Tom's final soliloquy, which ends the play, the faint music, the soft candlelight and the delicately tinted glass bottles are all poetic symbols, representing his memories of Laura. Says the playwright, "When you look at a piece of delicately spun glass you think of two things: how beautiful it is and how easily it can be broken."

TOM: I didn't go to the moon. I went much farther. For time is the longest distance between two places. . . . I left Saint Louis. I descended these steps of this fire-escape for the last time and followed, from then on, in my father's footsteps, attempting to find in motion what was lost in space. . . . I travelled around a great deal. The cities swept about me like dead leaves, leaves that were brightly colored but torn away from the branches. I would have stopped, but I was pursued by something. It always came upon me unawares, taking me altogether by surprise. Perhaps it was a familiar bit of music. Perhaps it was only a piece of transparent glass. . . . Perhaps I am walking along a street at night, in some strange city, before I have found companions, and I pass the lighted window of a shop where perfume is sold. The window is filled with pieces of colored glass, tiny transparent bottles in delicate colors, like bits of a shattered rainbow. Then all at once my sister touches my shoulder. I turn around and look into her eyes. . . . Oh, Laura, Laura, I tried to leave you behind me, but I am more faithful than I intended to be! I reach for a cigarette, I cross the street, I run into a movie or a bar. I buy a drink, I speak to the nearest stranger—anything that can blow your candles out!—for nowadays the world is lit by lightning! Blow out your candles, Laura . . .

1. What do you mean, Tom, when you say, "For time is the longest distance between two places"? Decide how much time has elapsed since you left home. What have you done since then? Where have you traveled? If you are now a writer, what have you written?

2. What do you, Tom, want to do? Why are you always on the move? Why do you want Laura to "blow out" her "candles"?

3. At times the sound of music "weaves in and out of your pre-occupied consciousness." In the original production a tune called "The Glass Menagerie" was played at appropriate moments throughout the play.

> This tune is like circus music, not when you are on the grounds or in the immediate vicinity of the parade, but when you are at some distance and very likely thinking of something else. * * * then it is the lightest, most delicate music in the world and perhaps the saddest. It expresses the surface vivacity of life with the underlying strain of immutable and inexpressible sorrow.

Try to "hear," faintly, a light tune such as the one described above.

"See" the pastel-tinted perfume bottles, which remind you of Laura's tiny colored-glass animals. They in turn bring to mind the image of Laura herself.

"Feel" her touch on your shoulder.

When you look into Laura's eyes, what do her eyes say to you? Think of the message that her image silently communicates when you pause, before adding, "Oh, Laura, Laura."

Visualize a girl or young woman whom you know in real life, someone you love. She should possess as many of Laura's inner qualities as possible—her shyness, sweetness, vulnerability, etc. She should evoke in you at least some of the emotions described below.

4. Your (Tom's) feelings about Laura are extremely complex. When you think of your sister, you are filled with nostalgia, ten-

derness, sorrow, guilt, resentment and remorse. You did not want to desert her, but you had to do so in order to save yourself.

It might be helpful for you, the actor, to work on some of these emotions indirectly, by recalling events in your own life which aroused one or more of these feelings in you. Concentrate on recalling everything you experienced then with your five senses. What physical actions did you perform? Why?

5. According to the stage directions, Laura and Amanda can still be seen, although dimly, during your (Tom's) narration. In pantomime, "almost dance-like," Amanda comforts her daughter. When you say, "Blow out your candles, Laura," your sister actually blows out the candles still burning in the candelabrum that had illuminated the living room during her conversation with Jim. The interior becomes totally dark. Thus your painful memory of Laura is finally blacked out, at least for the present.

6. You, the actor, should certainly read the entire play before performing this (or any) role. *The Glass Menagerie* is easily available, anthologized in many play collections. The subtleties of mood and character, the playwright's wit and his gift of language cannot possibly be conveyed in a plot summary.

This astonishingly beautiful soliloquy is one of the more difficult selections in this book and should be considered a relatively advanced acting project.

From *The Glass Menagerie* by Tennessee Williams.
Act II, Scene 8

INTRODUCTION

See pages 311–13 for a description of the play.
Both Tom and Laura knew Jim O'Connor slightly in high
school. Everyone in school knew Jim. "He had tremendous Irish
good nature and vitality * * * He was a star in basketball, captain of the debating club, president of the senior class and glee
club, and he sang the male lead in the annual light opera." Everyone thought he would go far after high school, but he is presently
holding a job not much better than Tom's: shipping clerk at the
warehouse. He is engaged to Betty, "a nice, quiet home girl * * *
Catholic and Irish," whom he must pick up later at the train de-
pot. The playwright describes Jim as "A nice, ordinary, young
man."

In high school Laura worshiped Jim from afar. They took chorus together and had a speaking acquaintance. Always friendly, he
was one of the few people who spoke to her.

Laura still adores Jim secretly. She once showed her mother her
treasured pictures of him in her high school yearbook. When she
learned that "Jim" from the warehouse was this same Jim O'Connor, she panicked, became ill and could not come to the table
when Tom brought him home for dinner on this warm spring evening. She remained in the living room, resting on the day bed. At
the end of the meal all the electric lights went out suddenly. Tom
had used the money for the light bill to pay for membership in the
Merchant Marine. Amanda gave Jim a candelabrum with lighted

candles to bring into the living room; with overwhelming southern charm she suggested that he keep Laura company while she and Tom do the dishes.

Jim takes a quick swig of wine and joins Laura. (Amanda has refurbished the time-worn living room for this occasion. There is a new floor lamp, a colored paper lantern concealing the broken light fixture on the ceiling, new chintz covers on the chair and day bed, and new sofa pillows.) "JIM's attitude is gently humorous." While this incident is "apparently unimportant, it is to LAURA the climax of her secret life." Jim puts the candelabrum on the floor in the center of the room. Under it he places a newspaper to catch the drippings. They sit on the floor. He offers Laura chewing gum, which they both chew. Gradually "* * * Jim's warmth overcomes her paralyzing shyness." Laura reminds him of their past acquaintance in high school. They sang in chorus together. Laura recalls always arriving late, and having to "clump" up the aisle with her brace, the whole class watching. Jim assures her that he never heard any clumping, never even noticed. Laura takes out her yearbook and shows him his picture in *The Pirates of Penzance*. She confesses that she saw all three performances in the hopes that he would sign her program. He autographs it now, immensely flattered. Laura admits to him that she quit school after receiving bad grades on her final examinations. Jim asks her what she has done since high school. She tells him that she had to drop out of a business course because of "indigestion," and that she now keeps busy with her glass collection. She turns away, "acutely shy."

On the right side of the stage (the actor's right) is an armchair. To the (actor's) right of the armchair are shelves holding Laura's glass menagerie. On the left side of the stage is a day bed. On the right of the day bed is a small table. Laura is standing by her menagerie. Jim is seated on the day bed. He has been smoking, leaning back and smiling at Laura.

A portion of the scene has been converted into a monologue. Deletions are indicated by asterisks.

JIM: [*Puts out cigarette. Abruptly*] Say! You know what I judge to be the trouble with you? [*Rises from day-bed and crosses right*] Inferiority complex! You know what that is? That's what they call it when a fellow low-rates himself! Oh, I understand it because I had it, too. Uh-huh! Only my case was not as aggravated as yours seems to be. I had it until I took up public speaking and developed my voice, and learned that I had an aptitude for science. Do you know that until that time I never thought of myself as being outstanding in any way whatsoever!

* * *

Now I've never made a regular study of it— [*Sits armchair right*] mind you, but I have a friend who says I can analyze people better than doctors that make a profession of it. I don't claim that's necessarily true, but I can sure guess a person's psychology. Excuse me, Laura. [*Takes out gum*] I always take it out when the flavor is gone. I'll just wrap it in a piece of paper. [*Tears a piece of paper off the newspaper under candelabrum, wraps gum in it, crosses to day-bed, looks to see if* LAURA *is watching. She isn't. Crosses around day-bed*] I know how it is when you get it stuck on a shoe. [*Throws gum under day-bed, crosses around left of day-bed. Crosses right to* LAURA] Yep—that's what I judge to be your principal trouble. A lack of confidence in yourself as a person. Now I'm basing that fact on a number of your remarks and on certain observations I've made. For instance, that clumping you thought was so awful in high school. You say that you dreaded to go upstairs? You see what you did? You dropped out of school, you gave up an education all because of a little clump, which as far as I can see is practically non-existent! Oh, a little physical defect is all you have. It's hardly noticeable even! Magnified a thousand times by your imagination! You know what my strong advice to you is? You've got to think of yourself as *superior* in some way! [*Crosses left to small table right of day-bed. Sits.* LAURA *sits in armchair*]

* * *

Why, man alive, Laura! Look around you a little and what do you see? A world full of common people! All of 'em born and all of 'em going to die! Now, which of them has one-tenth of your strong points! Or mine! Or anybody else's for that matter? You see, everybody excels in some one thing. Well—some in many! You take me, for instance. My interest happens to lie in electrodynamics. I'm taking a course in radio engineering at night school, on top of a fairly responsible job at the warehouse. I'm taking that course *and* studying public speaking.

* * *

Because I believe in the future of television! I want to be ready to go right up along with it. [*Rises, crosses right*] I'm planning to get in on the ground floor. Oh, I've already made the right connections. All that remains now is for the industry itself to get under way—full steam! You know, *knowledge*— ZZZZppp! *Money*—Zzzzzzpp! *POWER!* Wham! That's the cycle democracy is built on! [*Pause*] I guess you think I think a lot of myself!

SUGGESTIONS FOR THE ACTOR

1. Every movement onstage must be *motivated;* in other words, the character you are portraying must have a reason for rising, sitting, crossing *right* (walking across the stage to the actor's right), etc. If a movement does not fit your interpretation of what your character is thinking and feeling at that moment, then you must either change the movement indicated in the play script or else change your interpretation. Many of the stage directions in the above selection merely record the physical actions performed in the original Broadway production. You are not obliged to use all of them. Some of the movements indicated in the script, however, are important because they shed light on your (Jim's) personality. For example, you throw your gum, wrapped in newspaper, under the day bed when Laura is not looking. Why? What is the significance of this bit of stage business (physical activity)? What does it tell you about the character you are playing? Laura thinks of you as a storybook hero; does this little action fit her conception of you?

2. Piecing together the clues provided by the playwright, we, the audience, may think of you (Jim) as warm, kind, outgoing, romantic by nature, sometimes inconsiderate although usually

well-meaning, industrious, ambitious, unusually self-confident but
not exceptionally intelligent. You certainly lack Tom's command
of language despite your public-speaking course; you normally
speak in clichés. You have a sense of humor but you fail to catch
the absurdity of your remark about common people: "Now which
one of them has one-tenth of your strong points! Or mine! Or
anybody else's for that matter?" You think you "can sure guess a
person's psychology," but in fact you fail to sense the severity of
Laura's emotional problems. You think a little good advice is all
she needs to cure her of a "lack of confidence."

How do you (Jim) think of *yourself?* How does your own impression of yourself differ from the audience's impression of you?

3. Has the thought occurred to you (Jim) that you may have
been invited to dinner to meet Laura? You mention this possibility later in the scene. If this idea has already crossed your mind,
then why don't you tell Laura that you are engaged instead of taking the chance of arousing her false hopes?

4. What do you (Jim) think of Laura? What are your feelings
toward her? The warmth of your smile "lights her inwardly with
altar candles." She has never looked so lovely as this evening. "A
fragile, unearthly prettiness has come out in Laura; she is like a
piece of translucent glass touched by light, given a momentary ra-
diance, not actual, not lasting." Later in the scene you momentarily forget yourself and you kiss her.

If possible, have an actress play Laura opposite you, even
though she does not speak. The actress will have to invent Laura's
"inner monologue": her secret thoughts while she listens to you.
The actress will have to decide when Laura turns back to face
you.

5. The playwright tells us a good deal about your (Jim's) high
school days, but you, the actor, will have to imagine for yourself
your (Jim's) home background, office life and your relationship
with Betty. Visualize the members of your family, your fellow
workers and your fiancée.

6. Your (Jim's) last line, "I guess you think I think a lot of
myself!" reflects a sharp "transition," or inner change. The remark
is preceded by a pause. What are you thinking during that pause?
Why do you make the comment? How do you want Laura to respond?

From *Manchild in the Promised Land*
by Claude Brown

See the "Introduction" to *Manchild in the Promised Land,* beginning on page 132.

CLAUDE: I used to feel that I belonged on the Harlem streets and that, regardless of what I did, nobody had any business to take me off the streets.

I remember when I ran away from shelters, places that they sent me to, here in the city. I never ran away with the thought in mind of coming home. I always ran away to get back to the streets. I always thought of Harlem as home, but I never thought of Harlem as being in the house. To me, home was the streets. I suppose there were many people who felt that. If home was so miserable, the street was the place to be. I wonder if mine was really so miserable, or if it was that there was so much happening out in the street that it made home seem such a dull and dismal place.

When I was very young—about five years old, maybe younger—I would always be sitting out on the stoop. I remember Mama telling me and Carole to sit on the stoop and not to move away from in front of the door. Even when it was time to go up and Carole would be pulling on me to come upstairs and eat, I never wanted to go, because there was so much out there in that street.

You might see somebody get cut or killed. I could go out in the street for an afternoon, and I would see so much that, when

I came in the house, I'd be talking and talking for what seemed like hours. Dad would say, "Boy, why don't you stop that lyin'? You know you didn't see all that. You know you didn't see nobody do that." But I knew I had.

SUGGESTIONS FOR THE ACTOR

1. You, Claude, are filled with excitement as you talk about the Harlem streets. This excitement rises almost to a fever pitch as you recall coming back into the house from the street when you were a little boy and "talking and talking for what seemed like hours." What were you saying all that time? As an acting exercise, first try to imagine specifically and then describe aloud what you (little Claude) saw on the street one particular afternoon. Remember, violence may horrify you, the actor, but you, Claude, were used to it when you were small. You were no longer upset by the sight of violence, if you ever had been. You found it stimulating, just as so many children are stimulated rather than frightened by violence on TV or in the movies.

2. At the end of this monologue, when you say, "But I knew I had," what are you remembering? How you silently daydreamed about those fantastic happenings you saw on the street, because your father would not let you speak of them aloud any more? How you inwardly protested against being called a liar? What other possibilities can you think of for the inner thoughts behind those words, known as the subtext? Choose the subtext you prefer to use when you say your last line.

3. As an actor, you must find a way to create for yourself Claude's sense of excitement, in order to project that feeling to an audience. If you can easily identify with Claude's emotions, that's fine. But you, the actor, may not find the streets of Harlem or any other place as thrilling as all that. What then? You should then substitute a different image; in preparing the section of the monologue in which you speak of the Harlem streets, you should think of something or some place exciting to you. For instance, were you ever thrilled by the circus as a child? Maybe the high-wire act

once thrilled you the way seeing somebody "get cut or killed" thrilled little Claude. If so, try to recall in detail everything you saw, heard, smelled, touched and tasted at the circus on that memorable day.

The streets also represent home to Claude. You may need to use two different images. When you speak of the excitement of the Harlem streets, you need to visualize something or some place that thrills you. When you speak of the Harlem streets as your real home, you may need to picture a place that in real life gives you a feeling of comfort and well-being. If you were to run away from a place you hated, where would you want to go? You may choose to visualize your real home, or you may prefer to think of some other place, one you wish were your real home.

When you speak of Carole, Mama and Dad, you, the actor, should visualize real people, perhaps members of your own family. You should "hear" their voices too. What was Mama's tone of voice when she gave you instructions? You may wish to imitate her voice and manner to some extent as you recall what she said, even though you do not quote her directly. Imagine your little sister Carole's words and gestures when she coaxed you to come upstairs. What was your reaction at the time? Did she annoy you? Did you pay any attention to her or were you concentrating on something else? Visualize your (Claude's) father and "hear" his tone of voice. Did he sound angry? Amused? Baffled? You may want to imitate his manner when you speak his words. When he refused to believe you, what was your reaction? What did you want to do to him?

4. More often than not, you (the actor) are able to emphasize the key words in your speeches without special effort. If you clearly understand the meaning of what you are saying, if you know your subtext, that is, the thoughts behind your words, as well as all the surrounding circumstances of the character you are playing, and know what led up to each moment, you will most often stress the right words automatically. But some complex thoughts and groups of thoughts are likely to give trouble unless you do make a conscious effort to stress the important words. Part of this monologue may demand such preparation. Remember that ordinarily a word or phrase used before need not be stressed when repeated. The new word, the new idea should be emphasized.

Also, if you are contrasting two words, two ideas, both should be stressed.

In the first sentence of this monologue, "I used to feel that I belonged on the Harlem streets and that, regardless of what I did, nobody had any business to take me off the streets," the word "streets" is used twice. The second time it is used, it should not be stressed. In the phrase "to take me off the streets," the important new concept is the word "off."

In the second paragraph, look at this group of sentences: "I never ran away with the thought in mind of coming home. I always ran away to get back to the streets. I always thought of Harlem as home, but I never thought of Harlem as being in the house." Which pairs of words (or phrases) are being contrasted? (For example, in the second sentence the word "home" is contrasted to the phrase "in the house.") All these pairs should be stressed. The word "Harlem" does not deserve emphasis because it was used previously. Keep in mind, however, that these rules must not be followed blindly. Sometimes a repeated word, an old idea, *is* stressed for a reason. Just be sure that you (that is, the character you play) have a reason for stressing the word. In the last sentence of the second paragraph, "I wonder if mine was really so miserable, or if it was that there was so much happening out in the street that it made home seem such a dull and dismal place," the key words being contrasted are "really" and "seem." (Was my home *really* so miserable or did it only *seem* to be?) When you say the words "dull" and "dismal," think of something boring and depressing, so that your voice, face and body will convey a dull and dismal feeling to the audience.

From *Narrative of the Life of Frederick Douglass, an American Slave, Written by Himself*, edited by Benjamin Quarles

See the "Introduction" to *Narrative of the Life of Frederick Douglass,* beginning on page 156.

FREDERICK: I never saw my mother, to know her as such, more than four or five times in my life; and each of these times was very short in duration, and at night. She was hired by a Mr. Stewart, who lived about twelve miles from my home. She made her journeys to see me in the night, travelling the whole distance on foot, after the performance of her day's work. She was a field hand, and a whipping is the penalty of not being in the field at sunrise unless a slave has special permission from his or her master to the contrary—a permission which they seldom get, and one that gives to him that gives it the proud name of being a kind master. I do not recollect of ever seeing my mother by the light of day. She was with me in the night. She would lie down with me, and get me to sleep, but long before I waked she was gone. Very little communication ever took place between us. Death soon ended what little we could have while she lived, and with it her hardships and suffering. She died when I was about seven years old, on one of my master's farms, near Lee's Mill. I was not allowed to be present during her illness, at her death, or burial. She was gone long before I knew anything about it. Never having enjoyed, to any considerable extent, her soothing presence, her tender and watchful care, I received the tidings of her death with much the same emotions I should have probably felt at the death of a stranger.

1. Why are you, Frederick Douglass, speaking these words aloud at this moment? You, the actor, will have to invent a reason. One possibility: Perhaps you (Frederick) are addressing an audience at a public meeting. When, where and why is the meeting being held? Your purpose is to convince everyone that slavery is evil. If you, the actor, use this motivation, then you must be aware, as you speak, of the effect of your words upon your listeners. Communicate with real people—speak to your actual audience as you perform. Observe their reactions as you talk. Are they shocked? Angered? Convinced? You (Frederick) speak the truth, and your emotions are deeply felt, but nevertheless you are expressing your feelings for a conscious purpose—to arouse your audience to indignation so that they will abolish slavery.

2. What are your (Frederick's) memories of your mother? Since she was with you only in the dark of night, your memories would probably not be visual ones. You might recall her soothing voice, the warmth of her body, the touch of her hand. Use some early memories of your (the actor's) own mother putting you to sleep. For example, can you recall a lullabye that she sang to you at night? Any other bedtime rituals?

3. You (Frederick) are not mourning the loss of a loved one. Your early separation from your mother hindered the natural development of your affection for her. You feel deprived—you were never allowed to love your mother or to be greatly comforted by her love for you.

Have you ever felt bitterness or any other strong emotions because you were deprived of something vital to your well-being? If so, try to recall everything that you experienced with your five senses at the time of that terrible deprivation. What did you *do?* What do you think little Frederick did?

In a New York *Times* article (August 14, 1977) by Margaret

Croyden, the famous actress Anne Bancroft describes the manner in which she prepared to portray the role of Israel's former Prime Minister Golda Meir:

> She had come [to Israel] to meet Mrs. Meir, she said, not only to watch her move, learn her mannerisms and listen to her talk but to find a passion in her own life that would match that of Mrs. Meir, "something that would be a clue to my playing the role so that I would have a handle to hang on to every night. * * * When I work, I have to find a personal image that is similar to the person I'm relating to in the play. If you don't lock into something extremely personal within yourself, the play will have gone by without your having felt anything. So I have to find out what Israel is to Golda, and what Golda's passion is all about. And then I have to find something for myself that is equal.

From *The Rimers of Eldritch* by Lanford Wilson.
Act II

INTRODUCTION

This intriguing play is more experimental in form than are most of
the other works represented in this anthology. A mystery gradually unfolds, but the events are not shown in chronological sequence. The audience learns both the crucial question and its answer as one would solve a jigsaw puzzle, by fitting together small
bits and pieces. The audience must discover not only "Who done
it?" but "Who done *what?*" Geographical "place" is not treated in
the standard fashion either; incidents which occurred at different
times and places are often presented on stage simultaneously.
Through this highly effective dramatic technique, the playwright
reveals unexpected, sometimes startling *connections*—similarities
or contrasts—between the various characters and events.

The locale of the play is Eldritch, present population about sev-
enty, one of the many nearly abandoned towns in America's Middle
West. The time is the present.

The play takes place during the spring, summer, and fall of the
year, skipping at will from summer back to spring or forward to fall
and from one conversation to another. All the characters are onstage
throughout the play * * * grouping as needed to suggest time and
place.

Robert Conklin is eighteen years old, a recent high school grad-
uate. Before the evening of the crime, Robert had spent much of
his time with Eva Jackson, a crippled girl of fourteen. Their rela-

tionship had been innocent. They would take long walks in the woods together, exchanging confidences. Robert's older brother "Driver" had been the town hero. A racing-car driver, he had been killed in a car crash. As far as most of the townspeople were concerned, Robert could never measure up to Driver in any way. The old town hermit, however, an outcast taunted, mistreated and yet feared by many of the town's inhabitants, knew that Robert was a more decent person than his brother. Skelly Mannor knew that because he knew everything—the old man learned the truth about everybody by peeping through windows.

Robert and Eva were likable young people, and yet this is what really happened:

The two of them were walking through the woods as usual on the evening in question, Eva resentful over her mother's constant unjust accusations. Her mother had never believed Eva's assertion that her long walks in the woods with Robert had always been completely innocent. She had even slapped Eva for lying. Eva decided that she might as well actually do what she was being accused of doing. She said to Robert, "Let's do" (make love). Robert wanted to go back; he told her that she didn't know what she was talking about. She then provoked him recklessly, telling him that his brother could perform but that he couldn't, that he was too young, ashamed, afraid. Infuriated, he threw her on the ground and tried to rape her. Eva now wanted him to leave her alone, but he wouldn't stop. At the same time Mary Windrod, an old woman, heard the commotion outside, from her upstairs bedroom; she told her strong, middle-aged daughter Nelly to go out and see what was happening. Nelly took up a shotgun and opened the door. Just then old Skelly ran to Robert and Eva from the woods, calling out, "Don't hurt her." He threw Robert off Eva. When Skelly saw Nelly Windrod, he ran toward her, crying, "Help her!" Assuming that the old man was attacking Eva, Nelly aimed the shotgun at Skelly and killed him.

Afterward Robert avoided everyone, including Eva, although she confirmed his lie about what had happened.

At the murder trial the jury finds Nelly "Not guilty." The judge asks Robert to tell the court, in his own words, what happened. (Robert must have been called as a witness prior to the verdict, but in the play the verdict is delivered first.) The judge says, "We know this has been a terrible shock to you—." Robert then offers this false testimony.

ROBERT:—I'm okay, I think. See—Eva and I were walking. We do quite frequently. Just wandering through the woods, talking. And we noticed that it had begun to get dark so we thought we had better start back—and we were heading back toward the main street, that would be west. And Eva thought she heard something behind us and we listened but we didn't hear it again so I assumed we were hearing things. Or it was our imagination. And it got dark pretty fast. And we were just coming into the clearing right behind the mill. Windrod's mill. And uh, we heard something again and this time we saw something behind the trees and we started running. More as a joke than anything —and then he started running too. And it was Skelly, and I wasn't afraid of him, but I knew he'd never liked my brother, and he started running too. He must have been following us all the time: everybody knows how he spies on people; I guess just as we broke into the clearing—and he came from nowhere. [*Crowd reaction*] And he took us by surprise and he pushed me —he hit me from behind; I don't know if I passed out or not. [*Crowd murmur*] He's immensely strong. [*Crowd murmur*] And I heard a ringing in my ears and I saw what he was trying to do, and everything went white. And he pushed me.

SUGGESTIONS FOR THE ACTOR

1. How much of your lie, and which portions of it, did you (Robert) plan ahead of time? Which parts, if any, are you inventing on the spot? If some parts of your story were not prepared before-hand, then you, the actor, should think of them right now, on the witness stand, *as if* for the very first time. Imagine that you do not yet know what you are going to say next. You (Robert) would probably not speak those unplanned parts of your testimony as

smoothly or glibly as you would recite the rehearsed portions. You would be more likely to hesitate, then come up with an idea, then stop to think again.

2. Why do you lie on the witness stand? How do you justify this lie to yourself? What would be the dire consequences if you were to tell the truth?

We all try to justify our own behavior to ourselves. No one wants to think of himself or herself as a bad person. You (Robert) should find it relatively easy to rationalize, to justify this lie. After all, in your shoes most people would do exactly what you are doing; most people are not heroes. Skelly is dead. How can your false accusation hurt him now? As far as you are concerned, he was a contemptible person anyway. You may have convinced yourself that *you* cannot destroy Skelly's reputation—he had ruined his own reputation long before you were born.

Do you nevertheless have qualms of conscience about accusing the dead man? Do you have any such feelings while you are giving false evidence? If so, when? Exactly what are you thinking at these moments?

3. Why did you (Robert) attack Eva? Before that evening what had been your attitude toward her? What is your attitude toward her now? Do you try to justify your act of rape in your own mind? Do you succeed? If so, how do you manage to do that? If not, then how do you regard your misdeed? When you see Eva in court, what do you want to do?

4. You (Robert) must make the judge and jury believe your story. Even though the judge treats you kindly, he and the jury would probably be quick to notice inconsistencies in your testimony. You are always aware, as you speak, of the reactions of the judge, jury and other townspeople. When the crowd reacts to your words, you in turn react to the crowd. Perhaps their sympathetic response encourages you to add the violent details sure to evoke their further sympathy.

It would be helpful for you, the actor, to address particular members of the audience as if they were the judge, jury and other Eldritch citizens. You might even assign parts of judge, jury and townfolk to the members of the student audience, and instruct them to react in character to your testimony.

5. After your performance, you and the audience may wish to discuss this ethical question: Was Robert's lie immoral? If so, why? If not, why not? What do you think *you* would have done in similar circumstances?

Some Hints for Blocking a Scene

Directing is not the subject of this workbook for actors. Nevertheless in all probability you will have to "block out" your own scenes in an acting class or workshop. In other words, you will probably have to establish the positions of your "set props"—chairs, tables, etc. (perhaps by marking the floor with tape or chalk), plan your positions "onstage" and your basic movements. You may even be called upon to direct scenes performed by others. These few hints regarding one of the numerous functions of a director, blocking a scene, may therefore prove useful to you. Remember, these are only traditional guidelines, certainly not rules; feel free to disregard any of these four principles when you have a reason for doing so. None of them should be followed automatically, without careful consideration of the special problems and circumstances of your scene.

1. If we think of the conventional, proscenium stage (which the audience views only from the front) as roughly divided into six playing areas, the "strongest" areas (those receiving the greatest attention from the audience) are likely to be the center areas. Downstage center is generally considered the strongest area, especially when only one or two actors appear onstage. Up left and up right are commonly thought of as "weaker," less noticeable areas than down left and down right. The terms "left" and "right" always refer to the *actor's* left and right.

2. When the character you play makes a strong statement, comes to a crucial decision, feels a powerful emotion, a strong movement is frequently appropriate and effective. Movements toward the audience are traditionally considered more emphatic

Up Right (U.R.)	Up Center (U.C.)	Up Left (U.L.)
Down Right (D.R.)	Down Center (D.C.)	Down Left (D.L.)

AUDIENCE

Acting Areas of the Stage

than movements away from the audience; movements toward the center more emphatic than movements away from the center.

3. Rising is usually considered a stronger, more emphatic movement than sitting down.

(For a fuller description of the above principles and for other directing concepts, see "A Primer of Stage Directing for the Beginning Actor" in *Working Up a Part* by H. D. Albright [Boston, Houghton Mifflin Company, 1947].)

4. A completely symmetrical stage set or stage picture is more likely to suggest comedy than drama to the audience, even though the audience may be quite unaware of the psychological reason for their expectations.

It is worthwhile to know these four principles whether or not you make use of them all in a particular scene. Professional directors do not necessarily follow all these guidelines. The following two precepts, however, are *strict rules:*

Every member of the audience must be able to see and hear

every vital action and reaction of every character in the scene. The only exception I can think of is a scene performed "in the round." In that physical arrangement, some members of the audience are bound to miss some significant visual points. But a good director of theatre-in-the-round will use various means to make the important points so that no member of the audience loses the thread of the action.

Secondly, I have stressed throughout this book that *Every movement an actor makes onstage must be motivated: The* CHARACTER *must have a reason for moving.*

Actor's Check List

Whenever you begin to prepare a role, if possible read the play several times, once for a general impression (theme, main conflict, etc.), at least once to learn all you can about the character you are playing and his world, and perhaps once to put back together all you have analyzed. Then invent answers to the following questions about the character you play. Use whatever clues the play provides, but often you will have to use your own imagination as well. (If your selection is taken from a work other than a play, then substitute the word "book" for "play," and the word "selection" or "chapter" for "scene" in the questions listed below.)

THE CHARACTER YOU PLAY

In each question, "you" refers to the character portrayed.

What is your main objective (what do you want most) in this play?

What do you say and do to reach your main objective?

What do the other characters say about you and how do they behave toward you?

How does the playwright (or author) describe you?

What are your relationships with the other characters in the play?

How do you get along with others?

Describe each member of your immediate family and your relationship with each of them.

Where have you lived in the past?

Where do you live now? In what section, country, part of the world? What is the climate?

In what period of history are you living?

Describe your home, including your own room, in concrete detail.

Describe a typical day in your life.

Act out a typical or else a crucial moment in your life, a situation not shown in the play itself.

What are your physical characteristics?

Age	Height
Weight	Posture
Typical gestures	Typical movements
Voice and manner of speech	Physical traits developed
Any physical handicaps	through customary activities
(caused by ———)	(such as the grace of
Typical manner of dress	dancer Agnes de Mille, or
	the resonant voice of orator
	Frederick Douglass)

What is your most noticeable personality trait? (For example, Dru's domineering manner in *The Young and Fair*—see pages 5–16.)

What are three less obvious personality traits? You, the actress, will probably have to invent some of these characteristics out of your own imagination. For example, the play *The Young and Fair* tells us that Dru loves to go to parties and dances. You, the actress playing Dru, may also decide that you, the character Dru, are an expert bridge player. The play makes no mention of any such ability, but it would be in keeping with what we do know of Dru's personality. Inventing as many such traits as possible helps an actor to create a flesh-and-blood, three-dimensional character.

What kind of life have you lived until now? Describe your background in terms of home environment, social life, ethnic group, religion, economic level, education, jobs you have held and organizations to which you belong.

What do you value most? What ethical standards do you live by? To what extent are you aware of your own values and code of ethics?

SPECIFIC CIRCUMSTANCES OF THE SCENE

After reading the play as a whole several times if possible, you will begin to focus on the scene you are going to perform. At that point, answer these questions about the particular circumstances of the scene. Again, the word "you" refers to the character you play.

Where were you and what were you doing before this scene began? Describe everything you did today, from the moment you woke up until the beginning of the scene.

Where are you now? Imagine the setting in vivid detail. What is the weather? How do your surroundings affect you and influence the way you behave?

When is this happening (time of day, day of week, date, season, year)? How does the time influence your behavior?

What is your physical condition as the scene opens? (Describe your appearance. How are you dressed? How do you *feel* physically? For instance, are you hot or cold? Tired? Hungry? Thirsty? In pain? Be specific.)

Describe your relationship with each of the other characters on-stage.

What is your main, over-all objective throughout this scene? (What, chiefly, do you desire?) Why? What obstacle is in your way? What do you want to do to your obstacle? (An obstacle can be anyone or anything hindering you—it can even be something inside yourself, such as fear or your conscience.) What are your smaller objectives? (What do you want at each moment?)

Is it urgent for you to get what you want right now? If so, why? What actions do you perform to get what you want?

What are you thinking at every moment of the scene? Your inner thoughts need not be precisely the same at every rehearsal and performance, so long as they are always appropriate. Your honest reactions will depend on what is truly communicated to you by the other characters, unless you are alone onstage. You, the actor, should think your character's inner thoughts at home and in rehearsal, but you should feel free to change or add to these thoughts spontaneously, as you perform.